SUCCESSFUL
BOWHUNTING

SUCCESSFUL

BOWHUNTING

by M.R. James

Editor/Publisher of
Bowhunter® Magazine

A Blue-J, Inc. Publication

Acknowledgements

The author wishes to thank the following individuals for their assistance in the preparation of this book: Fred and Dora Burris, whose excellent wildlife photographs appear throughout Part II; Max Greiner, Jr., whose original painting "Change of Heart" graces the cover; Dr. C. Randall Byers, Records Committee Chairman of the Pope and Young Club, whose trophy information contributes to the book's completeness; William H. Nesbitt, Executive Director of the Boone and Crockett Club, whose permission to publish the big game scoring forms adds insight and understanding; Jim Dougherty and G. Fred Asbell, whose encouragement and kind words are much appreciated; Cathy Dee, whose critical questions and advice during the manuscript stage tightened and improved each completed chapter; and thanks to the entire "Blue Crew" for lending their talents in the design and publication of this book. Special thanks, too, for the many warm memories provided by David James, as fine a bowhunting companion—and son—as any man could have.

Library of Congress Catalog Number: 85-73440

ISBN 0-93-653100-2

For Janet—Who Understands

Contents

Part II

Part 1

Foreword

Bowhunting is important to me.

Bowhunting isn't just something I do for a few special months every fall, bowhunting is **what** I do—full time—year 'round—every day. I'm lucky.

I make my living in the archery community as a bowhunter, a manufacturer and distributor of bowhunting products, a consultant to others in the archery/bowhunting industry, and as a writer of sorts on the subject. I spend a very great deal of my time working with organizations founded to protect, preserve and cherish bowhunting. I take it very seriously and have since I was a teenager chasing cottontails through the southern California foothills.

I have come to look at bowhunting as an honest expression of the need in some men to hunt. By selecting restrictive equipment as an equalizer in a pursuit once necessary to survival but now only necessary to our spirit, it provides a trial of our ability to get back into the wilderness, into ourselves. It provides us with a fair and honorable confrontation with a quarry who knows only the honesty of life and death. Success honestly achieved is an admirable accomplishment. Done illegally, immorally, it is meaningless.

Participation in bowhunting has grown significantly since my cottontail hunting days. This has been good for the sport resulting in hunting opportunities far beyond what was available to a bowman then. For example, today's bowhunters have almost ten times the big game hunting days of any other method. This is not a right, this is a reward for having grown intelligently, for proving our equipment's capabilities, and being respectful

of the privilege. We must take care that as bow-hunting — and we as bowhunters — continue to mature we do not forget the essence of our sport and jeopardize the future.

It is because of what bowhunting is to me that I am pleased to be able to comment on the qualifications and character of the author of this book, M. R. James.

As a successful bowhunter in terms of game brought to bag and tagged, he is eminently qualified to write with authority on the requirements necessary for successful bowhunting. But the water is deeper than that. M. R. James is one of those completely honest men who has taken up the bow for all the right reasons, a man for whom hunting ethics—The Rules of Fair Chase—are a way of life. A man to whom the pursuit of game, the flight of an arrow, the companionship of fellow bowmen and the beauty of a mountain sunrise are privileges worth caring and fighting for. M. R. James does not squander such privileges and he writes about them as well as any man who ever came to full draw.

Jim Dougherty
Tulsa, Oklahoma

Preface

Bowhunting

Does any other single word evoke more anticipation and challenge in a hunter? It's been called the ultimate hunting challenge—with good reason. There's something about going after wild game while armed only with one of man's oldest known weapons, confronting an animal one-on-one in its home territory and then loosing an arrow—swift and silent—at a furred or feathered target that no traditional means of hunting can equal.

Bowhunting success, when measured solely in terms of downed game, remains relatively rare despite technological advancements that have turned modern hunting bows into complex-appearing, futuristic arrow launchers. Entering the decade of the 1980s only one American bowhunter in ten got his deer.

But bowhunting success should never be weighed by punched tags and meat on the table. Rather, its appeal—indeed, its **magic**—is found in the many enjoyable, rewarding experiences encountered in the field. It's the hunting, not the killing, which makes for lasting memories in the minds of true sportsmen. Of course, the legal taking of any highly prized game animal is a fitting climax to any hunter's quest. And when the arrow flies true and the animal is down, the flush of pride and accomplishment a bowhunter feels is likely unsurpassed by any other sport hunter.

To succeed as a bowhunter, a person should realize that attitude and ability are of nearly equal importance. True, mastery of the bow is necessary. But, ideally, finely honed shooting skills should be complemented by a thorough understanding of quarry and self. Bowhunting, at its best, is discovery. It is understanding. Both demanding and rewarding, bowhunting is like a fine, properly aged wine: its distillation process cannot be rushed and it must be savored one slow sip at a time to be fully appreciated.

Not surprisingly, bowhunting is not for everybody. Some people have neither the physical attributes nor the proper mental attitude necessary to become good bowhunters. Patience, for example, is one absolute requirement and it seems we live in an increasingly impatient world. This fact—plus the simple truth that there is no shortcut, no easy way to bowhunting success—discourages some people. In all honesty, it's probably just as well. Unless you **feel** the sport, chances are good you'll never make it as a bowhunter.

Another barrier for many is found in the fact that bowhunting is largely a solitary sport. In today's highly gregarious society and increasingly crowded world, only a few seek solitude and escape; many more revel in the constant companionship of others. While there is much to be said about sharing the hunting trip or camp with good friends, the best moments found in bowhunting are those when hunter and hunted meet in the eternal test of skill versus instinct with life or death hanging in the balance.

A third obstacle is, in truth, a sad commentary on contemporary America. Modern man, his outdoor senses often dulled by life in an urban world of metal and concrete, his mind swimming with demands of workplace and nuclear family, often has little time or inclination to hunt. And even those who may try to heed the primordial stirrings within their souls quickly learn they are uncomfortable when suddenly alone in an alien world of shadowy woods and quiet hills. A few are actually afraid of being alone, even if only for a brief time.

Finally, bowhunting is largely a mental game. Once the mechanics of shooting are mastered and the basics of elementary woodcraft accomplished, it's up to the individual. He must find the necessary time. He must work to face his quarry in a close range situation where, if he chooses and luck is on his side, he will kill. This, to some, is an unpleasant if not impossible task.

No, bowhunting is not for everyone. And therein lies a major reason for its appeal. Those of us who know and love the sport share a common bond, an understanding, a difficult-to-explain yet unmistakable oneness of spirit.

Is bowhunting for you? That's a question only you—and time—will be able to answer. If not, there is no need to be either remorseful or overly concerned. There are many other outdoor activities you may choose to pursue. But if you bowhunt you will be participating in a unique adventure, one which offers no guarantees yet promises potential satisfaction and enjoyment few sportsmen ever experience.

This book is written especially for bowhunters. It covers every important aspect of hunting North America's game with the bow and arrow; however,

it does not attempt to offer instruction which will raise your score at the local archery range or advise you which model bow is best, fastest or whatever. It's about hunting, written by a serious hunter. The emphasis is on game animals and generally successful bowhunting techniques for the various species.

Successful Bowhunting cannot make you a better bowhunter. It can help, though, by providing a treasure trove of no-nonsense information, by making you aware of time-tested techniques which work and by offering thought-tickling ideas which, when put to use by bowhunters, will open new vistas of opportunity. The rest is up to the reader.

To many people the term "bowhunter" is synonomous with "deer hunter." Indeed, most of the so-called "bowhunting books" published today are insightful deer hunting books. Also, the truth of the matter is that most bowhunters are deer hunters first and foremost. This is fine. This book, like the others, contains ample information for deer hunters. But bowhunting is much more than a single season, one dimensional sport. Today there is no huntable species of game on earth that has not been successfully hunted—or could be—by adventuresome men and women who prefer the hunting bow to a high powered rifle. Although primarily a North American sport, bowhunting is now regarded as having worldwide potential. For example, in 1984 the first international conference on bowhunting was held in Sweden with representatives from five of the seven continents in attendance. Additionally, it's been estimated that today over 2 million bowhunters actively pursue game each year in the United States and Canada. The future of bowhunting, at this writing, offers considerable potential.

Successful Bowhunting explores the potential that is available to anyone—young or old, rich or poor, beginner or veteran hunter—who wants more out of life and more out of bowhunting.

Speaking personally for a moment, it was challenge which led me to archery and to bowhunting in the late 1950s and early 1960s. Growing up in southern Illinois, I can't remember a time I didn't have a bow or two around the house. All too well I recall the time I discovered how not to carry a wooden longbow on a bicycle (spinning spokes can shorten a bow's tip in less time than it takes to tell). I also remember pint-sized pests—from gophers to groundhogs—being constantly harrassed by a skinny, freckled-faced youngster with more determination than shooting skill. But in time the persistence paid off.

From varmints and small game in season—squirrels and rabbits in particular—I turned attention to the whitetail deer inhabiting the hills and hollows of Illinois' Shawnee National Forest. A stout recurve replaced the limber "kid's bow" that had been the scourge of Wabash County's woodland critters for many years. I quickly discovered that despite their size, deer are as easy to miss—perhaps easier—as any grizzled woodchuck I'd ever loosed a shaft at. But I didn't care. The mere sight of a mature buck, glinting antlers aloft, breath clouding and coat gleaming in the misty aura of an autumn sunrise, was reward enough.

Later, as a college student in Indiana, I downed my first buck on a grey November evening while bowhunting in Warrick County's grown-over stripmining pits just north of Evansville. Like other important "firsts" in any person's life, it was a moment forever etched into my memory.

Seasons slipped by and I discovered that it was far too long between opening days to be satisfied with deer hunting alone. Other species drew my attention—bear and boar, pronghorns and elk, Western deer—muleys and blacktails—moose and

M.R. James and 1985 Idaho Bear

caribou, sheep and goats. Name it and I hunted it—or dreamed of it.

When the compound bow came on the scene I tried it and found, like any other hunting bow, it's only as good as the person using it. In an earlier book I called it "controversial" and perhaps "the ugliest bow ever devised." A full decade later I stand by those statements and will have more to say on that subject later in this volume.

In the early 1970s I had the good fortune to enter into a partnership with four men—Don Clark, Steve Doucette, Bob Schisler and Fred Wallace—who share my passion for bowhunting. Together we founded **Bowhunter Magazine**, a special interest publication for people who hunt with the bow and arrow. Within that same decade I was devoting myself full-time to bowhunting as Editor/Publisher of **Bowhunter**. This position has enabled me to travel widely, meet and share hunting camps with men whose names read like a contemporary **Who's Who of Bowhunting**. This association has taught me much, not the least of which is just how much the sport has to offer everyone. Bowhunting is—or could be—Everyman's sport.

Spend time around serious bowhunters and it's likely you'll be affected if not addicted. There's something about the feeling of using your muscles to draw an arrow, releasing and watching the shaft speed to a target. It's an intensely personal, immensely satisfying experience.

I know people who continue to bowhunt despite handicaps that would defeat less determined individuals. I know blind bowhunters who with the help of sighted friends take game each year. I know paraplegics who successfully hunt from wheelchairs and specially built carts. I know one-armed, one-legged shooters who use prosthetic limbs—some drawing and shooting the bow with their teeth!—just to be able to bowhunt.

Such is the spell of the sport. I know it well and understand its siren call. To those of you who doubt my words, be aware you've received fair warning. Bowhunting has a way of changing people, transforming them, hooking many hunters for life.

Try it. Discover for yourself what bowhunting is all about. You may love it, you may hate it. One thing is certain, regardless of the outcome, you won't forget it and you'll never be quite the same for the experience.

Good luck and good hunting.

M.R. James
Fort Wayne, Indiana

A History of Bowhunting

Saxton Pope and Arthur Young

1

Despite what my own youngsters and a few other wet-behind-the-ears whippersnappers may believe, I was not around when the bow and arrow was invented. The truth of the matter is no one can say for sure who fashioned the first bows and arrows just as no one can say with certainty just where these weapons originated. Some historians believe the Stone Age savages of Europe and Asia were the first to use crude archery tackle for hunting and self-protection. Other experts claim the bow was born elsewhere thousands of years before the dawn of the Mesolithic period.

Regardless, it is not really difficult to envision some skin-clad human ancestor searching for a missile—something better than a hand-thrown rock or club—that could travel fast and true to its intended target. Neither is it hard to imagine trial and error experimentation which led from hand-tossed spears to lighter missiles propelled by stick and sinew. At last, with the primitive bow and arrow, a hunter could stalk and shoot elusive game—even dangerous animals—from comparatively longer distances. With the birth of the bow came the hunter's basic weapon, a weapon that would reign unchallenged until the discovery of gunpowder many centuries later.

Bow and arrow hunting was practiced by Israelite and Assyrian, Babylonian and Scythian, Egyptian and Greek, Roman and Turk—all the oldest civilizations. And it is almost certain that when the first Indians followed the game herds across the Bering Strait to North America, they carried the bow and arrow with them.

All of these ancient people shared common knowledge of an effective hunting tool. Each shooter knew the strain of arm, back and shoulder muscles as the bow was pulled. Each sensed the power in the taut bowstring and heard the soft swish of a shaft speeding away at the instant of release. And each felt the deep satisfaction of watching a well-aimed arrow striking home.

Our long-dead kinsmen used the hunting bow to sustain life. It provided food and clothing and shelter—plus defense from enemies. It was a way of life. And it still is. True, the modern bowhunter no longer depends on the bow for physical survival. Now it is a temporary escape, a challenging sport. But each person who chooses to carry a bow afield in search of game is walking in the faint footsteps of forgotten ancestors and reliving a time in history when personal skills and simple weapons were all-important. No thoughtful person who bowhunts can help but remember and be affected by the memory and meaning of such a long and rich hunting heritage.

Although deer are the primary target of the modern bowhunter, virtually all species of the world's big game have been successfully hunted by archery enthusiasts. Later in this book I'll focus attention on North American big game and examine successful bowhunting techniques in detail. For the present let's see what has led many to consider bowhunting the ultimate hunting challenge.

Target archery interest in the United States was evident as far back as 1828. In that year an organization calling itself the Club of the United

Bowmen was founded in Philadelphia.

Interest in bowhunting in America can be traced to a pair of brothers from Georgia, Maurice and Will Thompson. The brothers fought for the Confederate States of America during the Civil War and found themselves denied the use and possession of firearms after the conflict. They began using the bow and arrow, making their own equipment and living off the land. In 1877 Maurice Thompson published **The Witchery of Archery**, a collection of writings credited with generating renewed interest in archery.

Early in the new century another twosome, Dr. Saxton Pope and Arthur Young, did much to revive bowhunting as a popular sport. Each had been influenced by the writings of the Thompson brothers and their friendship with men like Will "Chief" Compton and Ishi, the last of the wild Yana Indians of Northern California. They made numerous bowhunting trips together, collecting grizzly and Kodiak bears, moose, sheep, deer and other game. Pope's 1923 book, **Hunting With the Bow and Arrow**, promoted archery hunting. Across America some sportsmen began taking a serious look at the bow and arrow.

In 1934, thanks to the interest and efforts of men like Wisconsin bowhunter Roy Case, the first bow season for deer was held in the United States. In 1935 Oregon offered sportsmen both a separate deer season and a special bowhunting-only area. Pennsylvania and Michigan soon followed suit. By 1965 every state had special seasons and/or areas for bow and arrow hunters.

Noteworthy is the fact that Roy Case is the man generally credited with creating the term "bowhunter" to describe people who used archery tackle in the pursuit of game animals. An avid bowhunter for over half a century, Case continued to hunt deer in his native Wisconsin as the decade of the 1980s began.

But perhaps no name is more closely identified with the sport or more widely recognized than that of a lanky man from the Cumberland Valley of Pennsylvania. Fred Bear began bowhunting in Michigan in 1929 and in 1933 founded the archery

Fred Bear

company that still bears his name. His worldwide bowhunting adventures have been shared by millions through films, books and personal appearances. Modern bowhunters owe a debt of gratitude to Fred Bear's creative genius and promotional efforts. Like Case, he actively pursued his passion for bowhunting into the 1980s.

There are others, now deceased, worthy of mention. Howard Hill, perhaps the greatest instinctive bow shot who ever lived, brought bowhunting into the public eye through his films and shooting demonstrations. Ben Pearson, founder of the Arkansas-based archery company, did likewise. Bob Swinehart, author of **Sagittarius** and one of only a handful of contemporary bowhunters to successfully take Africa's dangerous "Big Five," gave additional credibility to the bow as an effective hunting weapon. Roy Hoff, Editor of **Archery Magazine**, fired the imagination of thousands of his loyal readers. And H. W. Allen, who patented the compound bow, offered bowhunters a new weapon for modern enjoyment of an ancient sport.

Roy Case

Washington bowhunter Glenn St. Charles, who founded the Pope and Young Club in 1961 as the record-keeping organization of all North American big game taken with the bow, is another man who has helped to bring bowhunting to its present level of popularity.

The same may be said of Jim Dougherty and G. Fred Asbell, two men closely identified with Pope and Young Club leadership. The writings and lectures of both—along with their continual promotion of bowhunting—have stirred the imaginations of thousands. Each has made the sport his life's work, Dougherty with his Oklahoma-based archery company and Asbell as the producer of some of the finest custom-made recurve hunting bows available today.

These men—and many other lesser known but equally involved bow and arrow enthusiasts—have contributed much to the growth of bowhunting. Today, with the hunting bow widely recognized as an extremely efficient and humane sporting weapon, bowhunting is an increasingly popular outdoor pastime.

Bowhunting Basics

2

It's generally agreed that bowhunting is a specialized sport requiring special knowledge and equipment. Above all else, it is personally challenging. And when approached with the proper attitude and understanding, it can be immensely rewarding.

Keep in mind that ultimate bowhunting success should never be measured solely in terms of animals hanging from a camp's meat pole. While dead game—both trophy-class and meat animals—is a basic and honorable hunting goal, most serious bowhunters revel in the challenge of the hunt itself. The kill, if and when finally made, is often anticlimatic. What really counts is the personal satisfaction derived from pitting oneself against wild game while armed with one of man's oldest known weapons.

Successful Bowhunting is written to help the reader better understand and collect North American big game. Make no mistake about that. At the same time it must be realized that if killing animals is the foremost objective, there are long-range firearms available which make the task considerably easier.

As already noted, only about one bowhunter in 10 will tag his deer each year. Yet bowhunting popularity continues to grow in virtually all areas of the country. I, for one, am convinced the reasons are found in the sport's unique challenges and rewards.

Beginning bowhunters and those who may be frustrated after several fruitless seasons afield should realize there is no real shortcut to success.

Bowhunting is a sport which must be experienced season after season to be fully understood and appreciated.

No amount of money spent on equipment and clothing can make a person a bowhunter. As I've written in the past, there may be instant coffee but there's no such thing as an instant bowhunter. **Bowhunter** is a title that's earned, not bought.

Likewise, no amount of archery practice can adequately prepare a person for the pulse-pounding moment when the quarry stands well within effective shooting range. But proper practice and preparation are essential. Without them no bowhunter should attempt to hunt game. Until the bowhunter understands what his personal abilities are, what his equipment will or will not do and how game is to be hunted, he should not venture afield.

Shooting a Hunting Bow

Whatever your choice of bow—compound, recurve or longbow—the basics of drawing, anchoring, holding, releasing and following through remain essentially the same.

Without question, it's best to learn the fundamentals of shooting while practicing at short distances by releasing arrows at a stationary target. Repetitious practice develops a shooting style that prepares a shooter for bowhunting, where most targets are located at unknown distances—perhaps moving or standing at odd angles—and when the shot must be taken under less than ideal conditions.

Practice also familiarizes the shooter with his equipment and his own ability. Learning one's effective shooting range is important. If you learn to consistently place arrows in your target at 25 yards but cannot maintain your accuracy at 35 yards, never attempt shots beyond your ability. Animals are not paper targets where a miss or bad hit means nothing at all. All responsible bowhunters strive for quick, humane kills and avoid shots which could result in crippled game. The best insurance is accurate shooting within your effective shooting range.

Game animals have little appreciation for proper shooting form. In fact, at times it seems they do whatever possible to present only shots which put the bowhunter in an awkward or unorthodox shooting position. But regardless of whether you're kneeling, crouching, twisted half around, seated or standing, your shooting mechanics must remain the same. The mechanics are:

Draw length—Each arrow must be pulled to the same release point every time the bow is shot. Consistency counts. Unless the shooter takes full advantage of the bow's poundage and power at his normal draw length, consistent arrow flight is impossible.

Anchor point—This is the stopping point of the draw. Most often it's located on a shooter's face near the mouth, cheek or chin. A common anchor point is the corner of the mouth although some shooters prefer a higher anchor near the eye which allows them to sight down the shaft the way a shotgunner looks down the barrel of his 12 gauge. A consistent anchor point ensures the arrow is being drawn the same length as each shot is taken.

Holding—Pausing to aim before the instant of release is usually necessary for consistent accuracy, particularly if bow sights are used. The shooter, having reached full draw and having anchored solidly, concentrates on the target while aligning the proper sight pin or envisioning the arrow's line of flight. Some veteran bowhunters, especially those using recurve or longbows, have mastered "snap shooting." They release the arrow the instant their fingers touch their anchor point. Although this is not

Practice in hunting garb, under conditions likely to be encountered in the field, will help a bowhunter learn his capabilities.

recommended for beginners, it's noteworthy that consistent repetition of what many consider to be a shooting flaw enables some snap shooters to be remarkably accurate.

Releasing—Prior to releasing the arrow, the shooter maintains two points of contact on the bow—the handle and the bowstring. As the shooting fingers relax, the only pressure point is where the palm of the bow hand touches the bow. Unless the bowstring is released and the bow held—never gripped tightly—consistently shot after shot, accuracy is difficult to achieve. Ideally, when the moment is right for the shot to be made, a slight relaxation of the fingers allows the bowstring to be pulled free by the energy stored in the bow's limbs or wheels and cables. Jerking or pulling the shooting hand away at the instant of release can destroy accuracy.

Following through—Until the arrow clears the bow, it's vital for a shooter to follow the same basic mechanics or suffer the consequences of poor shooting techniques. Even as the shaft speeds to its target, shooters should try to maintain the same physical position as at the moment of release. Ideally, only after the arrow has hit should the shooter drop or lower his bow arm. And more often than not, if the tenets of good shooting form are adhered to, the shooter will be wearing a smile each time he recalls the flight of a well-aimed arrow.

Learning To Bowhunt

After conquering the techniques of shooting the hunting bow, consider yourself fortunate if you have an experienced friend who can assist you in learning to bowhunt. Having someone to hunt with, to answer your questions and to teach you proper techniques is generally the ideal situation. But even without the benefit of an individual teacher, a person can master the fundamentals if he is serious and willing to shoulder the responsibility himself.

One excellent starting point is reading books like this and magazines like **Bowhunter**. Reading is no substitute for hands-on experience but nonetheless it provides a solid base of information and understanding.

Another excellent program for beginning bowhunters is the standardized six-hour course developed by the International Bowhunter Education Foundation. Now offered across the

Jim Crumley of Trebark Camouflage Co. is one of the hundreds of manufacturers to attend clinics for bowhunters. Anderson Archery Corp. hosts one of the nation's largest clinics each June.

United States and in several foreign countries, the course teaches bowhunting fundamentals and responsibilities. It is designed to help participants become better, safer bowhunters in a minimum amount of time.

Bowhunting clinics—sponsored by national organizations such as the National Rifle Association and myriad state and local sportsmen's groups and retail dealers—are an increasingly popular phenomenon. Such clinics are dedicated to reaching and educating thousands of American hunters and to introducing the very latest in bowhunting equipment and lore. Here experienced professionals conduct educational seminars, answer questions and help those in attendance get off on the right track toward becoming better, safer, more ethical and more responsible bowhunters.

Many areas of the country have active, well organized bowhunting clubs which offer instructional bowhunting seminars and seasonal shooting competitions. Most clubs feature outdoor ranges and many host regular "bowhunting shoots" at paper, silhouette or 3-D animal targets set up in hunting terrain with shots taken at unknown distances. These shoots may prove to be a beneficial form of pre-season or off-season practice. In addition, such clubs are often ideal spots for making the acquaintance of veteran bowhunters who can provide firsthand advice on equipment, shooting and hunting techniques.

Regardless, ultimate dedication and involvement depends on the individual. A serious-minded bowhunter will continually learn from the information found in the latest books and magazine articles and his own preparatory experiences. Regular practice provides not only physical conditioning but a growing knowledge about and self confidence in his equipment and his own shooting ability. Reading gives details about various species of game, hunting methods and game law regulations. Actual hunting experiences—small game, varmints, roughfish bowhunts—make excellent practice for future big game hunts.

I, for one, am convinced that bowhunting is at least 90 percent mental and 10 percent physical.

Finding suitable sites for tree stands should be done well in advance of opening day during pre-season scouting trips.

Once the basics of shooting are mastered, the hunting itself becomes a test of man's mental faculties versus the animals' survival instincts.

A thorough knowledge of the game and hunting area are often prerequisites to consistent success. Pre- and post-season scouting trips will acquaint a hunter with his territory and help him locate new hunting areas while pinpointing game movements and concentrations. Where necessary, permission to hunt is obtained from landowners. Stand sites will be located and necessary licenses and permits will be obtained well in advance of opening day. Consequently, when the bowhunter finally goes afield, he is committed, confident and well-prepared. He is ready to bowhunt.

Understanding Big Game

Although the section containing information about the big game animals offers detailed information regarding the various species, some general comments are appropriate at this point.

Many big game animals depend on their nose, their ears and their eyesight—in that exact order—to detect potential or imminent danger. Keep the following thoughts in mind as you plan your hunt:

* Human odor—when encountered by an animal at close range—is often very alarming. Immediate alertness, overt nervousness and outright panic are typical reactions.

* Unnatural woodland sounds such as the human voice or metallic noises are sure to draw the immediate attention of game. Even the raspy sound of an arrow being drawn into shooting position, the slight creaking of a tree stand or an unseen stick cracking underfoot can tip your hand at a critical moment. All such sounds can spook game.

* Movement is readily detected. A hand brushing away a pesky insect, a head turning quickly, a bow being raised and drawn—all may attract an animal's attention. Even if the animal does not immediately run, more often than not it will be alerted to a hunter's presence. This makes getting off a good shot extremely difficult.

Because a bowhunter should be close to his target to obtain the most effective results, he must

Whitetails—America's most popular big game animal—are quick to detect odors, sounds and movements. Avoiding detection is a must.

continually guard against detection. Common sense combined with a few pre-hunt precautions can benefit you greatly. General advice and specific tips on avoiding detection are detailed in the following "Hunting Methods" section and elsewhere in this book.

Hunting Methods

The bowhunter, like any other hunter, has several basic methods of pursuing game. The three best options include hunting from tree stands, hunting from ground blinds and still-hunting/stalking.

Whichever method you choose, depending on the game and the situation, keep in mind that bowhunters should carefully select appropriate clothing and footwear. Soft, quiet, camouflaged or drab-colored clothes are ideal. Noisy, stiff or bulky outerwear should be avoided; it can alert game or interfere with your accuracy by snagging the bowstring as the shot is attempted. If weather permits, some bowhunters who choose to quietly still-hunt their game favor flexible lightweight boots, jogging shoes or even moccasins. Conversely, heavy insulated boots—too noisy for stalking—might be the choice of a cold weather bowhunter who spends long, stationary hours on stand waiting for his quarry to appear. Dress according to the weather and hunting techniques you choose.

Remember, special attention should be paid to camouflaging the exposed skin of a bowhunter's face and hands. Gloves, camo headnets, facemasks and special camouflage creams for the face and hands are available and quite effective. Eyeglasses, jewelry—anything that may reflect light—should be masked, covered or suitably camouflaged if possible. The same is true of hunting bows and other accessories.

Scent camouflage is another consideration. Preventative measures and commercial products designed to neutralize or cover human scent may be beneficial; however, cleanliness (clothing as well as body) often pays big dividends for the bowhunter who watches the wind direction and exercises good judgment.

A fully camouflaged bowhunter, hunting from an elevated stand, has the best chance of getting an up-close shot at deer.

When hunting, never carry car keys, loose change or other metallic items that could make noise and alert nearby game. Likewise be aware that a slamming car door, a sloshing half-empty canteen, a squeaky boot, rustling clothing, an arrow hitting against the bow's riser or another shaft—any unusual noise—can tip off game to your presence. And never forget that the sound of the human voice will often alarm game even at great distances. If you must talk to a partner or another hunter in the field, never speak above a whisper.

Tree Stand Hunting

Bowhunting from elevated positions on tree limbs or stands is undoubtedly the most effective and productive method of harvesting deer in many areas of the country. It should be noted that other big game species may be successfully hunted from elevated stands as well. The basic advantages of this method include the following:

* A bowhunter in a tree generally has a greater field of vision; approaching game is often easier to detect.

* Telltale human scent is maintained or dissipated at a level well above the ground where keen-nosed game may normally detect human presence. Regardless, stands should be situated so prevailing winds will carry a hunter's scent away from the game trail or feeding area.

* Most game animals, unless hunting pressure is heavy, do not expect danger from above and frequently are vulnerable to this hunting method.

* Movements and sounds which may be made in preparing for the shot are usually minimal and go unnoticed; the chances of alerting game are slim.

* If undetected, the bowhunter in a tree frequently has the luxury of selecting the best possible shot offered by the animal.

Of course, you should realize that certain disadvantages do exist. Selecting the proper tree, positioning the stand at the best height and angle and finding or creating adequate shooting lanes may be a puzzle or challenge to the beginner. In addition, some bowhunters simply are not cut out for the sit-and-wait method where patience and confidence in their location are necessary ingredients for success. Finally, there is the possible danger of a fall. Safety belts or lines should always be used by tree stand hunters. Also, special care should be taken when climbing in and out of the stand, especially in cold or wet weather.

If you plan to hunt from a tree, practice shooting from elevated positions—preferably from the tree stand itself—before the actual hunt. Many bowhunters in trees tend to shoot high. Generally this is caused by subtle changes in shooting form—including lowering of the bow arm—and one remedy is to take pains to maintain proper form. This is simple if the bowhunter bends at the waist instead of trying to shoot down while standing erect. Despite what some may claim, gravity has little effect on arrows shot at downward angles at short-range targets.

Whenever possible, use suitable tree limbs or portable stands. Permanent tree stands are illegal in some areas and are eyesores everywhere. Nails can and do damage trees. Never erect any stand without the landowner's permission and without first checking the laws in your hunting area. When creating shooting lanes, keep all trimming of leaves and twigs or small limbs to an absolute minimum. Do this well in advance of the season, if possible, and remove all trimmings. Screw-in or strap-on tree steps or blocks are ideal for getting up and down the tree. Never climb when carrying your bow; use a cord for raising and lowering equipment and hunting tackle. The reminder we continuously print in **Bowhunter** is worth remembering: "Bowhunting safety is no accident."

Locate your tree stand near the junction of two or more well-tracked game trails. Stands located overlooking feeding or watering areas may also be effective. Try to select a tree large enough to break the human silhouette. Also, be aware of the background and avoid being sky-lined or silhouetted against the sky where you're likely to be readily noticed by approaching game.

Always approach and enter your stand as quietly as possible to avoid alerting nearby game. Pay attention to where you step and don't walk where human scent might alert approaching animals. Never relieve yourself in the vicinity of your stand. A glass jar or plastic container with a screw-on lid can be used during long waits in the stand.

The height of effective tree stands varies greatly, from a low of six to eight feet to a high of 18 to 20 feet or more. The average is probably found somewhere between these two extremes; however, what's right for you will depend on several factors including the terrain, surroundings, prevailing winds, and species of game being hunted. Obviously, tree stand hunting may be successfully combined with baiting (if legal) and calling or attracting game by the use of scents or calls. You may want to investigate and try the various options. More information is offered in the sections dealing with effective bowhunting techniques for the various species.

Ground Blind Hunting

Ground-level blinds—even pit blinds constructed partially below ground—are generally considered to be another effective means of bowhunting for many big game species. The idea here is to locate your blind and conceal yourself near game trails or feeding areas where you expect game to pass or gather.

You must realize that wind direction is of paramount importance to the bowhunter using a ground blind. Because your scent is on the same level as your quarry, it may be easily detected. Also, most big game animals expect predators to attack from ground level. This means that they will be especially alert to any unusual movements, sounds or odors which could spell potential danger. Always keep noise and motion to an absolute minimum. This advice also holds true for entering and exiting ground blinds.

Be alert for natural blinds. Boulders, blowdowns, stumps—anything that will break the hunter's

Natural blinds in brush, rocks or deadfalls make ideal stand locations. Camouflage is essential and movements must be minimal.

telltale silhouette—are often ideal places to take a stand. Any blinds constructed of natural materials should be erected well ahead of the hunting season so game animals may become accustomed to these structures. When hunting private land, always obtain permission to construct a blind and keep all cutting and trimming to a minimum. Disturb the surroundings as little as possible. Animals quickly notice changes in their home areas.

A roll of lightweight camouflage netting, small enough to be carried in pocket or pouch, can be ideal for concealment. Strung between trees or hung over branches, the netting helps create an instant blind wherever an ideal location is found. There are also small, portable blinds being manufactured that come with framework, shooting windows and even ceilings. Such structures are more expensive than the camo netting. It's always a good idea to check out the legality of such netting or blinds before making the purchase.

Generally, shooting lanes will be limited with only certain shots available to any bowhunter in a well-concealed ground blind. Consequently, you may not have the luxury of time in choosing the best possible shot. Visibility may also be limited.

Since long periods of waiting for game to appear are more often the rule rather than the exception, comfort is essential. Standing, crouching and kneeling can be tiring. A stool, log or similar seat may be used; however, bowhunters using this method should practice shooting while seated. Camouflage is vital. Since you are eye-level with your quarry, keep all movements slow and deliberate. Jack-in-the-box, jump up and shoot tactics rarely work for bowhunters.

Pit blinds which are actually located below ground level can be very effective. The major problem is finding a natural depression in a perfect location or in digging a suitable pit. Besides being hard work, digging the pit blind limits the bowhunter to a limited area. Care must be taken to scatter or conceal the dirt from the excavation and, whenever possible, the pits should be dug well in advance of the opening day of the hunting season. They must be roomy enough to allow the hunter to draw and shoot his bow from a sitting or kneeling position. Most pit blinds are ringed with brush, weeds or other natural materials which help camouflage the ambush site.

Still-hunting/Stalking

Still-hunting and stalking game is widely regarded as the most challenging method of hunting with the bow and arrow. It may well be the most rewarding as well.

A still-hunter moves through his hunting area very slowly and silently, doing at least two to three times as much looking and standing as walking. The idea here is to hunt into the wind and to spot your quarry before it sees you. When game is sighted the still-hunter usually attempts to intercept or to stalk closer to the animal, closing the distance and getting

Any bowhunter who is able to consistently tag big game taken by stalking has to be regarded as an exceptional hunter.

into position for a good shot. Knowledge of the hunting area is essential.

Unlike the hunter who chooses to wait for the animal to approach his selected shooting area near a ground blind or tree stand, the still-hunter must move to the animal and remain undetected. With most big game species, this is no easy task. Not only must you keep tabs on the breeze, you must remain unseen and unheard—often by several sets of eyes and ears—as you work into position for the ideal shot. On rare occasions you may encounter an animal feeding or walking in your direction. In such cases it's best to stay put and take the shot as the animal passes within good bow range. Remember, any time you can see the animal's eyes, it can see you if you draw attention to yourself by moving or making noise.

Good camouflage is a must. All movements should be made in slow motion and you must remain motionless while the animal is looking in your direction. Avoid dry leaves and dead sticks underfoot and be alert for sudden shifts in wind direction. Still-hunting is undoubtedly the least productive of the three basic bowhunting methods. Regardless, when an animal is taken by the stalking bowhunter it is usually a well-earned, well-deserved trophy.

Other Hunting Methods

Driving game—a method where groups or lines of hunters attempt to push animals past waiting hunters at predetermined locations—is a workable but generally poor bowhunting method. Frequently the game is alarmed and offers only a running shot which could result in a miss or—far worse—a bad hit and a wounded, unrecovered animal.

Road hunting—driving or riding motor vehicles slowly along rural or remote roadways and trails in hopes of spotting and shooting at game—is generally illegal and always unethical. Never use any motorized vehicle to approach, herd or harass game animals. Never attempt to shoot while standing in or on a motor vehicle.

Bowhunting game from canoes or other types of

boats, where legal, is an effective way to hunt certain big game species. Typically, boats are used by bowhunters as a means of transportation to remote areas, islands or for bowfishing expeditions. But floating or paddling silently along inland waterways can be a viable bowhunting method.

Horseback hunting is another option and pack-in trips are common in some Western states and on hunts for certain species. Horses are used to carry bowhunters and camping gear into backcountry hunting areas. Occasionally bowhunters will ride until game is sighted, then dismount and attempt to stalk within good bow range.

Backpack bowhunting has gained popularity in recent years. Carrying his camp, food and hunting tackle, the bowhunter hikes into remote hunting areas in search of game. Once the animals are located, he usually employs still-hunting/stalking techniques or hunts from natural blinds.

Remember, learning to bowhunt takes time and dedication. Proper preparation is the key.

Knowledge of your equipment and its limitations are essential. You must also know yourself and your personal abilities. Reading books and articles will help as will obtaining firsthand advice from experienced bowhunters and by attending Bowhunter Education clinics. Practice under simulated hunting conditions and scout your hunting areas—if possible—well ahead of opening day. Avoid taking any shot beyond your effective shooting range. Keep in mind it is your responsibility as a bowhunter to track and recover all wounded game.

The thoroughly prepared bowhunter who looks on each trip afield as a learning experience as well as an adventure is already well along the road to bowhunting success.

Bows, Arrows and Broadheads

3

"What bow do you shoot? What arrow? What's your favorite hunting head?"

These are common questions wherever bowhunters gather to swap stories, compare notes and exchange ideas about everything from the latest equipment to sure-fire techniques for taking a big game trophy. I, for one, am always glad to provide information and voice an opinion about my own bowhunting gear. Fact of the matter is I'm downright flattered when someone asks what tackle I use and why, or asks for my assistance and advice in helping them select a good bow, shaft or broadhead.

At the same time I feel obligated to remind the questioner that bowhunting is a highly personal sport. What works for one won't necessarily work well for another hunter. It's fine to get advice but the final decision should be based on what's right for the person buying and using the bowhunting tackle. With this thought in mind, let's take a brief look at what's available.

Hunting Bows

A good hunting bow can represent a lifetime investment and therefore should be selected only after careful consideration. Over the course of several seasons—and countless practice sessions—a hunting bow becomes an important extension of any shooter. In the long run your own success or failure as a bowhunter will depend largely on the bow you use and the confidence you have each time you release an arrow.

Over the past two decades, I've shot a representative sampling of just about every model and type of bow to come on the scene. I soon learned most bows are only as good as the person using them. A good bowhunter will take game regardless of the bow he or she carries afield. The quest for the perfect bow that will transform anyone into a "super hunter" is doomed to failure from the outset. No such bow exists. You may as well search for the Fountain of Youth or the Holy Grail. Your chances of success are about equal.

Regardless, be warned that some people would have you believe there's really nothing to selecting a hunting bow—you find one you like the looks and feel of and you buy it. I'm always surprised how many people—especially novice bowhunters—accept such advice without question. I'm also surprised at how many people buy a bow simply because some noted bowhunter—or some buddy—shoots the same model. Such haphazard selection may on occasion result in a satisfied shooter; however, I encourage you to avoid reaching for your wallet until you've found a bow that satisfies you.

Shop around. Visit dealers. Read available literature. Talk to bow owners. Keep your eyes and ears open—while maintaining an open mind—and try to remain as objective as possible. Above all, don't rush your purchase.

Basically, you'll be deciding on one of three types of hunting bow—the straight-ended longbow, the recurve or the compound. Both longbows and recurves have been around in various forms for centuries; however, the compound is a recent technological discovery which today ranks as the unquestioned sales leader of the bow marketplace. But even if a compound bow is your preference and final choice, it's wise to check out the advantages and disadvantages of all three types. The best place to begin is at the nearest qualified archery dealer or pro shop.

I don't think any beginner should ever buy a bow sight unseen. The risk of disappointment is simply too great. At the same time it's dangerous to trust the judgment of some sales clerk who knows little or nothing about bowhunting or the equipment used in the sport. You can get burned. Badly. To get what you want—what you really need—it's best to deal with people who speak the language and can provide sound, helpful advice. Find a qualified dealer. Ask your questions. Express your goals. Listen objectively, sorting out fact from opinion and prejudices. Then decide for yourself.

On several past occasions I've written that buying a hunting bow is a lot like buying an automobile. I still believe it. There are many models available—from economy types to the expensive luxury models—and the problem is finding one which suits your needs, wants and budget.

Generally speaking, you can expect to pay between $100 and $300 or more for a hunting bow. If you add sights, a quiver, camouflaging, string silencers, a spare bowstring and other accessories, expect to fork over more money.

The stick bows—longbows and recurves—were extremely popular in the early years of our sport, the years I call B.C. (Before Compounds). Simple yet efficient and deadly in the hands of a competent bowhunter, these weapons accounted for a batch of game. From the old hand-made bows of lemonwood and osage orange to the mass-produced fiberglass and laminated wood bows of today, stick bows enjoyed tremendous popularity. Today some bowhunters favor these hunting bows and in recent years there has been an obvious resurgence in their popularity. Some feel this is a backlash against the seemingly endless technological advancements in

G. Fred Asbell is one veteran bowhunter who prefers the recurve. His company, Bighorn Bowhunting Co., makes the Bighorn recurve.

modern bowhunting. Others believe it is simply an increased awareness of what many veteran bowhunters have known all along: **Stick bows are uncomplicated, highly effective hunting tools**. Any beginner or bowhunter unfamiliar with stick bows should take a close look at the recurve and longbow, shoot them if possible and compare their performance to the compound. It's guaranteed to be a real eye-opener for many.

Time was when a bowhunter's choice was somewhat limited when it came to purchasing a compound. Those of us who have been around the sport for quite a spell can recall the days when only two companies—Allen and Jennings—manufactured those "strange looking, newfangled compounds." And although some bowyers and archers felt the ugly "confounded mechanical contraptions" were only a passing fad, it wasn't long before every major bow manufacturer was climbing on the compound bow bandwagon. Check out any current archery catalog or national publication and you'll see more compounds pictured and advertised than any other bow.

With the advent of the compound bow in the late

1960s came considerable criticism and many unfounded advertising claims. Diehard recurve and longbow shooters felt the compound just might lead to the ruination of the sport. Many devotees of the stick and string school said no true bow had cables, pulleys and wheels. A few unjustly claimed that shooting a compound bow was like shooting a crossbow. Overzealous advertisers, anxious to cash in on the compound craze, announced heretofore unheard of arrow speeds and claimed their compounds would shoot twice as fast as a recurve bow of the same draw weight. Most of this copywriting hype was pure baloney.

The fact is, despite what critics and promoters would have people believe, the compound is simply a modern bow with inherent advantages and disadvantages. It is no super weapon; it does represent a modernization of the bowmaker's art.

Early compound bows had two major factors going against them, their looks and mass weight. Even today, despite production improvements and refinements, some think of compounds as ugly, aesthetic atrocities. They're also heavier than stick bows. This latter fact may serve the shooter somewhat insofar as additional stability is concerned; however, a long day afield toting a compound is often an exercise in endurance compared to the much lighter recurve or longbow.

On the other hand, there's no question in my mind that a compound bow is easier to draw, hold and shoot than any other type of bow. This is due to the bow's unique relaxation or let-off factor in the draw. As a compound user pulls the bow string toward the anchor point, peak force is reached approximately mid-way through the draw. The bow then "relaxes" to a much lesser draw weight at the shooter's anchor point, thanks to the compound's complex system of wheels and cables. Many of today's compounds will relax as much as 50% of draw weight. Simply put, this means a bowhunter shooting a 60 pound compound may be holding only about 30 pounds at full draw.

To the bowhunter who normally shoots a heavier pulling bow than his target-punching counterpart, this let-off factor is a definite plus. Often a hunter

will draw down on an animal only to have the potential trophy stop one step short of offering a clear shot. It's much easier to hold a compound at full draw than either a recurve or longbow of comparable draw weight. To me and many other veteran bowhunters, this is the biggest advantage the compound has to offer.

One major disadvantage is the unwieldly nature of the compound. Any bowhunter who has made a backpack hunt or pack-in trip on horseback can attest to the fact a compound user faces many more problems than, for example, the stick bow enthusiast toting a take-down recurve or longbow. If you do much backwoods or wilderness bowhunting, the portability factor should be considered before you reach a final purchase decision.

The beginner should take a long look at the various types of compounds offered and shoot as many different brands as possible. There are relatively simple two-wheel models and complex multi-wheel models offered. There are compounds that are easy to tune and others that require constant attention to remain shootable. There are compounds with circular pulleys and others with programmed, odd-shaped elliptical wheels called "cams" by today's shooters. These so-called "cam bows" are generally regarded as faster-shooting compounds (many are noisier, too). There are even bows which look like a cross between compounds and recurves. Space limitations will not allow an in-depth report of technical data here. Besides, reading about the different types of bows is not the same as shooting them, handling them, comparing them first hand. And that's where you come in. You must make the final decision regarding which bow you'll buy. And if you're like most bowhunters, you'll want a well-built, reasonably fast hunting bow that's a pleasure to handle and to shoot. Again, the final judgment is yours.

What about the subject of arrow speed? Are compounds twice as fast as recurves or longbows in delivering the arrow? As previously noted, most claims are figments of some copywriter's imagination or the results of rigged tests wherein

All of the author's hunting bows—compounds and stick bows alike—are in the 60-75 pound range. He feels that's enough for North American big game.

light target arrows were shot out of heavy hunting bows to achieve super speeds. Personal testing of a number of compound and cam bows gives these bows a slight edge in speed over recurves and straight-ended bows; however, in most cases the difference is not all that significant. And make no mistake about it, there are longbows and recurves that will outshoot compound bows of comparable weight when the same arrow is used.

Speed, of course, can be important to a bowhunter aiming at game with lightning-like reflexes. But we should keep in mind that most bowhunting shots are taken at close range—30 yards or less—which boils down to something under 90 feet, less than the difference between home plate and first base on a baseball diamond. Is it really significant that at such ranges one bow delivers the broadhead-tipped hunting arrow at 204 feet per second while another bow shoots the same arrow at "only" 192 fps? Think about it.

Personally, I prefer a fast, flat-shooting bow. But "fast" is relative. Any experienced shooter can tell whether a bow is fast-shooting or not without needing a chronograph to register arrow speed. Too many people get needlessly concerned over arrow speed. I'm far more concerned with a bow's feel and performance as I shoot than with its exact arrow velocity.

Most knowledgeable bowhunters will agree that a hunting bow should have a pull of at least 50 pounds. With practice, slightly built women and youngsters can learn to handle a compound bow of this draw weight. All it takes is time, determination and dedication. The compound's big advantage is the shooter will be holding much less poundage once the bow relaxes. Stick bows of the same minimum draw weight will probably require more time and effort to master but some shooters feel it's worth the extra effort. That's a decision only you can make.

I personally believe that compound bows with adjustable draw weights are ideal for the beginner. As an example, a bow capable of being adjusted to any desired weight between 50 and 65 to 70 pounds makes an ideal hunting/training weapon. Most men can quickly learn to shoot a 50 to 55 pound bow with ease (the national average for a hunting bow is said to be just under 60 pounds) and, as his proficiency increases, he will probably want to "crank up" the bow's weight somewhat. He can do so with the adjustable compound simply by making a few turns of an Allen wrench rather than going out and buying a new bow of heavier poundage.

Speaking of heavier bows, there are some hairy chested bowhunters who go around proclaiming that they shoot only "man-size hunting tackle"— bows pulling 80, 90, even 100 pounds or more. A few of these macho types look down their noses at using less than super-heavy gear. Should you bump into any of these he-man hunters, keep the following points in mind: All of my hunting bows—compounds and stick bows alike—are in the 60 to 75 pound range. I've owned and shot heavier tackle but I've always gone back to the bows I'm most comfortable with. Personally, there's not one animal on the North American continent—from brown bears to bison, moose to mountain lion—that I'd be worried about hunting with my 60 to 70 pound bows. And trust me when I say there are far more bowhunters around—from Fred Bear professionals to Joe Average—who feel as I do than the handful of hunters who claim only quiche-eaters use normal weight hunting bows. So don't overbow yourself.

By all means, shoot the bow you intend to buy. Few people buy a car without a test drive and, generally speaking, bows for hunting are a much more personal buy than the family automobile. So ask the dealer to allow you to try out the bow on the shooting range. If he refuses your request, you have two options. Either find another dealer who will comply or find the same model bow (borrow one from a friend or an understanding bowhunter at the local range) and try it for yourself. Regardless, it's always wise to personally test the bow you're thinking about buying.

Finally, you might just want to check out the bow's warranty. Most bows come with a limited warranty which protects the buyer against defects in materials or workmanship. Your dealer can answer questions and assist you in completing the warranty form at the time of purchase.

If you've exercised some common sense judgment and done your homework—and legwork—well, you can rest assured your bow is the one you want with all the characteristics that satisfy you. You will be making a purchase from a dealer you can trust. Your bow will be a name brand weapon, perhaps even custom made, guaranteed and worth the price tag it carries. And with these assurances, you can head home confident that your final choice in a hunting bow has been the right one. Find the bow— longbow, recurve or compound—that you like best and buy it. That's the bow that's best for you.

Hunting Arrows

If you want to be a successful bowhunter, you'll use arrows matched to your hunting bow and to you. Selecting a good bow is important, but using proper arrows is an absolute must.

At one time hunting archers used wood arrows because that's all that was available. This, of course, is no longer true. Modern hunting arrows come in a variety of materials—fiberglass/graphite composites, aluminum alloy and wood. Each has good and bad points worth mentioning.

Mass-produced wood shafts are often the least expensive (a fact especially appealing to the beginner or bowhunter on a limited budget) but they can and do warp if not stored properly and they are not overly durable. Glass and graphite fiber shafts are long-lasting, rugged arrows but tend to be heavier than other types. Graphite shafts are light but expensive, and composite shafts made of glass and graphite solve the weight/cost production factor. Finally, aluminum arrows are unmatched for accuracy but generally cannot take the in-the-field abuse of glass or graphite shafts. Usually the better grades are more expensive, too.

Whatever your choice of arrow material, the arrows must be matched to you and your hunting bow. Many dealers have a measuring arrow (an extra-long shaft marked in inches) which you draw and hold to determine what length arrows you require. If no measuring arrow is handy, find a yardstick. Place one end against your chest about where your second shirt button is located and extend both arms, holding the opposite end of the yardstick between your palms. Your draw length is measured at your fingertips.

To get good groups with broadheads, arrows must be matched to hunter's bow and draw. Practice at 3-D game targets is a good idea.

Note: Most hunting arrows are cut one-half to one full inch longer than your draw length to accommodate the hunting head.

Next, find arrows matched to the weight of your hunting bow. Arrow spine (stiffness) is critical for accurate shooting. For example, arrows spined to be shot from a 50 pound bow may wobble or fishtail in flight if shot from a 60 pound bow. Also, equipment may be damaged by shooting arrows spined for a lighter draw weight than is recommended for your bow. It can be dangerous to the shooter, too.

Most arrow manufacturers have charts which help with proper shaft selection. These charts list various bow weights and draw lengths plus suggested shaft sizes. Most dealers have them or you can order them directly from manufacturers. **Note**: More than one size shaft may shoot well from your hunting bow.

Some hunters want a lighter arrow for flatter trajectory while others prefer heavier shafts for greater durability and penetration.

Once you know what arrow is right for your shooting style and hunting bow, you may order correct shafts from a dealer or manufacturer. Later you may even wish to make your own hunting arrows. But at the outset it's generally best to rely on your nearest dealer or pro shop.

Most arrows come with three feathers or plastic vanes, two of the same color and one odd-colored vane or dyed turkey feather. The odd-colored feather is called the cock feather and always points to the shooter's fingertips when properly nocked. Generally, the feathers or vanes are mounted on the shaft at a slight angle which causes the arrow to rotate in flight and maintain a straight course to the target. This is called helical fletching. Some bowhunters prefer four-fletch arrows for greater stability (little if any arrow speed is sacrificed by using four feathers or plastic vanes rather than three). Mostly it's a matter of personal preference.

Plastic fletching is very popular among wet weather hunters even though vanes reportedly cause slightly more air drag when shot than turkey feathers. Bowhunters who prefer feathers often apply various waterproofing compounds to their fletching before venturing afield. Again, the choice is often based on personal likes or dislikes. The same thing is true of colors of the fletching itself. Some bowhunters use and like light-colored fletching because it's easier to follow the flight of the arrow and to determine the hit. On the other hand some hunters want total camouflage and use only drab-hued colors.

Speaking of camouflage, most arrows may be purchased in various colors. Bowhunters tend to use dark or drab-colored shafts and avoid bright or shiny arrows which could alert keen-eyed game.

Hunting Heads

No discussion of hunting bows and arrows would be complete without an examination of the business end of the arrow—the broadhead. In truth, there are many excellent designs and brands available although broadheads generally come in one of two basic designs—fixed-blade heads and replaceable blade heads.

Both types typically come with from two to four cutting edges although some five- and six-bladed broadheads have been and are still being used by a few bowhunters who believe "more is better." Some heads are lightweight and fragile-appearing while others are heavy, sturdy and extremely durable. But all good hunting heads—no matter what the hunter's ultimate and personal choice—share a common characteristic. **They are all razor-sharp**.

To do its job, a broadhead must penetrate hair, hide and tissue. It must also create massive hemorrhage. No bowhunter should ever shoot a hunting arrow at any game animal unless the broadhead is honed to a shaving edge. Because arrows kill by hemorrhage, very few animals hit with an arrow drop on the spot (brain and spine shots are exceptions). Most run off and die on their feet or in nearby beds. A bowhunter seldom has the good fortune to see the animal go down within sight. This often means a tracking job and a good bloodtrail is the

answer to a bowhunter's prayers. A razor-sharp head is the best insurance of massive hemorrhage and a quick, humane death.

To help understand the basic broadhead types and their individual features, let's look at half a dozen popular heads beginning with three fixed-blade models.

Bear Super Razorhead: At one time the Bear Razorhead had undoubtedly accounted for more big game than any other broadhead made. Even today the Super Razorhead remains a popular choice among bowhunters who like its design and easy-to-sharpen stainless steel primary blade. The main blade features two cutting edges. Additionally, a small, replaceable auxiliary "bleeder blade" fits into a slotted ferrule for additional cutting capability. The chisel point is rounded for additional strength and the end result is a solid, well-flying head. The cutting width is one and two-eighth inches and the weight is 125 grains.

Zwickey Black Diamonds: Long a favorite of many serious bowhunters, the Black Diamond broadheads—both the Delta and the Eskimo—are spot welded to the tip for extra strength. No separate

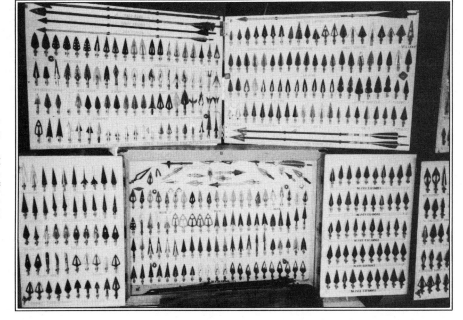

There have been hundreds of hunting heads produced over the years. Some bowhunters collect broadheads. This display is a small part of the collection of Michigan bowhunter, Floyd Eccleston.

inserts are required since the four-blade models are stamped from the existing steel of the main blade. The Deltas are available in both two- and four-blade models with a cutting width of one and three-eighths inches and a weight of 125 grains. The slightly smaller Eskimos come in both two- and four-blade models and weight choices of either 125 or 110 grains. Deltas are favored by those using heavier pulling bows. Although somewhat more difficult to sharpen than the Razorhead, the Black Diamonds seemingly hold a razor edge longer and fly accurately with either vanes or feathers on the shaft.

Rothhaar Snuffer: Perhaps the best three-blade broadhead available, the Snuffer is copper-welded for extreme strength and features a design that allows sharpening two blades at a time. Bigger and heavier than most broadheads, it is meant to be shot by serious bowhunters from heavier hunting-weight bows. Its cutting width is one and one-fourth inches and the weight is 145 grains.

All of these heads—and other brands requiring sharpening by hunters before use—should never be used for hunting until all cutting edges are honed shaving sharp. Even the Bear Super Razorhead which comes "factory sharpened" needs some

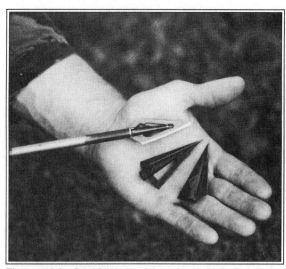

Three poplular fixed-blade heads are (from left) the Bear Super Razorhead, the Rothhaar Snuffer and the Zwickey Black Diamond Delta.

attention.

Note: Once a head is shot — whether at game or in practice — it must be resharpened before being used for hunting. **Never**, under any circumstances, shoot an unsharpened broadhead at game.

There are many broadhead files, stones and sharpeners on the market. Some bowhunters, especially many who favor the fixed-blade heads, consider the sharpening ritual as an important part of their pre-hunt preparation. Others who have difficulty using a stone and file to produce a razor edge may favor the broadheads with replaceable blades.

Anderson 245 Magnum: Probably the most expensive replaceable-blade broadhead available, this quality four-blade head has heavy stainless steel blades (.027) yet weighs only 125 grains. Its cutting width of one and one-half inches creates a huge wound. Like most such heads, it has a tip of tool steel that must penetrate up to one-half inch before cutting action begins. A 243 Mini Magnum—a slightly smaller version of the 245—is offered along with two three-blade models.

Rocky Mountain Supreme: This is another big broadhead for bowhunters who favor heavy tackle. The four-blade model weighs 160 grains and like

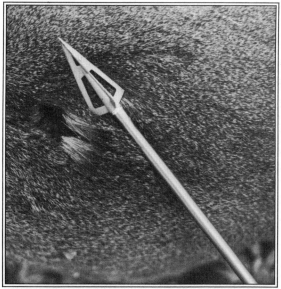

Long a favorite of the author, the Snuffer is a big, deadly three-blade broadhead that can put down game in a hurry.

the Anderson 245 has a cutting width of one and one-half inches. A three-blade version weighs 150 grains. The stainless steel blades are .020 inches thick and vented for good arrow flight. Regular Rocky Mountain broadheads are also offered in three- and four-blade designs in weights of 130 and 140 grains.

Thunderhead 125: Here's a three-blade broadhead featuring .027 thick presharpened blades behind a hardened, high carbon steel point. Weight is 125 grains and the cutting width is one and one-eighth inches. The Thunderhead is manufactured by New Archery Products, the same company which produces the popular and efficient Razorbak four- and five-bladed broadheads. And for bowhunters wanting larger broadheads, there is the two-blade Thunderhead 150 and the three-blade Thunderhead 160. Each has a cutting diameter of one and three-eighths inches.

Two other replaceable-blade broadheads are worthy of mention. One is the Satellite-2, a four-blade broadhead composed of a heavy primary blade (.036) which is sharpened to the point to assure instant cutting action. The smaller insert blades are standard Satellite blades. But unlike other Satellite and most other replaceable-blade broadheads, its

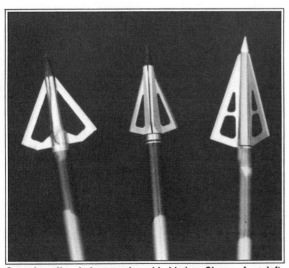

Some broadheads have replaceable blades. Shown, from left, are the Anderson 245 Magnum, the Thunderhead 125 and Rocky Mountain Supreme.

sharpened tip design must be considered an advantage. The second is the Blazer from Bohning Co., Ltd. Its strengthened, high carbon and stainless steel blade construction is a plus and the blade design also allows the head to begin cutting on contact. This four-blade head weighs 140 grains and, like the Satellite-2, is worth a close look from those wanting a different kind of replaceable-blade head.

Note: At the time of this writing Bohning is planning the unveiling of the first Teflon™ impregnated broadhead, a head whose design and material is intended to facilitate penetration. Called the Blazer Max, it has heavy (.032) blades and weighs 165 grains.

Think about this. The tips of most replaceable-blade heads are pointed but have non-sharpened steel tips which must push through hair and skin before the razor-sharp blades can begin to do their job. It's logical to assume that this "punching" action affects penetration to some degree due to the friction caused by the non-cutting tip. For this reason some veteran bowhunters discourage the use of such broadheads on heavy-haired or thick-skinned game animals.

I have successfully hunted and killed several big game species using the broadheads previously mentioned; however, I tend to favor the fixed-blade heads which feature points with immediate cutting action.

Some years ago Steve Albertson, a bowhunter and an archery shop owner in Warsaw, Indiana, opened my eyes to the difference the tip of the arrow can make in penetration. Using a baby scales, a block of wood and a cut-off shaft—along with a deer hide—Steve conducted a series of tests with popular broadheads sold in his store. The results are non-scientific but noteworthy.

Steve found a sharpened Black Diamond Delta required only one-half pound of pressure to completely penetrate the deerskin while a Snuffer needed four and one-half pounds and a Razorhead chisel-point (with insert) needed 10 pounds of pressure. Meanwhile several replaceable blade broadhead types with tool steel tips required 20 to 24 pounds of pressure to achieve complete penetration. This simple test dramatically illustrates the difference between broadheads which cut on contact and those with tips which must punch through hair and hide before the slicing action of the blades begins. Again, since arrows have only so much energy created by the thrust of the bow, it stands to reason the less used on penetrating the hide the more power remaining to penetrate internal organs and create an exit wound. It's definitely something to ponder.

Whichever type and model of broadhead you settle on, keep in mind that your heads must be as sharp as a new razor blade to do their job effectively. Even unused replaceable blade heads need to be touched up with a stone or file from time to time after being carried afield. And **never, never** reshoot a replaceable blade broadhead without resharpening it or replacing the insert blades. It may still feel sharp to the touch, but it's not sharp enough to hunt with.

With the array of sharpening tools available to bowhunters, there's simply no excuse for venturing afield with dull broadheads. And it's an excellent idea to always carry a file or stone with you when hunting for on-the-spot resharpening or retouching chores.

Note: The best, easiest to use sharpening devices I've found are those hones offered by TruAngle™. Several models, each designed by bowhunter Tim Roberts to hold precise angles while sharpening the full length of the blade, are offered at a reasonable price. The individual hones accommodate most two-, three- and four-blade broadheads used today.

One final word on the subject of hunting arrows. Always practice with broadheads before venturing afield to hunt. Broadheads and field points, even if they are of the same weight, tend to fly differently and a bowhunter must discover these differences before the hunt. Then and only then should you resharpen the heads or replace the blades and go hunting with confidence. It can mean your success or failure as a bowhunter.

Bowhunting Accessories

4

The modern bowhunter has a veritable treasure trove of equipment and information available—everything from the bows and arrows themselves to a vast and often confusing array of accessories. Additionally there are enough instructional pamphlets, periodicals and books on the market to satisfy almost any reader's curiosity on nearly any bowhunting subject you can name. This is both good and bad.

On the positive side is the obvious fact that no longer does the beginning bowhunter have to go through a long period of trial and error, in-the-field experimentation. Many of us can remember when such was not the case and how our own initial ventures were clumsy—often comical—attempts to collect game with our bows.

But times have changed. The sport has grown. Some individuals and companies, more interested in the bottom line of their ledgers than bowhunting, have seemingly attempted to make bowhunters out of every man, woman and child in the United States. They've confused archery with bowhunting—and there is a very real difference! Archery is shooting at paper targets, for fun or in serious competition. Bowhunting is hunting big and small game with archery tackle especially designed for that purpose.

Attempting to kill an animal with any weapon is no casual pastime. Whether using a bow or a firearm, the responsible hunter realizes he must always do his best to kill in a humane, ethical manner. This requires a combination of ability, attitude and opportunity. And regardless of what some zealous wheeler-dealers would have people believe,

bowhunting is not for everyone.

People who kill things for fun are sick individuals. To the serious bowhunter, the **hunting** is fun; **killing** is often the satisfying culmination of the hunt—but it is not fun! This is a distinction the anti-hunters and some ad agency copywriters fail to comprehend.

Regardless, men and women who are aware of the obligation they must assume when entering the sport are at a distinct advantage over we bowhunting greybeards who learned things the hard way. They won't become instant bowhunters or overnight successes simply by making an investment in the necessary equipment; however, they have at their disposal a greater variety of gear and literature to help them get started than at any time in the history of bowhunting.

Reading is an excellent way to acquaint would-be bowhunters with the sport and the equipment used. Books such as this one—and magazines like **Bowhunter**—offer the perceptive reader valuable information and advice. But reading is only a first step.

Next comes a visit to an archery/bowhunting pro shop or to a sporting goods store where knowledgeable personnel can answer questions and where the individual can handle bowhunting equipment and determine which gear best suits his needs. Matching equipment to the individual is vital. Bowhunting is an intensely personal sport and ill-suited or mismatched equipment is a primary reason many beginners become disillusioned and discouraged.

The best advice I can give to any man or woman getting outfitted for bowhunting is this: **Select what's right for you. Sure, listen to advice, check out the options—but make the final decision yourself.**

Don't rush your purchases. Don't buy brand names because of slick ads or hard-sell sales pitches. Don't buy equipment solely on the say-so of a hunting buddy. **You** must be satisfied. The equipment must suit **you.** If it doesn't—well, you've got problems and chances are good you'll be disappointed with both the equipment and its performance.

In reality all any bowhunter needs is a hunting bow and arrows equipped with razor-sharp broadheads. Modern bows fall into two basic categories—the "stick bows" which include longbows and recurves and "compounds." The previous chapter contains an in-depth examination of bows and bow selection, arrow types and broadheads. Since these essentials have been explored in detail, the balance of this chapter focuses attention on various accessories and what some contemporary bowhunters label as "gadgets."

Someone has called crossbows "the ultimate bowhunting gadget." Many bowhunters and bowhunting organizations have fought attempts by manufacturers and pro-crossbow hunters to effect legislation which would allow the use of crossbows during the general archery seasons in various states. They generally agree the crossbow is a primitive weapon but insist it is more comparable to the muzzleloading rifle or slug-loaded shotgun in accuracy and range than to the hunting bow.

At the time this is being written in the mid-1980s, the crossbow is a subject of considerable controversy in many bowhunting circles. Most states do not allow crossbow hunting for big game animals and the Pope and Young Club will not recognize animals taken with crossbows as arrow-killed trophies. Regardless, certain manufacturers—spearheaded by Precision Shooting Equipment of Arizona and Barnett Archery Company of Florida—are actively seeking legislation to make crossbow hunting legal throughout the United States. While they have

Bow quivers are the most popular way to carry hunting arrows, although some backquivers—like this Catquiver—do the job well.

recorded some successes, their efforts have been thwarted in states like West Virginia and Michigan thanks to resistance led by well organized state bowhunting organizations. More battles are sure to occur in this ongoing controversy.

Besides bows and arrows, equipment which is generally considered basic includes a quiver, shooting glove or tab and an arm guard. In addition, a spare bowstring equipped with a nocking point and string silencers is always a good idea. Bowstringers are musts for stick bow shooters.

Bow quivers are without question the most popular means of carrying arrows into the field. These quivers are mounted to the bow and typically hold half a dozen or more arrows separately and securely. All good bow quivers have hoods or similar protective covers to guard against accidental cuts by razor sharp hunting heads. Arrows snap into rubber slots and may be removed with very little motion.

Back quivers, popularized in Indian and Robin Hood movies, are favored by some bowhunters. Most such quivers hold more arrows than bow quivers; however, two major disadvantages exist:

the arrows are often loose and tend to rattle or rustle as the hunter walks, alerting keen-eared game and dulling heads which must remain sharp to be effective. Also, an arrow being withdrawn from a back quiver requires considerably more motion than one being removed from a bow quiver. Some back quivers—like the St. Charles and Catquiver models—hold arrows individually and have protective hoods. Some hunters combine the bow quiver and back quiver, especially on wilderness hunts where running short of arrows could spoil the day.

Belt and hip or side quivers are another possibility. These slip on a belt and are worn on the side, sometimes tied down like a holster, or in back. They are viable options to those bowhunters who simply do not like the additional weight of a quiver and arrows mounted to the bow.

Shooting gloves or tabs are used by the majority of bowhunters. These leather devices protect the shooting fingers and aid in obtaining a smooth release. Some bowhunters favor release aids, mechanical devices which attach to the bow string. Frankly, releases are more popular in target archery circles where machine-like shooting precision is

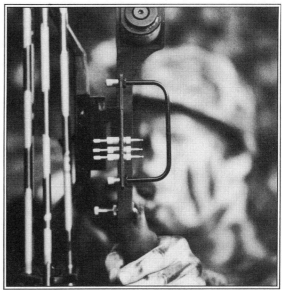

Bow sights, like this Cobra multiple-pin model, are favored by some bowhunters who know shooting distances to the target.

necessary. Many veteran bowhunters feel release aids simply "get in the way" and are "one more thing to worry about" in that pulse-pounding moment when a game animal steps into view.

Arm guards strap to the bow arm and keep the bowstring from slapping your forearm or catching on the sleeve of your camo shirt or jacket. This is especially important in cold weather hunting when bulky clothing is worn. When a bowstring catches on your sleeve, the arrow's flight will be erratic.

Arrow rests come in a wide variety of shapes and sizes at a wide range of prices. Some models are extremely complex, equipped with small wheels or rollers that turn as the arrow is drawn or released. Others consist of a small rubber, metal or plastic arm that is mounted to the sight window with adhesive backing or fitted into built-in slots. Some rests have small holes to accommodate adjustable tuning buttons designed to fine tune arrow flight.

Position is all important. An improperly mounted arrow rest will cause arrows to fly erratically. Consequently, it's vital for the bowhunter to make certain the arrow rest is correctly positioned. Bows come from the factory equipped with arrow rests

David Powers, one of Idaho's top bowhunters, uses a release, string peep, sights and stabilizer on his 74-pound Golden Eagle hunting bow.

already in place; however, rests can wear out and need to be replaced. A spare rest should be part of each bowhunter's gear package; it's as important as an extra bowstring.

Many modern bowhunters use sights—another accessory popularized by target archers—and there are dozens of various models available. Most have several fixed pins set at 10-yard increments. Each setting allows for arrow drop at different distances. Other sights are adjustable and at least one model—the pendulum sight—adjusts automatically as the shooter raises or lowers his bow.

While instinctive shooters rely on intuitively accurate range estimation, sight shooters—called freestyle shooters—must **know** the distance to the target. Many bowhunters who use sights and hunt from a blind or stand frequently pace off distances to various points within good bow range. Some even mark the distances with stakes, surveyor's tape or natural objects like dead limbs or rocks. This enables the shooter to know how far the animal is and to select the proper sight pin.

Pins usually do not work well on moving or flying targets. Also, many veteran bowhunters—especially those who prefer to still-hunt and stalk their game—shoot by "feel" or instinct. They let their senses tell them how far the animal is and how to elevate or lower their bow arm so the arrow will fly true. Such hand-eye coordination takes practice but is not as difficult to master as some beginners might imagine.

Lighted sight pins are another variation/option. Operated by miniature batteries, these pins have tips which light up for increased visibility in poor shooting light. Some shooters insist they're just the thing for insuring accuracy on overcast days. Others believe they tempt the user to shoot before or after legal shooting hours and feel they should be outlawed nationwide.

Rangefinders are another option for either the freestyle or instinctive shooter. Using a double image principle, the devices give accurate readings of distance when the images merge. These are not always practical in stalking situations where movements must be kept to a minimum; however,

Ranging, Inc., produces quality rangefinders which accurately measure the distance between the shooter and the target.

they can assist the stand hunter who is able to determine distances without leaving his concealment.

String peeps are small rubber or plastic sighting aids which fit within the strands of the bowstring. Each has a tiny hole which the shooter peers through at full draw, lining up on the proper sight pin before releasing the arrow. They basically serve the same purpose as the rear sight on a rifle.

Another bowstring appendage some shooters use is a kisser button. This plastic disc fits on the string and touches the shooter's mouth when he reaches full draw. It serves to insure against changes in draw length or form. Peeps and kisser buttons are more popular with target archers than bowhunters.

No bowstring should be without a nocking point. If properly installed, it guarantees that each arrow fits on the string in the same place for each shot. This is vital for good arrow flight. Arrows should always be nocked below the nocking point which is installed one-eighth of an inch or slightly more above an imaginary line running from the shelf or arrow rest to the bowstring. A bow square can quickly determine the proper nocking point and commercially produced nocking devices—usually of the clip-on or heat-shrink variety—should be fitted in place before shooting begins. Minor adjustments—raising or lowering the nocking point—may be necessary for correct arrow flight.

Most bowhunters attach string silencers to their bowstrings. These devices are usually made of rubber—common yarn is another ideal noise-dampening attachment—and are designed to reduce the **twang** commonly associated with releasing an arrow. Usually string silencers are fitted to the bowstring above and below the nocking point approximately half way to the string's tip. Some compound shooters add noise dampeners to the bow's cables as well as the bowstring.

Brush buttons and bow tip protectors are rubber attachments favored by many stick bow shooters. Brush buttons fit on the string just below the loops and keep leaves, weeds and twigs from snagging the bowstring as the hunter moves through brushy terrain. The bow tip protector fits tightly over the lower end of the bow limb and holds the string in place as well as protects the bow tip.

Stabilizers—weighted rods mounted to the riser or bow limbs and designed to help balance the

Rubber string silencers—like the Catwhiskers model—dampen bowstring noise at the instant of release. Yarn also works effectively.

bow—are another target archery innovation adopted by some bowhunters. They are viewed as a fine tuning device by some bowhunters seeking consistent accuracy. Most stabilizers mounted to hunting bows are camouflaged and shorter than those used by target shooters to allow for manueverability in brush and confined stands where movement is limited. Today's compounds come with threaded holes to accommodate stabilizers, but relatively few bowhunters use them.

Bow slings are leather straps which are attached to the bow's handle. The shooter inserts his bow hand through the sling's loop to prevent the bow from being dropped as the arrow is released. Since many shooters do not grip the bow and keep their hand open as the arrow is drawn and released, bow slings can save wear and tear on the equipment.

Bow holders generally come in two types. One U-shaped model fits to the hunter's belt and is designed to hold the bow horizontally as the bowhunter stands or walks. The other model is a bracket which attaches to the tree stand itself and holds the bow vertically. Some compound bows, especially when laden with a full complement of quiver and arrows, are quite heavy—or seem so after a long day afield. Bow holders are designed to ease the strain of holding or carrying the bow for long periods of time. Many hunters on stand simply hang their bow from a convenient branch or peg during the wait and pick up the bow only when game is sighted.

For those who prefer to keep their bow in hand, a small cloth pocket or loop sewn just above the knee is ideal. The lower limb's tip is slipped into the pocket/loop to alleviate the strain of holding the bow for long periods of time.

Arrow holders keep the nocked shaft in position on the string. These flexible rubber devices fit onto the bow's riser and clip to the arrow itself. As the bowhunter begins his draw, the clip slips free and allows the arrow to be drawn into shooting position. Most bowhunters waiting on stand prefer to wait with an arrow nocked and ready. Arrow holders save strain on the index finger which typically holds the nocked arrow in place.

Specially designed head pullers are handy for retrieving errant broadheads from trees, fallen logs or stumps. Any bowhunter who has spent time with a knife hacking and chopping to free a buried broadhead can appreciate the relative ease with which a head puller extricates the broadhead.

Bow cases and arrow carriers are important accessories, especially during transport to and from the hunting area. Some states require that a bow be cased and—in the case of recurves and longbows—unstrung in a motor vehicle. Regardless, a bow case can protect against damage and is worth consideration. Two basic types of cases are available. One is a soft, frequently lined case that protects against nicks, scratches and little else. When the bow is inserted and the case zipped closed, it provides a modicum of protection and meets the legal obligation where bow cases are required. But for the best bow insurance, the hard cases of molded plastic are difficult to beat, especially on long distance trips by land or air and on pack-in or fly-in trips where bow damage could result in an aborted hunt.

The best hard bow cases hold not only the bow but usually carry a dozen or more hunting shafts and offer compartments for necessary accessories. Some sort of protection is a must for arrows, even

The author's custom-designed bow case holds a compound bow, two dozen arrows and a quiver plus accessories. Similar bow cases are manufactured.

if it's only the cardboard box the shafts came in. Special arrow carriers—some holding two dozen shafts—keep nocks, fletching and hunting heads well-protected during transportation. Never, under any circumstances, should arrows be tossed loosely into a container. Responsible bowhunters use only arrow carriers that hold individual shafts securely in place.

My own bow case/arrow carrier is a large, heavy, specially constructed box-like contraption that looks like a cross between a band instrument case and an oversized suitcase. One padded compartment holds my compound bow and quiver while the other has room for two dozen arrows and the usual assortment of accessories. It's drawn a lot of strange looks from airline personnel—and a lot of envious looks from bowhunters. I had it specially made for me back in the early 1970s and aside from some external wear and tear, it's as good as new. The cost, as I recall, was something like seventy-five dollars—a pretty penny back then—but I consider it one of the best bowhunting investments I've ever made. Bowhunters who are handy with woodworking tools could easily design a similar case. For those of us not quite so handy, commercially produced cases and arrow carriers are available in several sizes and shapes at various prices.

A good knife is another valuable bowhunting accessory. Hunting knives come in two basic types—lock-back folding models and the popular fixed-blade belt knives. And despite what some may believe, bigger isn't necessarily better when it comes to choosing a hunting knife. A sharp, sturdy blade of four to six inches in length will handle any field dressing chore there is. In fact, some veteran bowhunters and guides opt to use a favorite pocket knife for dressing and skinning game. A small folding saw or belt hatchet is always handy for cutting through the pelvic bones on any big game animal. But perhaps more important is a lightweight, pocket-sized hone or fine-grained stone which can be used to keep a fine edge on a skinning knife.

A compass is almost always a wise investment for

A good compass can be used to locate stands or game as well as prevent a bowhunter from becoming "turned around."

of monofilament fishing line and several hooks, insect repellent, water purification tablets and similar survival gear. Such items may never prove necessary; however, they take up relatively little space and their presence can help put a person's mind at ease. "Be prepared" is a motto not limited to scouting groups.

Personally, I never venture afield without at least one 35mm camera and several rolls of film. Bowhunters frequently miss out on the once-in-a-lifetime photo opportunities simply because they neglected to carry a camera with them. Not only can a pocket camera be used to take photos of the proud hunter and his or her trophy but the scenery, hunting camp, companions, wildlife, sign, vehicles, terrain and other memorable moments or scenes can be captured with the click of a shutter. Today's photo market is flooded with a wide variety of fully automatic cameras that weigh next to nothing and are small enough to fit in a shirt pocket. There's a model in every price range and I feel any bowhunter who leaves his camera at home or in camp is cheating himself—as well as family and hunting friends—out of the opportunity to record and to share priceless outdoor moments.

any bowhunter. Not only can it prevent getting "turned around" in the woods or back country, it can help relocate remote stands or hunting hotspots. A compass also helps make sense in the reading of topographical maps and the working out of blood trails. Any good pin-on or pocket model must be considered an insurance policy no bowhunter should be without.

Another typical pocket or pack accessory is a reliable flashlight or small lantern. Many bowhunters are afield well before first light and return long after dark. Locating a tree stand or hunting area—or returning to a vehicle or camp when it's darker than the insides of a black bear—is infinitely easier with an artifical light to find the way. In heavily hunted areas a small light also doubles as an insurance policy against shadow-shooters. Even the dumbest, most overzealous arrow-flinger knows deer and other big game can't carry flashlights. And when it comes to working out a blood trail in the dark, a reliable light can pay big dividends.

I generally carry a small first aid kit in a jacket pocket or my fanny pack. In it are several different sizes of band-aids, some sterile antiseptic pads, a whistle, smoke cartridge and a cigarette lighter. Others I know also include a snakebite kit, a roll

A bow square helps locate nocking point and arrow rest position which in turn insures proper arrow flight.

Compact, lightweight binoculars can be a wise investment for the serious bowhunter who learns to use the glasses while afield.

Probably more important than a camera is a pair of small, lightweight binoculars. Many longtime bowhunters would never think of leaving on a hunt or scouting trip without toting their favorite binocs. My own choice of optics is the Bushnell Custom Compact 7x26 model; however, there are many excellent types and brands that are small, quick-focusing and sturdy enough to endure normal field abuse. When checking out binoculars, it's wise to look for light, fast-focusing binocs that provide adequate magnification while brightening the image area. Good glasses are seldom cheap.

Again, bows, arrows and broadheads are all a hunter really needs to get started in the sport. All other accessories—with the possible exception of a quiver, armguard and finger protection—are optional "gadgets" that may or may not be of interest to the bowhunter. Only individual experimentation and preference will dictate which extras become a part of the bowhunter's equipment list. Over the years the list may grow or shrink depending on the personal needs of the shooter.

Planning the Bowhunt

5

As already mentioned, advance planning and proper preparation are keys to most productive hunting trips. Whether you're hunting close to home or half-way across the country, always allow plenty of time to thoughtfully organize the time to be spent actually seeking game. Lay the groundwork early and later you'll be ready for an enjoyable, rewarding bowhunt.

On any out-of-state hunt, preparations should ideally start at least a full year in advance. State fish and game departments will provide sportsmen with license application forms, detailed regulations and other literature which can assist in planning. Some states offer a limited number of licenses and conduct drawings to determine who will be allowed to hunt. Obtaining the necessary forms and meeting application deadlines is an important first step for hunting several species.

In contacting state or provincial game agencies, be specific with your request for information. Name the species you want to hunt and ask for particulars concerning archery season dates, license costs, application forms and deadlines. Some game departments even maintain a list of licensed guides and outfitters which will be sent upon request.

If a guide or outfitter is to be used, plan on investing time and money in postage and telephone calls asking questions and checking references. Good guides and outfitters are often booked up a year or more in advance and the earlier you contact them the better. More later on about selecting and employing the services offered by these outdoor professionals.

Even when hunting close to home within the boundaries of your own state, certain steps can guarantee that you'll be prepared when hunting season rolls around. These include:

* Obtaining permission to hunt private land. This should always be done far in advance of the opening day. County maps and plat books, generally available at county courthouses, may be invaluable in identifying good hunting sites. Maps will show roads, public lands, waterways and section lines. Plat books provide even more detailed information about property lines and usually contain the names of landowners.

* Contacting your state wildlife agency. Conservation officers and wildlife managers, although normally reluctant to recommend specific areas, generally have information on public hunting lands and game densities. Officials can also provide particulars about special hunts, application requirements and regulations.

* Talking to locals. Rural mail carriers, sporting goods or archery dealers and members of area conservation/hunting clubs can answer questions and offer general advice.

* Getting more particulars. Many bowhunters complete their pre-hunt preparations by obtaining topographic maps and aerial photos of the hunting areas. Topo maps depict landscape features including land elevations, wetlands, roads, buildings and other identifying characteristics of the terrain. The maps themselves are inexpensive and free index maps of areas east and west of the Mississippi

River are available by writing the U.S. Geological Survey, Western Branch of Distribution, Box 25046, Federal Center, Denver, CO 80225 or Eastern Branch of Distribution, 1200 South Eads Street, Arlington, VA 22202. Another map to consider is a U.S. National Forest Map. Aerial photos, obtainable from the U.S. Department of Agriculture and private survey firms, complement area maps by offering even more visual details. Information about aerial maps is available from the U.S. Department of Agriculture. Photography Division, Eastern Laboratory, 45 South French Broad Avenue, Asheville, NC 28801.

Once you've done your preliminary homework, it's time to get out into the field and familiarize yourself with the territory. This is also an excellent time to check out game populations in the hunting area. As you walk around, be alert for tracks, scat, beds and feeding areas as well as animals themselves. If you locate a heavily used game trail, note it but remember that hunting pressure can cause animals to change normal travel patterns. Look for stand sites or still-hunting areas that indicate feeding, watering or breeding areas. Such locations often produce season after season.

Even if you're familiar with an area you've hunted from seasons past, don't ever take it for granted and spend your pre-season scouting time sitting at home. You just might arrive opening day to find last year's hotspot obliterated by a housing development or logging operation.

Many of the most successful bowhunters I know spend the entire year "scouting" favorite hunting locales. Even if they get their game early in the season, they swap a camera for a bow or just remain afield to observe game with binoculars. Post season scouting helps, too. In areas where foliage disappears and the landscape is revealed, an alert hunter can locate signs which help him keep tabs on game while familarizing himself with the land. Fresh snowfall always provides the opportunity to read sign and learn more about the animals' habits and movements.

If it's legal, many hours of valuable in-the-field practice may be enjoyed by the bowhunter who

Checking bowhunting equipment needs to be done well in advance of the hunt itself. It's important to be fully prepared— and fun, too.

carries his hunting bow with him on scouting trips. Practice at backyard targets may develop good form; however, stump shooting and hunting small game or varmints hones a bowhunter's skills better than any other method.

Part of the enjoyment of any hunt is sharing the adventure with someone. While bowhunting itself is generally an individual undertaking, there is much to be said for sharing the planning, the travel, the hunting area and the success or failure of the adventure with a companion. Perhaps the best place to begin looking for a hunting partner is within your own family. Father/son hunting teams are as old as sport hunting itself and in recent years more and more husband/wife duos are found in hunting camps. Sharing time in the field can solidify—or destroy—any relationship.

Careful consideration should be given to the selection of a hunting partner. In some areas, off the beaten trails, it is unwise to hunt alone and in an emergency situation a person's survival could depend on a companion. It could be disasterous if a partner proved undependable or cracked under pressure. And regardless of where the hunt takes place, a chronic complainer can spoil the best of outdoor experiences. Other people to avoid are those who shirk responsibilities, those who may be jealous of the success of others and, of course, game law violators.

The ideal hunting partner is someone who shares your own enthusiasm and hunting philosophy, someone whom you trust and enjoy being with. On a short hunt a companion may make the ride to and from the area somewhat shorter. On longer trips a partner or partners can defray travel expenses, share responsibilities and make the experience more meaningful simply by being there.

Many beginning hunters, faced with limited time and limited budgets, opt to try less expensive do-it-yourself bowhunts in neighboring or distant states and provinces. While some are successful—both in terms of the overall experience and in game tagged—many learn the hard way that many "cheap hunts" are not so inexpensive after all.

I have known bowhunters who hesitated to pay a guide or outfitter to hunt on private land or be packed into remote regions where game is plentiful

Scouting hunting areas may be combined with hunts for small game or varmints. This is excellent practice for big game bowhunts.

and less pressured than in more accessible areas. They've made perhaps half a dozen or so annual trips and generally returned complaining about the scarcity of animals, abundance of other hunters and how they wished they were rich so they could get in on some good hunting.

Well, if they were to sit down and figure up what the five or six "cheap hunts" cost them, they may be surprised to learn they could have made several "rich man's bowhunts" for the same money.

Granted, guided hunts are generally costly—and getting more so every year—but in good areas you often have a better chance of getting your trophy without the hassles and total time spent on the do-it-yourself hunts. "You get what you pay for" is an old admonition that applies as much to bowhunting as well as to shoppers in search of a good deal.

In some regions and when hunting certain species, bowhunters must be accompanied by a licensed guide. This is done for such practical reasons as keeping hunters from becoming lost in wilderness areas and out of dangerous situations involving animals that, in fact, could kill them. It also gives game agencies control over equal distribution of hunting pressure in various regions and—providing the guide/outfitter is honest—prevents game law violations that may occur through ignorance or intent.

Make no mistake about it. Dishonest guides exist. Like any other group of professionals, guides and outfitters have their share of bad apples. But there are many more honest than crooked professionals around. All it takes to locate them is some preliminary work and common sense, precautionary follow-up.

A good guide or outfitter offers several obvious advantages. First, he knows the area, where to find the game being hunted and how best to go about getting it. Second, he makes it possible—by providing transportation to and from the camp and hunting areas, by tending to the cooking and other camp chores and by packing out and caring for the game that is tagged—for the bowhunter to spend all of his time trying to collect a trophy animal and enjoying his hunt.

This is not to lead anyone to believe that a guide/outfitter is a slave or hired hand. He's at best a knowledgeable hunting partner who is being paid to help you, not wait on you hand and foot or make trophy game appear on command. Realize that when you employ his professional services you're booking a hunt and not buying an animal. Do this and you're well on your way to establishing a relationship that will often last a hunting lifetime.

Just as the guide or outfitter has certain obligations to his clients, each bowhunter should do his part to ensure that he's mentally and physically prepared. The mental preparation includes developing a positive attitude while the physical aspect centers on conditioning. All too often bowhunters arrive in hunting camp sadly out of shape, physically unable to get around in game country. A lack of conditioning and an inability to shoot well are two common complaints voiced by professional outdoorsmen of their clients.

Getting into condition takes time for most out-of-shape hunters. Individuals who postpone pre-hunt conditioning programs are often the same people who dig out their bow just before leaving. One or two practice sessions is seldom enough to hone rusty shooting skills. The serious-minded bowhunter who regularly practices and works out—and faithfully follows a pre-hunt plan that thoroughly prepares him—has a definite advantage over others who follow hit or miss methods of getting ready for a hunt.

It's important to listen to a guide or outfitter when he suggests clothing and equipment. Most people have a natural tendency to pack too much gear. While many veteran bowhunters have learned what's needed and what safely can be left at home, many beginners need assistance and should not be bashful about asking for help. Some guides and packers commonly provide check lists for their clients.

Basic gear generally includes clothing, personal items, a sleeping bag and pad, hunting tackle and, if the hunt is not outfitted, food and a shelter of some type. It's a good rule of thumb not to pack too much clothing. Fresh socks and underwear may need

daily consideration; however, most bowhunters wear the same hunting clothes to the field day in and day out. If this is the case, it's a good idea to have a set of camp clothes handy to change into when not hunting. Clothing absorbs cooking odors and other smells of "civilization." Hunting clothes—including footwear—are best kept separate.

Raingear is worthy of special mention. No bowhunter enjoys getting soaked and a rainsuit or poncho should always be carried afield. Many such waterproof garments are noisy and may alert game at critical times. Some bowhunters wear rainsuits **under** their hunting clothes to muffle noise. Also, even though it's usually more expensive, wool is an excellent choice for bowhunters since it retains warmth even when wet. Additionally, it can't be beat as the most quiet clothing available today.

Footwear is another vital area. Sore feet can quickly spoil any bowhunter's dream trip and special attention must be paid to what you wear. Cotton or nylon socks are a good beginning when teamed with heavier woolen socks. Next, sturdy but lightweight and waterproof boots with a non-skid

Bear guide Wayne Bosowicz explains the ideal bowhunting shot to a young client. Advice from good guides should be heeded.

sole are favored by many of today's bowhunters. Pacs, with rubber bottoms and leather or synthetic tops, are another favorite where lots of walking is involved. Rubber-soled boots are also a favorite of bowhunters who do not wish to leave a scent trail entering their stand area. Cold weather hunting mandates insulated footwear and no smart bowhunter ever heads for the woods wearing brand new boots, especially if he plans to do much walking. Always take time to break in footwear before the hunt begins.

Since getting a restful night's sleep is essential to one's comfort and endurance, another wise investment is a good sleeping bag. Down-filled bags, especially those with removeable liners, are often worth the extra cost. Temperatures vary widely during North America's big game seasons—from warm and mild to cool or freezing cold—and down-filled bags are probably the best overall buy. An air mattress (rubber is better than plastic) or foam pad and a pillow complete the bedroll.

A smart bowhunter typically makes a list of his gear and checks it off as it's packed in the duffel bag. A first aid or toilet kit—as well as items such as a canteen or bota bag, camera and film, flashlight, binoculars, knife and sharpening stone, notebook and pen, daypack or fanny pack, game bag and a plastic bag for the heart and liver, rope or cord— all have their place in a bowhunter's pack. None does any good at all if left at home and a checklist prevents the possibility of such an oversight.

Another check that goes hand in hand with settling on a guide or outfitter involves obtaining and checking out references. Common sense says no one is going to list names of disgruntled or dissatisfied clients; however, a person should ask for several names—of unsuccessful as well as successful hunters—and talk to these people. A telephone call is best and it's wise to have a list of questions ready before dialing. If you write to the reference, always include a stamped, self-addressed envelope for a convenient response. Again, a telephone call is simpler with the results being immediate. When the overall cost of the hunt is considered, the price of a few long distance calls represents a small part of the total investment.

Some professional guides and outfitters actually offer a contract to their clients detailing services provided and costs involved. Others simply spell out particulars in a letter. Either way, it's always best to have everything in writing to avoid misunderstandings and problems later on.

Keep in mind that many outdoor professionals receive hundreds of inquiries each year and typically book only a handful of hunters. Much of their business comes from repeat clients. Most don't have the time to individually answer each and every question in each letter they receive. Personally, I write only to request a brochure and price list, mentioning the time of year and game I'm interested in hunting. After receiving the information, I call and talk to the guide or outfitter if I'm interested in pursuing a possible booking. This is when I ask my specific questions and take note of answers. After references are checked, I always confirm things in writing before making a deposit.

Most guides and outfitters ask for a partial payment—one quarter to one-half is common—to confirm the booking and reserve specific dates. A cancellation can result in a partial or full forfeiture of the deposit so be sure you understand the terms. Never send any money until you are satisfied with the agreement and are willing to make the commitment to go on the hunt.

In all honesty, the planning portion of any hunting trip—besides being essential for the best possible chance of success in the field—is a very rewarding venture in itself. Getting mentally and physically ready while anticipating the long-awaited adventure is the next best thing to the hunt itself.

When to Shoot

6

One of the most critical decisions you will make as a bowhunter is determining the precise moment to release an arrow. Often the success or failure of the hunt—or even an entire season—is ultimately judged by this single act. Therefore, all bowhunters should recognize the necessity of learning the most effective time to shoot.

On the surface, when to shoot may seem to be an easy decision for any hunter to make. "Take the first good shot you get" is typical advice passed along from veteran to beginning bowhunter. But what constitutes a **good** shot? You must keep in mind that each individual—and each hunting situation—is different. What's **good** for one person might be **risky** or **poor** to another. Learning when to shoot depends on a number of factors including personal shooting ability, hunting experience, distance and target position, personal ethics and proper equipment to name but a few considerations. The knowledge actually comes from within. In fact, only one person—you—can judge when the time is right to release.

Mental and physical preparedness is the key. As a conscientious bowhunter, you would never venture afield without a thorough understanding of your hunting equipment, your personal proficiency, and pertinent game laws. By the time opening day arrives all basic shooting skills have been mastered through long hours of off-season practice. You've acquired at least a fundamental knowledge of game animals—from habits to anatomy to habitat—by both armchair research and in-the-field scouting trips. Recognizing the value of expert advice, whether garnered from primary or secondary sources, you use it to complement your own first-hand knowledge. Finally, in your own mind you believe that when that bowhunter's moment of truth arrives, you will release your arrow confident of placing the shot well and registering a quick, humane kill.

Bowhunting Considerations

It is the ethical bowhunter's responsibility to do everything possible to ensure clean kills in the field. This is best accomplished by understanding bowhunting tackle and practicing the principles of effective bowhunting. Always keep the following thoughts in mind:

* Compared to high-powered hunting rifles, muzzleloaders and even slug-loaded shotguns, the hunting bow is a short range weapon. Most bowhunting kills are made at 25 yards or less. This means getting close to the quarry—well within the limits of an individual's effective shooting range—and making an accurate shot.

* A hunting arrow propels a razor-sharp broadhead towards an intended target. Arrows have neither the velocity nor the shocking power of a bullet and are easily stopped or deflected by not only large bones, tree limbs and brush but even almost-invisible twigs and leaves. A clear shooting lane to each target is essential.

* A broadhead is designed to kill by creating massive hemorrhaging. To be most effective, ade-

quate penetration must be achieved and major arteries or veins severed. Sharp broadheads penetrate better than dull heads and do much more internal damage.

* A bowhunter should always aim for the heart-lung-liver area of any animal. It's the largest vital target area and a hit here will usually result in a short blood trail and quick kill.

* It is easy to miss a big game target. Successful bowhunters always resist the temptation to shoot at the entire animal—even at point-blank range. Instead they select a single, small spot on the animal's body—an imaginary aiming point over a vital area—and try to place their arrow in this exact spot.

* Unless accidentally struck in the brain or spine, arrow-hit animals rarely drop on the spot. Typically, wounded animals run or walk for a distance before succumbing. This means that more often than not a bowhunter must follow a blood trail from the point of the hit to the point of recovery. Since sharp broadheads facilitate bleeding, this is another case for using only keenly honed hunting heads. An ample blood trail makes the tracking and recovery task much easier.

* Most experienced bowhunters will wait 30 to 60 minutes before taking up the blood trail unless adverse weather conditions or unusual circumstances threaten to obliterate it. If not pressured, arrow-hit game may pause to rest as the effects of the arrow are felt. Often wounded animals lie down and die peacefully near the area of the hit. However, if immediately pushed or frightened by human voices or other sounds, even mortally wounded animals can cover considerable ground. There are exceptions to the sit-and-wait-before-tracking rule, of course, depending on the weather and position of the hit. For example, leg-hit game should be pursued immediately in hopes of getting a finishing shot. Paunch-hit game should be given even more time—four to six hours—to succumb.

Remember, it is a bowhunter's responsibility to do everything humanly possible to recover wounded game. No ethical bowhunter will abandon any search until the game is recovered or until he is absolutely convinced the hit was non-vital. The ethical bowhunter also takes only shots that will result in the best chance for success. "Be sure or don't shoot" would be a good motto for every bowhunter to adopt. He owes it to himself, his sport and the game he pursues.

Animal Position

It would be impossible to learn when to shoot without first understanding the importance of animal position and arrow placement. Even though these aspects are examined elsewhere in this book, they cannot be overemphasized.

The best shots a bowhunter can take are those offered when the animal is standing in a quartering away or broadside position. Both the classic broadside shot and the shot at quartering animals are preferably taken at stationary or slowly moving targets. A double-lung hit must be regarded as an ideal goal of any bowhunter.

Unfortunately, animals do not always cooperate with you and position themselves well. At such times a bowhunter must determine whether to wait for a better opportunity, or to release his arrow immediately. Keeping in mind that all risky shots should be avoided, there are several effective positions where a well placed arrow will result in a

Here's an ideal bowhunting shot. The mule deer is walking slowly, quartering away from the shooter. Always aim for the heart-lung area.

Head, neck or any frontal shots are risky for bowhunters to take. Chances of a poor hit are great and generally these shots should be passed.

quick, clean kill. There are also several shots which should be avoided under normal circumstances.

The head or neck shot may be an effective choice for the firearms hunter, but no conscientious bowhunter should ever attempt such a marginal shot. The brain is a relatively small target which is surrounded by arrow-stopping bone. Forget it! And while the neck offers several vital areas—spinal column, jugular vein and carotid artery—these too are relatively tiny targets, well-hidden within a large area of non-vital muscle. Generally, fatal neck shots by bowhunters are accidental hits where the sharp broadhead just happens to sever something vital. Avoid them!

Frontal shots may prove lethal providing the arrow penetrates into the heart-lung-liver area and does sufficient damage. But the chances of a poor hit are too great to warrant taking this shot under

average conditions. The cardiovascular area is protected by heavy bone structure. Shots, unless perfectly placed, may imbed in the brisket, chest or shoulder area. The result may be a non-lethal hit and a lost animal. Another negative factor is that when an animal is facing you the chances are greater he is already alerted to your presence or will spot you at the instant of release and spin away. This greatly increases your chances of making a poor hit. Front-facing shots are seldom worth the risk involved.

Another questionable shot for the ground-level bowhunter is one where the animal stands facing away, presenting its rear to the shooter. True, an arrow which cuts the femoral artery on the inside of either hind leg, or which penetrates through the rear to the chest cavity, will result in certain death. And even the shot that flies high could luckily strike the spinal column in the animal's neck. But heavy hip, pelvic and leg bones can impede arrow penetration and result in a non-fatal wound. The rear-end shot is risky at best—avoid it! Unquestionably, broadside and quartering away shots are preferable.

The broadside shot is popular—for good reasons—and offers the bowhunter the biggest target area. However, it is important to understand that concentration on that single, small spot is necessary. A properly placed arrow will often slice

Running shots should be avoided unless the animal is already wounded. Few bowhunters have the ability to accurately hit moving game.

The bull elk is standing in an excellent position for a fatal shot. The cow in the background is offering a very poor opportunity for a killing shot.

through both lungs, the heart or the liver—all fatal hits. But an arrow too far forward can imbed itself in the shoulder region and stop short of inflicting a mortal wound. Also, an arrow too far back can result in a dreaded paunch or intestinal hit. An arrow that hits high might miss the lungs and aortic artery, resulting in a sparse blood trail and an animal that may not be recovered.

Beyond doubt, one of the most deadly bowhunting shots occurs when the animal is facing away at a 45 degree angle. A broadhead, angling forward into the vitals, will do considerable damage within the chest cavity. When an animal is standing in this position, virtually the entire kill area presents itself to the shooter and the animal is in the most

vulnerable position possible. Even an arrow that is slightly off target—high, low, back or forward— stands a good chance of inflicting a fatal wound entering or exiting the body.

Resist the temptation to shoot at running game unless the animal is already wounded. Few bowhunters have practiced enough to develop the skill necessary to place their arrow in the kill area of a rapidly moving target.

Proper Practice

Ask any bowhunter about the first shot he ever attempted in the field—he'll tell ya...there's a world of difference between a paper target and a flesh and blood animal. While shooting at stationary, in-animate targets from known distances may help you master proper archery technique and form, you should realize that there are better ways to prepare for hunting big game.

Perhaps the best way to practice for bowhunting is to go stump shooting. Alone or with a hunting partner, walk through woodlands and fields, selecting rotting stumps, clumps of grass, a fallen leaf, a shadow—anything that offers a good, safe shot—and try to place your first arrow in that predetermined target.

Always practice with your hunting equipment and, if possible, dress in the same clothes and footwear you will wear when actually hunting. Shoot only one arrow from any one location (bowhunters seldom get more than one shot at the same target). Stand, kneel, crouch and sit when making your shots. Shoot uphill, downhill, between trees and over brush, learning to concentrate when making your release.

Wear your hunting clothes during practice sessions and use the same equipment you'll use for hunting. Small game, like gophers, can keep your shooting eye sharp.

As hunting season approaches, test shoot your broadheads (hunting heads generally fly different-ly than field points) and practice with them ex-clusively. Shoot at lifesize animal targets (silhouette targets are ideal), picking a spot and placing your arrow in the kill area from different shooting posi-tions and varying distances. Keep practice sessions short, enjoyable. Frequent periods of brief practice are usually more beneficial than extended, infre-quent sessions.

Such practice under realistic bowhunting condi-tions helps concentration and hones the ability to judge distances accurately. Remember to practice at different times of day and under different weather conditions.

Safety Tips

* Before shooting, be certain of your background. Ask yourself, "Is there an adequate backstop? Where will my arrow go if I miss my target?" If you can't be certain, don't risk a shot. Never shoot at skylined game and never shoot an arrow straight up. Don't ever dry-fire your bow.

* Always check your bowhunting gear for possi-ble danger signs (frayed bowstrings, bent or cracked arrows, weak or twisted bow limbs, cracked or split nocks, etc.). Don't attempt to use faulty equipment. Replace it immediately. Failure to do so can be dangerous to you and to others.

* Don't climb trees, fences, natural or manmade barriers or anything while holding your bow. Many bowhunting injuries are self-inflicted. Falling on your equipment can result in a serious—even fatal—injury. And never carry your arrow nocked on the bowstring unless you are approaching an animal in the final stages of a stalk. This is a dangerous prac-tice if others are present, and remember that falls and self-inflicted cuts are possible as well.

* Always select and use a bow quiver which holds arrows securely and features a protective covering for the broadheads. Exposed, razor sharp hunting heads are potentially dangerous. If a back, belt or hip quiver is used, never ride horseback or put

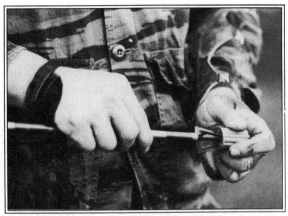

To avoid nasty cuts when handling sharp broadheads, always use a broadhead wrench to tighten or loosen heads.

magnifies all shooting mistakes; get close and pass up all risky shots. Release your arrow when you **know** the time is right.

The bowhunter who is both mentally and physically ready to hunt is without doubt the one who stands the best chance of success.

yourself in a position where you could accidentally fall on the quiver.

* When field dressing game, always be especially careful if you failed to locate your broadhead or its blades (if replaceable-blade heads are used). They might be lodged in the animal's body and result in nasty cuts to the unwary hunter.

* Where it's legal, always carry a small light when entering or leaving the woods before daylight or after dark. Bowhunters can avoid being mistaken for game animals by other hunters—even poachers—in the same area.

* When transporting bows and arrows, use appropriate cases or containers. This protects equipment against damage and potential problems in the field.

* Be extremely careful when sharpening broadheads or inserting replacement blades in certain types of hunting heads. A slip can result in a severe cut. Use appropriate tools and caution. Always handle broadheads with respect.

Expect the unexpected and always be prepared. No single bit of advice, if heeded, can go farther toward ensuring success afield.

Know yourself, your equipment and your quarry. Understand the importance of animal position and arrow placement. Remember that distance

Tracking and Recovering Game

7

One of the biggest criticisms leveled against bowhunters is they hit and fail to recover far too many animals. This leads some critics to believe that bowhunting equipment is ineffective—a completely ridiculous conclusion. Others believe the majority of bowhunters do not have the skill to shoot accurately or to follow and recover a wounded animal. This latter claim is difficult to support or refute.

Undeniably, as in all forms of hunting—whether scattergunning for upland game birds or using a large bore rifle on big game—some game will be hit and lost. That's a fact of hunting life. And while one unrecovered animal is one too many, the anti-hunters tend to exaggerate facts. Listen to them and you'd be led to believe that after bow season the woods are full of "porcupine deer," animals walking around with numerous arrows protruding from various parts of their anatomy. That, to put it bluntly, is porcupine poop.

Some studies have been conducted and the results are generally encouraging. Few arrow-killed deer are actually found rotting in the woods after bow season. Also, an examination of gun-killed deer at check stations (with metal detectors and careful visual inspection) in some heavily hunted states—immediately following the annual archery season—has led to the conclusion that very few checked animals show evidence of arrow wounds. Perhaps more importantly, those few that were found were generally in excellent health, having recovered fully from the broadhead wound.

Such findings are important because many critics equate "lost" game with "dead" game. Undeniably,

some animals do die of their wounds, but many arrow-hit animals recover fully—undoubtedly wiser for the experience. The reason should be obvious. A sharp broadhead cuts cleanly, rupturing blood vessels around the wound. Researchers have found this creates a numbing effect with relatively little pain. If there is not sufficient blood loss—about one-third of the total blood volume—to cause the animal's death, the clean, surgical nature of the wound—with minor damage to surrounding tissue and the nervous system—lends itself to quick healing and complete recovery. Chances of infection and a lingering death are slight.

Unfortunately, bowhunters sometimes help to perpetuate the myth of their ineptness with such public comments as: "I haven't got my deer yet but I've stuck a couple." Such stupid, thoughtless statements are sometimes lies. Some would-be bowhunters cover their own ineptitude with fabrications in a vain attempt to impress others. And even if the comment is true, no ethical sportsman ever goes around bragging about game that's been hit and lost. Such cases are reason for silent shame, not chest-thumping braggadocio.

Once you've released an arrow, you owe it to yourself, the animal and every other responsible bowhunter to follow up on the shot. First, you must check carefully for evidence of a hit. Even when you think you've missed, you should try to find and examine your arrow for any traces of blood. If the arrow can't be located, look for cut hair or drops of blood near where the animal stood. Be thorough in your search, especially when you can't find your arrow. Look for tracks and follow them a ways. Sometimes evidence of bleeding is not immediately found; continue your search along the animal's escape route until you're satisfied the shot resulted in a clean miss.

Second, if you see the arrow strike or later locate signs of a sure hit, you must immediately prepare yourself for the trailing and recovery portion of your hunt. Although each tracking job and blood trail is different, depending on the species of game and location of the hit, the following tips will increase your chances of locating the animal and putting your tag on the well-earned trophy:

* Mark both the point of the shot and the place where the animal was standing. If you're hunting from a blind or stand, the first part is easy. If you're still-hunting or stalking and make a shot, physically mark the spot. Many bowhunters carry toilet tissue, surveyor's tape or some similar marker. Using an extra arrow from your quiver works just as well. Next, make a mental note of where the animal stood and the last place you saw him. A compass reading can help pinpoint the direction of travel.

* Next, you wait. Keeping quiet, watch and listen. If not immediately pursued or alarmed by unnatural sounds following the shot, the animal may bed down nearby when the effects of the arrow are felt. Under certain conditions you may see or hear the animal moving—perhaps falling. Regardless, it's wise to wait between 30 minutes and a full hour before taking up the trail. Exceptions occur when adverse weather threatens to obliterate the trail, when open country allows you to keep the wounded animal in sight and when you actually see the animal fall and are certain it's dead.

* Walk quietly to the spot where the animal stood and confirm signs of a hit. Mark this location. Check the arrow, if found, for evidence of complete penetration (blood streaks from broadhead to nock) and clues to position of the wound. Greasy, whitish material on the shaft may mean a brisket hit (often non-vital). Greenish brown matter is evidence of a gut shot. Such hits can be fatal if sufficient time elapses before the search begins. Plan to wait four to six hours—even longer—before following the

blood trail of paunch-hit animals. Bright red blood with bubbles means a lung hit—a very good sign.

* Decide whether to take up the trail alone or get assistance. In the case of potentially dangerous game, it's usually wise to enlist the aid of a companion. When hunting with a guide, listen to his advice and follow his instructions. Never use more than three to four people on a blood trail. Too much help causes more problems than it solves.

* Refrain from rushing. It's natural to want to locate your game; however, it's best to proceed slowly, marking the blood trail as you go in the event you need to retrace your steps later. Never walk in the path itself; stay to one side. Don't obliterate sign. If the trail is spotty, take special care to find and mark all blood. A companion can assist here, hanging tissue or tying tape to limbs or brush as you continue your search.

* Check leaves and grass for blood but don't overlook rocks, logs, tree trunks or bare ground. If blood is scarce, look for scuff marks left by the animal's hooves or pads. Look back along your marked trail from time to time to help get a feel for the animal's line of travel.

* If you lose all blood sign, continue the search by following the general direction the animal was heading. Some bowhunters begin walking in a tight but ever-expanding circle from the last blood sign. Others use companions to fan out and search for clues. It's wise to conduct orderly searches whenever possible. Random wandering through an area in hopes of stumbling across the animal is a last resort.

Keep in mind that mortally wounded animals often follow the path of least resistance, avoiding natural obstacles and seldom traveling uphill. Look in and around water. Probe heavy thickets. Look under deadfalls. **Think** like the animal by putting yourself in its place. Allow instinct to take over.

If your arrow was well-placed, chances are good you'll locate your animal within the first 100 to 200 yards. But even hard-hit game possesses tremendous stamina so don't be surprised or discouraged if the trail is longer. And don't let the amount of blood fool you. Sometimes most of the bleeding is internal and a lack of good blood sign doesn't mean much. Naturally, we all like the kind of blood trail you can follow at a fast walk—but these are the exception. Sticktoitiveness is essential in recovering most arrow-hit game.

Note: String tracking devices are now manufactured and sold by several major archery companies. These units are designed to help bowhunters recover arrow-hit animals by following a trail of nylon line. The tracking spool itself, containing hundreds of feet of easily visible line, is mounted to the bow. The thin but sturdy line attaches to the arrow and plays out when the animal moves away after the shot. Ideally, all the bowhunter has to do to claim his trophy is to follow the trail of nylon string. At times, however, the line may tangle or break and there have been some reports of string trackers affecting arrow flight. While they can and do work quite well, any bowhunter planning to use a string tracker should thoroughly test shoot his choice of tracking device and remember there's no substitute for a keen-edged, well placed broadhead. String trackers are worth consideration as one possible answer to game recovery, not **the** answer.

Working out a blood trail is no time for rushing things. Easy-does-it is a key to tracking success. Persistence pays.

Night trailing is worth mentioning. If game is hit shortly before darkness falls, the bowhunter must make a decision of following after the brief waiting period or postponing the search until the following morning. In some cases a wait could result in meat spoilage and a ruined trophy. Threatening weather may be another consideration. The risk of pursuing certain species after dark is still another problem.

Really, if the arrow was well-placed, there's no reason to postpone the search because of darkness. Blood reflects light and Coleman lanterns or bright-beamed flashlights are valuable in night tracking. In most cases at least two people should be present to unravel the trail. Generally, the same rules of daytime tracking apply to after-dark searches.

If all your best efforts fail to find the animal, what can be done? Most responsible bowhunters search until they are certain beyond any reasonable doubt that the animal is not recoverable. If the blood trail peters out after several hundred yards without evidence the animal is even slowing down, chances are good the hit was non-fatal. If the trail is lost, and the hunter is convinced the hit was fatal, he may continue to search as long as he remains in the area. Scavenger birds and other varmints may help locate a lost carcass. The same is true of odor during warm weather hunting.

The Pope and Young Club will not accept trophies eventually located once the initial search has been abandoned. For example, if a hunter shoots a buck on the first day of his hunt, tracks it but loses the blood trail, gives up searching and resumes hunting, that's it. Even if he later locates the deer he shot, it is ineligible for entry in the record listing. Conversely, if he had continued the search over a period of several days—forsaking his hunting in a determined effort to find his game—he hasn't abandoned the search and could possibly enter it for consideration as a record book entry.

Such dedication is both commendable and deserving of recognition. If more bowhunters made every effort possible to take close shots well within their effective shooting range, to place each arrow in the heart-lung area and to doggedly follow every blood trail, very few animals would be lost. This, in turn, would give critics of bowhunting little reason to complain.

Field Care of Game

8

It always amuses me to hear people talking about the "wild taste" or "gamy flavor" of venison and other big game. If properly cared for in the field, the meat of virtually every big game animal can be transformed into mouth-watering meals. While the animal's age, condition and treatment by a chef are certainly contributing factors to the flavor of the meat, it remains any bowhunter's primary responsibility to promptly care for the carcass of all game killed.

Approach every animal cautiously. Make certain it's dead before taking hold of its antlers, horns or head. Move in from behind downed game, staying away from the hind legs which could cause injury should the animal suddenly begin to thrash about. Be especially cautious if the animal is lying in a bunched up position or if its head is up. Any animal capable of holding its head erect is in need of a follow-up arrow. Dead game generally lies sprawled where it fell.

If a tossed rock or jab with a sharp broadhead elicits no response, the animal is likely dead. The final test is to touch the animal's open eye with a stick or broadhead. Dead animals won't blink.

Note: Never cut the animal's throat. This is a sure-fire way to spoil any potential mount and to upset your taxidermist. Since arrow-killed game most often dies by bleeding to death, cutting the throat is wasted effort. In fact, cutting the throat of any dead animal is a total waste of time since the heart must be beating if blood is to be pumped out of the neck incision.

So what do you do first? Fill out and attach your game tag, of course. Next, time and weather conditions permitting, I urge you to take time for a few photographs. These make fine mementos of a memorable bowhunt. Resist the temptation to have an arrow protruding from the carcass. If the shaft is still in the body, remove it. And never stick or replace an arrow in the entrance wound. It adds absolutely nothing to the photo and tends to turn many viewers off.

Also be sure the tongue is not lolling out of the animal's mouth (replace it, if necessary) and avoid especially bloody photos. If possible, fold the animal's legs under it. By all means place your bow so it shows in the picture. On antlered game such as deer or horned game such as antelope, use two fingers to hold the ears erect as you grasp the animal's headgear or neck. Never hold the trophy solely by the ears. Treat all animals with the respect they deserve.

Shoot at least one roll of film before beginning the field dressing chores. Turn the animal's head slightly with each click of the shutter. Vary your own body position, too. If hunting buddies or a guide are handy, they can simplify the photo-taking process. Include them in the photos, too. If you have a camera with a timer and shutter-release button, you can set up the shots yourself even though it takes longer and involves considerable running back and forth between the camera and the carcass. But even photos of the animal and your hunting gear can make interesting shots if some thought is given to the composition of the picture.

Once the photo session is over, lay your bow aside

and roll up your sleeves. It's time to turn full attention to the field dressing chores. A well-honed knife, rope or cord, bone saw or hatchet and a hone for touching up the skinning blade are essentials. Some bowhunters carry paper towels or pre-moistened hand wipes in their packs along with a plastic bag for the heart, kidneys and liver. A few fastidious individuals even carry a pair of rubber or disposable plastic gloves to wear during the gutting process.

The size of some animals—moose or elk, for example—makes on-the-spot field dressing mandatory. Smaller animals such as deer or pronghorns may be moved to a better location. And in certain cases, such as when hunting game over bait or near a water hole, it may prove unwise to gut the animal near the bait or water. Blood smell and viscera may spook or alert approaching game for days to come.

Regardless, to begin the dressing process—with the animal on its side or back—an incision must be made from anus to the breast bone. Rope or cord may be used to tie legs apart and help position the carcass. (Animals lying slightly downhill are in an excellent field dressing position.) Some people start the cut in the area of the animal's soft upper belly while others begin at the genitals. Whether cutting up or down the body, the point to remember is to keep the cut shallow—perhaps one-eighth to one-quarter inch—and to avoid slicing the intestines or rupturing the bladder. Sliding two fingers along on either side of the knife's blade between the skin and intestines works well with practice.

If evidence of sex must be maintained on the carcass, leave the testicles or udder attached. Otherwise, slice the identifying tissues away and discard them. Next make a deep, circular cut around the anus, as if coring an apple. This frees the lower end of the intestine and facilitates the later removal of the rectal tube.

When a trophy is to be saved for mounting, the sternum and ribcage should not be split. Otherwise it's smart to open the chest by cutting through the cartilage to the base of the throat. Reach into the chest cavity and cut the liver free (if it is to be saved

for the kitchen). Locate the heart and repeat the extraction process. Next slice the diaphragm muscle free of the ribs and then reach up into the throat to cut through the esophagus and trachea. Then, laying the knife aside, firmly grasp the windpipe and feeding tube. Pull down hard to free the chest contents above the diaphragm. Finally, tug or pull—cutting when necessary—the stomach and intestines free. The bean-shaped kidneys will usually remain attached to the back wall of the animal but are easily located and removed. The freed intestinal mass may be pulled between or to the side of the animal's rear legs, completing the field dressing process.

Note: At times the pelvic bone must be split or sawed through to completely free the rectal tube. Any pellets or other fecal matter must be cleaned away. Failure to do so may cause tainted meat.

Besides excrement, an animal's blood and intestinal fluids can cause meat to take on a strong flavor; however, I'm convinced the prime reason for tainted meat is improper cooling to eliminate body heat. In the chapter dealing with elk, for example, there is special mention made of the potential problems along with suggestions for cooling elk venison for best culinary results.

If it's possible to elevate the animal in some cool or shady spot, do so as quickly as possible after the field dressing process is completed. Hanging allows blood to drain from the body cavity and air to circulate completely around the carcass. Remember, body heat is retained wherever the animal is in contact with the ground. Porous game bags are a wise early season investment and a sprinkling of black pepper will discourage ever-present blowflies. Never hang the animal in the sun. Propping the chest cavity open helps the loss of body heat.

Note: It's wise to always hang the game head up to allow proper drainage. Use a rope or stout cord and don't hang horned or antlered game by the throat if the trophy is to be saved for mounting (rope marks may later show in the cape). Always tie such animals by the antlers or horns.

With larger game, it may be necessary to quarter the animal at the kill site. And there are some bowhunters who opt to bone out the meat at the spot where the animal fell. They insist it's foolish to pack out bones and anything else which isn't edible or which isn't destined for the taxidermist. Even so, the hide, cape, horns and antlers of some animals often can amount to quite a load for one man...not to mention adding a backpack full of choice cuts. It's wise not to try to carry too much in a single trip. If a companion is nearby, enlist his assistance. But in the case of larger game, pack animals are a viable option along with the recruitment of willing hunting buddies. Paid guides and their associates generally provide packing services as part of the hunt package.

In bear country—especially where grizzly or brown bears live—a gut pile or cooling carcass are open invitations to a free meal. And in reality it's unwise to hang game in camp where a bear may be attracted by the tempting food smell. Common sense precautions can avoid possible confrontations between bowhunters and hungry bruins.

If the animal can be dragged or packed to camp or a waiting vehicle, this process is best accomplished by two or more people. On antlered and horned game, pulling the animals by their headgear is possible and much easier than using the forelegs. Care should be exercised not to bruise the meat through rough handling and not to spoil the potential mount by rubbing bare spots in the hide as the animal is dragged.

Some game is small enough for one person to drag or carry; however, it's best not to overexert yourself. The excited, out-of-condition bowhunter is a prime candidate for a coronary. And while bowhunting is a generally safe sport, it's still wise to tie fluorescent tape or cloth to any animal being carried. Care also needs to be taken to insure a game tag is not pulled free and lost enroute between the kill site and camp.

Commercial deer dragging harnesses and belts are now offered and may be worth investigation. Regardless, tying the front legs to the head of any animal being dragged from the woods prevents them from constantly catching on brush and other obstacles.

Once the camp or vehicle is reached, further consideration should be given to preserving the meat and hide. If a motor vehicle is used to transport the animal, be certain legal requirements are met and all tags are filled out and in place. In some hunting areas portions of the animal must be visible for easy identification by wildlife officers.

Don't ever tie the animal to the hood where the heat from the vehicle's engine may cause tainting problems. Carry the game on the roof or on the trunk and use a game bag, tarp or blanket to protect it. Don't skin the carcass before hot, dusty trips but, if possible, make sure the animal's body heat has dissipated before the journey. Never transport game in a closed trunk or unventilated trailers where air cannot circulate.

Note: Thoroughly cooled carcasses or game quarters may be wrapped in tarps, sleeping bags or other well-insulated material for transportation. On long hauls dry ice or large coolers filled with blocks or bags of ice can preserve the meat. Some bowhunters have constructed special insulated meat boxes for out-of-state hunts and include them as an important part of their gear season after season.

No chapter on field dressing game would be complete without some mention of whether it's necessary to remove the musk glands on deer and certain other hoofed animals. Some "experts" and stubborn old-timers insist this procedure is mandatory to maintain the quality of the meat. I for one believe it's best to leave the scent glands completely alone. Handling them before touching the meat can spoil the meat's flavor because odor and fluids may be transferred by touch. Ignore these scent glands and they'll have no affect whatsoever on the meat's flavor.

Skinning and Caping Game

If your trophy is destined for the taxidermist, you must be aware of certain skinning and caping techniques necessary to insure best results for a lifelike mount.

Simply explained, caping refers to skinning the shoulders, neck and head of any trophy animal. It is best accomplished by making a single incision from between the shoulders up the back of the neck to a spot just below the antlers or horns. Next a cut is made completely around the animal's body **behind** the shoulders. Then the shoulders and neck are skinned until the junction of the neck and skull is reached. At this point the head and hide may be freed by cutting or sawing through the neck vertebrae and twisting the head and cape loose. Unless you're proficient at skinning out the skull and turning the ears, this job is best left for the taxidermist. Salt the cape thoroughly and roll or fold the hide, hair side out. Store in a cool or shady place and get the head and cape to a taxidermist as quickly as possible. Keep in mind that spoilage may occur if the temperature ranges above 45 to 50 degrees.

Note: Some bowhunters with access to large coolers or a freezer preserve their hides or capes by freezing them. This preservation method works well. Just remember that the sooner any taxidermist receives the cape or hide for mounting, whether well-salted or frozen, the better the chances for an excellent mount. So if possible, talk to the taxidermist before the hunt and ask for instructions for preserving and delivering the trophy in the best possible condition. Follow his directions.

If a rug is to be made of the trophy—common practice with bears and cougars—or if a lifesize mount is planned, the skinning process is somewhat more involved. In these cases an incision is made from anus to sternum (on rugs the cut may continue to the animal's throat or chin). Additional cuts are made down the inside of each leg to a point just above the hoof or paw. The skin is then peeled and cut away from the body until completely free. The feet and head are then separated at the last joint and left attached to the hide. The tail may be cut free at the root or split up the underside to facilitate removal of the tail bone.

If warm weather or other reasons pose a serious threat to the skin it's probably best to remove the skull and feet from the hide. Special care must be paid to cutting around the animal's ears, eyes, nostrils and lips. The same is true for the area at the base of antlers and horns. Additional care is

In caping horned or antlered game, make an incision up the back of the animal's neck from a point behind the front shoulder.

needed removing the paw cartilage. It's best to cut as closely to the skull as possible and allow the taxidermist to do the final trimming of unnecessary skin. However, it is wise to remove as much clinging meat as possible before heavily salting the hide. Be sure to work salt into folds and creases in the skin before folding the hide, hair side out, for storage or transport. Do not store the hide in a plastic garbage bag unless it is bound for the freezer.

If the animal is not going to be mounted, the skinning process generally starts with the removal of the animal's front legs at or near the knee joints. A cut is then made through the tendons behind each hock joint and the animal is hung, head down, by hooks or a gambrel. Slit the skin around each hind leg just below the hocks, extending the cut down the inside of each rear leg. Take care not to cut into the meat itself and do not let the hair touch the exposed meat. Peel the hide down, pulling and cut-

Once the skinning chore is complete, it is ready to be cut up by a handy do-it-yourselfer or a knowledgeable butcher. Strict health laws sometimes make it difficult to locate a meat processing operation that will accept wild game; however, in certain parts of the country—especially many heavily hunted Western states—finding someone to cut and wrap game animals is relatively simple. Anyone initially attempting the process himself should refer to a diagram showing correct cuts and use a well-illustrated butchering guide.

There are some bowhunters who insist that venison and other wild game is best if properly "aged" before processing. They often let the animals hang, from several days to a week or more, in 40-degree or slightly lower temperatures and swear this makes the meat taste better. Others process the animals immediately with excellent results. In truth there is probably no one best way to age or treat game animals bound for the freezer. People have different tastes—and ideas—and only experimentation will determine what's right for you and your family.

Just remember the meat of most big game species can provide numerous meals for a period of several months. No bowhunter should overlook the culinary qualities of the big game trophies he pursues.

In skinning a bear or lion to make a rug or full-size mount, make the cut from sternum to vent and down each leg.

ting as necessary, until you reach the front legs. Make cuts from the knee joints down the inner leg to the chest. Free the skin from each leg and shoulder. Continue to tug and cut until the skin is hanging over the head with most of the neck exposed. Cut deeply and completely around the neck near the head, then saw or twist the head and hide free. The animal is now completely skinned.

Note: While pronghorn hides make poor leather, tanning the skins of deer and certain other game may make salvaging the hide worthwhile. Gloves, vests, rugs and similar items may be made from your trophy. Even the hooves can be transformed into bow racks, clothes hooks, table lamps, knife handles and many other items of interest to outdoorsmen. Any qualified taxidermist can explain various options and give an estimate of costs involved. The buoyant hair of several species of the cervidae family makes excellent fly-tying material.

Trophy Recognition

9

Mere mention of the word "trophy" conjures up many different images in the minds of bowhunters. To more experienced hunters, it often means an outsized, record book animal. A real wall-hanger. To beginners, it understandably may mean any legal animal—male or female—taken with the hunting bow.

Personally, I feel **any** adult big game animal—legally taken under the rules of Fair Chase—is a "trophy" to the bowhunter making the kill. For example, a few of my most unforgettable bowhunts ended with my tag being tied to an "average"

Although most bowhunters dream of a big-racked buck, many settle for a ''trophy'' of smaller proportions.

animal. Some of these trophies came much harder than certain Pope and Young animals I've managed to collect over the years. Therefore no one is ever going to convince me such big game animals are not true trophies.

The definition of a bowhunting trophy—like beauty—lies in the eye and mind of the beholder.

But admittedly it's also human nature to appreciate recognition for outstanding accomplishments. And when it comes to recognizing the top North American big game trophies taken with the bow and arrow, the Pope and Young Club stands head and shoulders above any other bowhunting organization.

The Pope and Young Club

Officially founded in Seattle, Washington on January 27, 1961, the Pope and Young Club came into being thanks to the efforts of Glenn St. Charles. St. Charles, an avid promoter of bowhunting since the 1940s, had two basic objectives in mind for his newly formed organization. First, he sought to improve the image of the bowhunter by proving the bow and arrow could be both humane and effective in harvesting big game animals. Second, he wanted to record and recognize for posterity the outstanding examples of North American big game animals taken with the hunting bow.

Actually, the Pope and Young trophy compilations began in 1957-58 as a part of the National Field Archery Association's Hunting Activities

Committee. Grayling, Michigan was the site of the first Awards Program which was held as part of the 1958 NFAA Tournament. Initially there were 41 trophies listed and the top trophy in each category was declared the World Bowhunting Record.

Favorable response was immediate. As word of the new all-bowhunting record keeping organization spread, entries began to pour in. Official measurers were trained and requests for information came from interested bowhunters and state conservation departments alike. By 1960, when the second Awards Program was held in Grayling, it was apparent to St. Charles that there was a need for an independent organization—patterned after the time-tested Boone and Crockett Club—to record North American big game taken with a bow. The club would also promote sound conservation practices, quality bowhunting and fair chase practices.

Appropriately, the new club was named for bowhunting pioneers Arthur Young and Dr. Saxton Pope. St. Charles soon obtained the 1957-60 records compiled by the NFAA Hunting Activities Committee and the rest is history.

Today the Pope and Young Club holds two-year recording comparisons to honor the top skulls, horns and antlers collected by North American bowhunters. Data obtained during each biennial period is entered into the Club archives. Information

Part of each P&Y Awards Banquet involves the presentation of plaques for top animals. Randy Byers congratulates Noel Feather.

is now computerized and updated on a regular basis. At the time of this writing the Pope and Young Club has published two books of bowhunting records. The first appeared in 1975, the second in 1981. A third edition is planned for 1987.

Every two years the Pope and Young Club also meets to hold an Awards Program and Banquet. New World Records are declared and honored. Additionally, top specimens in each big game category receive deserved recognition. The Club's top honor, the Ishi Award, may be presented when a trophy is deemed deserving of special recognition.

Pope and Young biennial recordings are open to all bowhunters. Trophies entered must be taken with a hunting bow during legal seasons under Fair Chase rules. Official measurers, the backbone of the organization, are found throughout the country and scoring information or a list of measurers may be obtained by writing:

Dr. C. Randall Byers
P & Y Records Committee Chairman

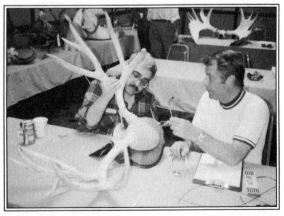

Pope and Young measurers Dr. Gene Altiere and Jim Dougherty score the World Record mule deer taken in Colorado by Bill Barcus.

1804 Borah
Moscow, ID 83843

To qualify as a Pope and Young trophy, animals must meet or exceed established minimum scores. Minimums may be changed from time to time at the discretion of the Directors. A complete list of Pope and Young Club minimum point standards appears elsewhere in this chapter.

No trophy may be officially scored until 60 days have elapsed from the date of kill. This period allows for normal shrinkage of skulls, horns or antlers and is often referred to as the "drying period" by trophy hunters and measurers. Each scoring form must be accompanied by three photos of the trophy—showing the frontal and side views—and a $25.00 entry fee. A signed Fair Chase affidavit is the final requirement. Each bowhunter whose trophy form is accepted and recorded will receive a colorful certificate suitable for framing. These certificates list the species, when and where the animal was taken and the official Pope and Young score.

As previously mentioned, the Pope and Young recordings are open to any bowhunter; however, the Club offers three classifications of membership to individuals wishing to join and support it. All new members are placed in the Associate category. To qualify, applicants must have legally taken one adult big game animal under the rules of Fair Chase. There is no limit to the number of Associates.

There is a limit of 100 Regular Members, each of whom must have taken at least one adult animal of three various species, one of which must be of record class. An Associate's advancement to Regular membership must be proposed and seconded by two Regular Members and at least three letters from Regular Members endorsing membership must be provided. Associates, if accepted, then move into Regular membership as openings occur.

Finally, the Senior membership category is available to Regular Members who meet the requirements. Applicants for Senior status must have served as a Regular Member for a minimum of five years. Also, they must have legally taken at least one adult animal from four species of North

Pope & Young Minimum Scores*

Alaskan Brown Bear	20
Black Bear	18
Grizzly Bear	19
Polar Bear**	20
Bison	80
Barren Ground Caribou	300
Mountain Caribou	265
Quebec/Labrador Caribou	300
Woodland Caribou	220
Cougar	13
Columbian Blacktail Deer	90
Sitka Blacktail Deer	65
Coues Deer (typical)	60
Coues Deer (non-typical)	66
Mule Deer (typical)	145
Mule Deer (non-typical)	160
Whitetail Deer (typical)	125
Whitetail Deer (non-typical)	150
Roosevelt Elk	210
Yellowstone Elk	260
Rocky Mountain Goat	40
Alaska/Yukon Moose	170
Canada Moose	135
Wyoming Moose	115
Muskox	65
Pronghorn Antelope	64
Bighorn Sheep	140
Dall Sheep	120
Stone Sheep	120
Desert Bighorn Sheep	140
Jaguar**	14

*These minimums may be changed from time to time at the discretion of the Club's Directors. **No entries accepted in this category until further notice.

American big game with three of these of record class and entered in the Pope and Young records. There is no limit to the number of Senior Members.

At the time of this writing the Pope and Young Club has some 2,000 members. Its Conservation Committee is actively supporting certain educational, field research and game management

The author, a Senior Member of the Pope and Young Club, poses with some of his bowhunting trophies.

programs. Both moral and monetary support is provided.

Bowhunters interested in joining the Pope and Young Club may obtain complete membership information by writing:

Naomi J. Torrey
P & Y Executive Secretary/Treasurer
6471 Richard Avenue
Placerville, CA 95667

The Boone and Crockett Club

Some bowhunters mistakenly believe that the Boone and Crockett Club is for gun-killed trophies only. In truth, the Club welcomes entries from any hunter no matter what his choice of weapon. The primary reason so few bowhunting kills are listed in the B & C records is because of the high minimum requirements.

For example, to be eligible for the Pope and Young listings a mule deer with typical antlers must score 145 points. To qualify for the Boone and Crockett records, however, a muley must score 195 points. Consequently, all of the bow-killed mule deer eligible for B & C recognition could be counted on one hand. It wasn't until 1985 that a bowhunter—Bill Barcus of Colorado—earned recognition for

This World Record whitetail, taken by Mel Johnson of Illinois, won both the Ishi Award and the Sagamore Hill Medal.

Bowhunters wanting a listing of minimum requirements and information about the Boone and Crockett Club should write:

William H. Nesbitt
B & C Administrative Director
205 South Patrick Street
Alexandria, VA 22314

The NRA

In January of 1984 the National Rifle Association began to offer its members who enjoy bowhunting an opportunity to earn awards for trophies deemed worthy of recognition.

Fourteen categories of North American big game are listed in the NRA Big Game Hunter Awards. Minimums are somewhat lower than Pope and Young requirements. Examples include a whitetail deer with "at least four points on the side," a black bear with a skull measurement of 16 inches, a moose with a tip-to-tip spread of 40 inches and a sheep with a three-quarters curl. In addition, the NRA has added wild turkeys to the list and any gobbler with a beard over eight inches long is eligible for an award.

Forms provided by the NRA must be used for all entries. Also required is one front-view photo and a $16.95 application fee. There is no time limit and applications may be submitted at any time for any animal taken in any previous year.

Outstanding bow and arrow trophies—those exceeding the Boone and Crockett minimums—are eligible for the prestigious NRA Leatherstocking Award Contest. These entries must be accompanied by an official Pope and Young Club or Boone and Crockett Club scoring form.

For NRA membership information and details on the NRA Big Game Hunter Awards, interested bowhunters should write:

National Rifle Association
Hunter Services Division
1600 Rhode Island Avenue, NW
Washington, DC 20036

taking a muley that scored over 200. The Barcus buck had an official score of 201 4/8. This new bowhunting World Record replaced a buck scoring 197 0/8, a mere two inches over the Boone and Crockett minimum. Yet this bow and arrow trophy and former bowhunting World Record had stood virtually unchallenged since 1969!

Regardless, more and more bowhunters are earning trophy recognition beyond the Pope and Young Club. Each season outstanding bowhunting trophies are taken that qualify for Boone and Crockett recognition and awards.

One bowhunter, Mel Johnson of Illinois, was presented with the B & C Club's highest honor—the Sagamore Hill Medal—for his bowhunting World Record whitetail deer. Johnson's huge buck scored 204 4/8. Shot in 1965, it still ranks as one of the top whitetails of all time.

Other Possibilities

Today there are literally hundreds of local and state or provincial bowhunting clubs which offer their membership various awards for bowhunting accomplishments. Certificates, plaques and trophies are awarded for everything from the biggest animal to the smallest, from a first kill to the funniest in-the-field happening. No matter where any bowhunter lives, chances are good there's a bowhunting club nearby—or as close as the nearest mailbox.

Sporting goods stores, pro shops and archery dealers frequently sponsor "Big Buck" contests and similar seasonal events for customers. A few national magazines offer awards or conduct contests for readers or carry advertisements detailing various opportunities for trophy recognition.

Some states keep meticulous records of bow-killed game and on occasion publish elaborate record books. In 1973 the **Colorado Bowhunting Records of Big Game Animals**, compiled and edited by Lee Kline for the Colorado Bowhunters Association, was published in a well-illustrated hardcover edition. In 1980 a similar book, **Bowhunting in Arizona**, appeared through the efforts of Tom Dalrymple and his Record Book Committee.

While such books are the exception—understandably so when costs and a coordination of efforts is required—many states maintain and record listings on a regular basis. For example, the California Bowmen Hunters started keeping records of big game animals taken within state boundaries in 1962. The Lone Star Bowhunters publishes a listing of state records of not only big game but bowfishing records, exotics and javelina/feral hogs as well. The Washington State Bowhunters publish quality softcover record books on occasion. The list goes on.

Having spotlighted exotics elsewhere in this book, it should be noted that at least one organization, the Texas-based Records of Exotics, keeps tabs on non-North American game trophies and offers awards to successful hunters. For details, write:

Records of Exotics
Box 502
Irving, TX 78025

Bowhunters successfully pursuing African game should be aware of **Rowland Ward's Records of Big Game**. First published in 1892, this record book now lists game animals taken with the bow. Details may be obtained by writing:

Rowland Ward's Records
Game Conservation International
P.O. Box 17444
San Antonio, TX 78209

Safari Club International (SCI) is still another organization which offers awards for bowhunting accomplishments. Details are available by writing:

Safari Club International
5151 East Broadway, Suite 1680
Tucson, AZ 85711

These and lesser known organizations give bowhunters everywhere the opportunity to receive recognition for their accomplishments. Some undoubtedly feel that recording organizations, contests and the like are unnecessary, that the personal satisfaction a bowhunter gains in harvesting a big game animal is reward enough. But unless the quest for recognition becomes obsessive and leads to cheating, lying and violations of game laws, there is probably no harm in continuing the practice. This is especially true if the bowhunter remembers the choice of entering into public competition is his or hers. Most bowhunting veterans agree the only real competition is between hunter and quarry in the recurring drama of life and death in the few truly wild places left on earth.

Part II

Midword

North America's bowhunters are fortunate.

While certain other parts of the world—Africa, for example—may harbor more species of native game, no place on earth offers the variety of wildlife **and the freedom to pursue it** found on this continent. This freedom of choice and the almost endless opportunities for pursuit combine to make North American big game hunting second to none.

True, hunting is becoming an increasingly expensive outdoor pastime. Equipment costs more. Transportation costs more. The required permits and licenses cost more—especially when out-of-state or out-of-country bowhunts are planned.

But the bottom line is unchanged: bowhunting can be a very affordable sport. Once the initial outlay of cash for basic equipment has been made, affordable bowhunting opportunities exist within a relatively short drive of any place in America.

Bowhunters successfully pursue deer within sight of the skyline of our largest cities. Backyard bowhunting is common in many suburban and rural areas. And while "getting away" or "packing in" remain viable possibilities for many sportsmen, the time and expense associated with trips to remote, inaccessible areas of the continent need not deter budget-conscious men and women who seek to share in the excitement of the sport.

Part I of this book centered attention on the history and basics of bowhunting. It detailed the need for physical and mental preparation. It stressed the planning stages, offered the various hunting methods and presented ideas for game recovery and trophy care. It, in essence, focused on methods for becoming a bowhunter.

Part II, which follows, deals with the North American big game animals bowhunters commonly pursue. Each chapter contains interesting details about the animals themselves; however, perhaps more important are the in-depth discussions of effective bowhunting techniques. A perceptive reader will garner many helpful hints while gaining a better understanding of the various ways to collect the species of his or her choice. Straight talk and no-nonsense advice are presented in the following species-by-species examination of North American big game.

Bowhunting, of course, is now a worldwide activity. No "Complete Guide to Big Game Bowhunting" would indeed be complete without some mention of opportunities in other parts of the globe. Additionally, brief attention is paid to certain species of game—the "exotics," for example—not native to the continent but certainly available to bowhunters. And passing mention is made of such species as turkeys and javelina which some feel deserve the "big game" title.

A primary goal of the section which follows is to offer an understanding of the animals most commonly pursued by bowhunters and to make readers safe, knowledgeable and successful bowhunters. It also is hoped the information will instill an appreciation of the wildlife itself and the most challenging of outdoor sports.

Black Bears . . . Woodland Ghosts

10

There is something about bears and bear hunting that holds a special fascination and appeal for many bowhunters. Perhaps it's the aura of mystery that surrounds these furtive woodland animals or maybe it's the element of gut-wrenching anxiety involved in pursuing large, potentially dangerous game. Whatever the reason or reasons, the black bear is without a doubt a highly prized and highly sought after bowhunting trophy.

A native North American, the black bear (*Ursus americanus)* prefers mixed hardwood and conifer forests—from high mountains to swampy lowlands—and today is found in greatest numbers north of the U.S.-Canadian border. Alaska has more bears than any state. In the contiguous forty-eight states, black bears range from Washington southward through Oregon and into California as well as east into the Rocky Mountain states where they are found as far south as Mexico. In the upper Midwest bears favor the timbered expanses of Minnesota, Wisconsin and Michigan. In the Northeast the bears range south and west from Maine into other New England states and down the Appalachian Mountains into the southern United States. Black bears also are found across the Gulf Coast states from Texas to Florida. Although it is impossible to take an accurate inventory of the present black bear population in North America, it is safe to estimate the number at 200,000 to 300,000 animals.

Distant ancestors to the modern black bear were thought to come to North America from Asia half a million years ago. And of the four species of bears found on the continent, only the black bear is actually increasing in numbers. The reason is obvious. Unlike the belligerent, aggressive big bears—the grizzly, Alaskan brown and polar bears—the black bear learned to fear humans. Instead of confronting man—and inevitably losing the fight—the black bear won by retreating and adapting. Although black bears will attack on occasion as when cornered, wounded or pressured, they generally avoid all contacts with humans and often choose to run rather than fight.

Black bears are considerably smaller animals than the bigger bear species and lack the prominent shoulder humps. They have a straight profile like the polar bear rather than the concave profile of a brown or grizzly bear. And it is important to note that the term "black bear" may be misleading since these bears have several color phases. Most eastern, southern and northern black bears are indeed a glossy ebony shade; however, in much of the West—excluding Washington State—the black bears are frequently brown, blond or red and are often referred to as "cinnamon" bears. The bluish-coated glacier bear of southeast Alaska is still another color variation. In British Columbia there's even a rare white subspecies called "kermode bears," and rarely a true albino black bear is reported. Many black bears have small triangular, diamond-or V-shaped patches of white hairs on their chests.

Not surprisingly, many bear hunters tend to overestimate the weight of their trophies. This is due to pride and the animals' long, lustrous body hair. Average-sized bears weigh perhaps 150 to 250 pounds with big boars going as much as 400 pounds or more. Truly exceptional specimens—some weighing over 600 pounds—have been reported. The biggest black bear on record was a Wisconsin giant that supposedly went 802 pounds.

Boars typically stand two to three feet at the shoulder and measure four to six feet from nose to stubby tail. Sows average one-fourth to one-third less.

Black bears walk on the soles of their feet and leave distinct pad marks that bowhunters quickly come to recognize. Claws may not be apparent in tracks unless the ground is soft. A bear's front foot is four to five inches long while the hind foot is six to seven inches. Tracks with a width of five or more inches are regarded as above average.

Note: Black bears have five toes on each paw, each equipped with a non-retractable claw of one to two inches in length. Adult black bears are the only members of the *Ursidae* family capable of climbing trees with relative ease. Brown and grizzly bear cubs can climb trees and on occasion an adult of these species may clamber into low-limbed trees for one reason or another. Generally they don't bother and more than one hunter, hiker or camper has saved his skin by taking to the treetops when confronted by an angry bruin.

Black bears have large, rounded ears and a well-developed sense of hearing that helps in avoiding close confrontations with man. Their eyes are small, pig-like, and their vision relatively poor; all bears are believed to be nearsighted. They do have an exceptionally keen sense of smell and rely on the telltale odors to locate food and avoid danger. Bears also have a highly developed sense of taste and their weakness for sweets is well-documented. More about this later in the discussion on baiting.

Seemingly always hungry, bears are not picky eaters and will pass up very little which is edible— from insects to meats, grass to fruit and farm crops, plus about everything in between. Upon first emerging from the winter dens, they drink a considerable amount of water and then devour sprouting grasses, spring buds and even inner bark of pine trees. Once their digestive systems are

functioning again, they turn to meat, digging up rodents and killing the young of other big game species they happen across. Bears also turn to scavenging, feeding on winter-killed animals. They sometimes track, kill and eat old, sick or crippled animals. Garbage dumps and food left unattended by campers or picnickers will also lure black bears.

Ripening berries attract bruins like magnets and in years of good mast crops they gorge themselves on acorns—especially the white oak variety. Bears also raid orchards, farm fields and the unattended hives of beekeepers. With the approach of fall, they may go into feeding frenzies as they build body fat and prepare for winter.

In areas with heavy human populations the black bears are mostly nocturnal animals. They prefer to feed late in the day, throughout the night and into the early morning hours. Then the bears retreat to heavy cover to rest during the heat of the day.

Boars are solitary animals and have nothing to do with other bears except during the breeding season in June and July. They travel a great deal, ranging across a home territory that has been estimated to include up to 100 square miles. When the sows come into heat, the boars seek their company and display considerable affection during the courtship. Sows reportedly come into estrous only once each season and breed only every other year.

Cubs are born in winter dens each January or February. At birth they are tiny, blind and nearly hairless animals weighing perhaps half a pound. They find their mothers' teats by smell and begin to nurse almost immediately. By the time the sow and her cubs leave the den in March or April the newborns weigh four to five pounds. Twins and triplets are common.

Sows are very protective of their young and will not hesitate to defend them. Many outdoorsmen can relate hair-raising tales of confrontations and narrow escapes from sows with cubs; most knowledgeable people living in bear country do whatever is necessary to avoid the overly protective females. Small sows even battle big boars that may be encountered if they feel their cubs are threatened.

Boars are known to kill and eat cubs on occasion.

Cubs remain with their mother throughout the first year and often den together during the winter months. The family group may part the following spring or remain together until the breeding season. Female black bears usually do not breed until their third season. Black bears often live past their mid-teens with some old-timers reaching their twenties.

Bears are normally quiet animals although "bear talk" may be overheard at times. Cubs bawl, whimper and cry to attract mama's attention and growl during mock battles with their siblings. Sows cough and grunt in response to their young and growl when angry. Boars make the same sounds and roar or pop their teeth when threatened or upset. Mortally wounded bears emit an eerie death moan that once heard is never forgotten.

Bears normally walk from place to place with the odd, shuffling gait of their species. When pushed they can move with surprising speed for large animals, running at speeds of 25 to 30 miles per hour.

Black bears do not really hibernate. They can be roused from their winter sleep by an intruder or a prolonged period of warm weather. Bears seem to prefer dens with north-facing openings and many create cozy nests of leaves and branches. Caves or crevices in rocky cliffs, blowdowns or deadfalls and natural depressions in heavy cover are all ideal denning sites. Across their northern range, bears head for their dens as early as late September or early October. In some warm southerly ranges bears do not "hibernate" at all.

Tracks are the most common and easily recognized bear sign. Droppings are also a clue not only to the presence of bears but to their dietary preferences. Scat is generally loose when the bears are feeding on grasses, berries and fruit; however, it is thicker and composed of ropy fecal plugs when meat or solid food is being consumed. Berry seeds, grass, hair and other undigested matter may be apparent in the bear scat.

Other signs include hair on favorite rubbing trees or rocks where they relieve itches by scratching themselves. Bears also mark their territory by raking trees with their claws, standing on their hind legs and reaching as high as they can to claw soft-barked trees. In areas of the West there are many white-trunked aspen trees marked forever with the claw marks of a climbing bear. These scars in the bark turn black upon healing and offer mute testimony to the fact the tree is in what was or is bear country.

Bears also turn over rocks and tear apart logs or stumps in their search for insects. They also expend considerable energy digging for bite-sized mice and ground squirrels. Evidence of their continuous quest for food is obvious in other forms, especially where bruins have clambered into chokecherry or fruit trees and broken branches during feeding binges.

Bear biologists—and many hunters—rate the black bear near the top when it comes to intelligence and elusiveness. Such testimony serves to increase the respect and appeal bowhunters hold for America's favorite bear.

Effective Bowhunting Techniques

There are four basic methods of bowhunting black bears—stalking/still-hunting, baiting, coursing with hounds and calling.

Calling black bears is the newest and—quite likely—the most exciting hunting method. Here the caller typically imitates injured rabbits or birds or he mimics the bleating sound of lost fawns. Bears, ever on the lookout for a free meal, may come to investigate the sounds.

This technique likely started by accident when predator callers—after coyotes or bobcats—found to their surprise that hungry bears also responded to their calling. Reports of face-to-face encounters between bears and callers undoubtedly led some more adventuresome hunters to actually try calling bruins. They quickly learned the method works.

As noted, this technique offers considerable excitement because the bear is actually stalking the hunter. The mere thought of a big bruin pinpointing the source of the caller's cries and coming to investigate is enough to make some bowhunters look to less adventuresome methods of collecting a bearskin rug for their dens.

Real or imagined danger aside, there are two major disadvantages to the calling method. First, the bear is already alerted and using his finely honed senses to find the "meal." A bowhunter moving into shooting position or drawing his bow is likely to be detected by sight or sound and the chances of getting a good shot are slim. Second, an approaching bear generally offers only a frontal, head-on shot; this is perhaps the poorest shot any bowhunter can take.

The use of tree stands can work to a bowhunter's advantage; however, bears have excellent hearing and can quickly locate the exact source of the distress calls. Bear are not stupid and may become suspicious of injured rabbit or lost fawn cries emanating from some tree. Perhaps a better technique involves a team—one caller and one shooter—with the concealed caller situated on the ground and the shooter in an elevated stand nearby.

Small game cries are likely to pull in a bear at any time of the year. Lost fawn calling naturally works best in the spring.

Still-hunting and stalking bears is unquestionably the most difficult and challenging bowhunting method. Locating a bear to stalk is not easy; working quietly into good bow range without being detected is doubly difficult. Regardless, each year a number of bears—including some true trophy-class animals—are arrowed in this manner.

In open country, particularly in the West, bears may be spotted on grassy sidehills as they feed on tender greens or ripe berries. Feeding black bears often have their attention focused on filling their stomachs and may be approached by a careful stalker. Of course, the hunter must constantly keep tabs on wind direction and avoid making any noise which could alert the bear.

Patience is essential. Long hours—perhaps days or weeks—must be spent finding a bear. Even in prime bear country animals may be hard to locate due to nocturnal habits and their secretive nature. Good binoculars help since considerable time may be spent just sitting on high points and carefully glassing opposite slopes.

Exceptions to the bears-are-hard-to-find rule do exist. In Alaska and certain other parts of the continent where annual salmon runs attract hungry predators, bears may be found in abundance. These black bears are often so intent on fishing and gorging themselves they can be approached with comparative ease. Often the splashing of the fish and sounds of the rushing water combine to effectively cover any sounds made by the stalking bowhunter.

Each year some black bears are shot by licensed hunters in search of other big game, particularly those after deer and elk. As these bowhunters slip through woodlands or wait on stands in prime game coverts, they suddenly see a bear and manage to get off a killing shot. This, of course, is not bear hunting; it is bear shooting. While they may deserve credit for their marksmanship, they cannot know or understand the thrill or satisfaction of the bowhunter who sets out to locate a bear, stalk him and eventually succeed in tagging his trophy. There are surely few greater bowhunting challenges and rewards.

Where legal, hunting bears with hounds is a popular and surprisingly demanding pastime. As with all hound hunting sports, the fascination of chasing bears with dogs is centered on the thrill of the chase; the shooting is usually anticlimatic. First, it requires a hardy, hunt-wise pack of specially trained hounds capable of trailing, harassing and then holding a bear at bay until the hunters arrive. Second, the rugged terrain, dense foliage and unbelievable endurance of the bear and dogs make each chase a potential cross-country marathon.

A popular method of finding a bear to run involves daybreak drives along old logging roads or trails in 4WD vehicles with keen-nosed strike dogs chained to special platforms atop the trucks. When a bear is winded, the hunters bail out to check for tracks. These give a clue to the animal's size and direction of travel. If the tracks are fresh and the conditions right, the strike dogs are released. Other hounds are turned loose as the chase progresses until the bear is brought to bay on the ground or chased up a tree by the persistent hounds. If no roads crisscross a hunting area, horses are commonly used to locate and pursue bears.

Most bear-dog chases are at best something of a crapshoot with Lady Luck smiling on the bruin more often than the hunter. Often the scent plays out. Frequently the chase moves out of hearing. Sometimes the dogs are lost. On occasion inexperienced hounds jump deer, coyotes or other game and promptly forget about the bear. Still other times, especially if the bear has been chased by several dog packs, he simply refuses to tree or bay and alternates between walking or running and fighting, keeping on the move and never giving the hunters an opportunity to get close. Such "walking bears" may remain on the move from daylight to dark without ever allowing the hunters to approach close enough for a shot.

Rarely, chases are short-lived, with the bear treeing almost immediately. At such times the hunter moves in, dispatches the bruin with a well-placed shot and leaves with the mistaken idea that bear hunting with hounds is easy.

True, shooting a treed bear is not especially difficult. Neither is arrowing a whitetail that walks under a tree stand. It's the effort required to get into either position for a killing shot that makes the big difference. The deer hunter may scout the area, put up a stand and wait for the deer to come to him. The bear hunter may follow a yowling pack of hounds over some of the most God-awful wild country around in a chase that lasts for hours. If he has the physical and mental toughness to keep up and finally reach the place where the bear has been cornered, he's earned the shot.

Bears bayed on the ground—in deadfalls or among boulders—present a completely different picture. They're angry, usually ringed by dogs and offer very difficult targets. They're also tough to kill in this worked up state, even when arrows are well-placed. Houndsmen hate such situations and fret over the possibility of an errant arrow—or a shoot-through—hitting a valuable dog. Some frenzied

hounds get careless around wounded bears and get clawed, bitten or swatted—sometimes fatally—by the dying bear.

Angry bears have been known to charge approaching hunters and caution is always necessary when a bowhunter moves into shooting position. Sometimes the mere sight of a growling, teeth-popping black bear, hair bristling along its neck and back, is enough to make the bowhunter lose all interest in collecting a bruin with a bow.

A few black bears will develop a taste for livestock—especially pork and mutton—and make periodic raids on domestic stock. Such nuisance bears are the bane of hog farmers and sheep ranchers who welcome houndsmen and often point out recent kills. Fresh kills are excellent starting points for bear-dog chases. The same is true of garbage piles or baits purposefully set out to attract hungry bears.

Baiting black bears, where legal, is certainly the most popular and effective method of getting within bow range of a future bearskin rug. Hound hunting is generally a costly proposition since few bowhunters own their own dogs and must hire the services of a competent houndsman. Such services come high in most cases. But any hunter with garbage—or access to large amounts of "bear goodies"—is a potential bait hunter.

Establishing a bait involves more than walking out in the woods and dumping a pail of garbage. It generally involves planning, hard work and more than a little bit of luck.

Finding a good bait site involves acquiring a knowledge of the territory to be hunted. Topo maps can pinpoint likely locations for a bait but firsthand inspection is required. Ideally, the bait will be situated in heavy cover. Bears are extremely wary animals and may visit an exposed bait only under the cover of darkness. Good bait spots include remote, rugged mountain canyons near streams or water sources, low-lying areas adjacent to bogs or swamps, normal travel routes and natural feeding areas.

Often bait hunters establish several baits, perhaps

POPE AND YOUNG CLUB
NORTH AMERICAN BIG GAME TROPHY SCORING FORM
BOWHUNTING

To:
P & Y Records Office
1804 Borah
Moscow, ID 83843

BIG GAME   RECORDS

BEAR   KIND OF BEAR _____

SEX _____

SEE OTHER SIDE FOR INSTRUCTIONS		Measurements
A Greatest Length Without Lower Jaw (Measured in Sixteenths)		
B Greatest Width (Measured in Sixteenths)		
TOTAL and FINAL SCORE		

Exact locality where killed _____ County _____ State _____

Date killed _____ By whom killed _____

Present owner _____

Address _____

Guide's Name and Address _____

Remarks: (Mention any abnormalities) _____

I certify that I have measured the above trophy on _____ 19 _____
at (address) _____ City _____
State _____ Zip Code _____ and that these measurements and data are, to the best
of my knowledge and belief, made in accordance with the instructions given.
Witness: _____ Signature _____
           (To Measurer's Signature)

                     Pope & Young Club Official Measurer

                     MEASURER (Print)

                     ADDRESS

                     CITY   STATE   ZIP

wound, stemming the flow of blood. Hair absorbs much of the blood that is lost. Hunters shooting down from elevated stands must get a low exit wound for there to be any blood trail at all; this is another excellent reason for using heavier-pulling bows which are capable of punching an arrow completely through the chest cavity.

String trackers are popular in some bear camps. These devices mount to the bow with a line attached to the arrow. After the shot the yards of string plays out as the animal runs, leaving a trail for the bowhunter to follow to claim his trophy without worrying about a poor or non-existent blood trail.

Arrow-hit bears usually crash away from the bait, bowling through brush in a hasty, noisy departure. Mortally wounded bruins often roar or groan. As previously mentioned, an eerie gurgling or rattling death moan is common as the final breaths escape the dying bear's throat. This can alert the bowhunter to the fact his shot was well-placed and the tracking job is likely to be a short one. Blood trailing a wounded bear is often a spooky undertaking. Most often the shot is made shortly before dark which means the search must be made by lantern light or postponed until the following morning. Some gladly wait for daylight while others are reluctant to delay the search. Inclement weather and the fear of a lost trophy compel some hunters to begin tracking soon after the shot.

Following a wounded bear at night is no job for the faint-hearted. It is no time to be careless, either. Wounded bears can be dangerous and could attack if pressed. It's always a good idea to have two or three people working together on the trail. Where it's legal, one should probably be carrying a sidearm, rifle or slug-loaded shotgun.

In warm or hot weather, a delay in trailing and recovering the animal may well result in spoiled meat and a ruined pelt. Bears retain body heat and a carcass should be field dressed, hung to cool and skinned out as soon as possible. Bear meat—especially the roasts—is quite edible if properly handled and prepared.

Another incentive for following up the blood trail

soon after the shot is sometimes scavengers may find the carcass and destroy the hide. In areas of high bear concentrations, bruins are known to turn cannibalistic and eat a dead bear they come across.

Common sense and caution must be employed whenever attempts are made to locate a wounded bear. Usually a wait of at least an hour is suggested unless the hunter is certain the bear is down and dead nearby. And even "dead bears" should be approached cautiously. No trophy is worth a mauling—or worse.

Bear hunting over baits is usually a late afternoon and evening activity. Mornings and mid-days are often spent replenishing baits, relaxing, fishing or perhaps hunting another species of game found in the same general area. Many bear hunters and guides feel morning stands are a waste of time since the nocturnal bruins are likely to be at or near the bait by first light. They believe a hunter taking a morning stand is likely to do little more than spook the animal away from the bait site.

Generally speaking, baits should be approached quietly whenever possible. It is possible to find a bear already feeding and stalk close enough for a shot.

But some baiters take the opposite tact, making some noise each time they visit the bait site, rattling pails, talking or walking noisily through brush. Some bears grow accustomed to these sounds and learn some human activity means fresh food is being served. A few of these bears walk boldly to the bait almost before the "waiters" are out of sight. Such brashness can be the undoing of these bears when one hunter takes a stand at the bait while his partner leaves alone after freshening the set.

Because of the work involved in establishing a bait and keeping it replenished, many baiters are tempted to locate bait sites near roads. Such baits may be effective; however, some unscrupulous individuals may discover obvious baits and stake them out or use them to start their dogs on a fresh bear scent. There's nothing more discouraging than to have some claim jumper spoil a bait set and for this reason the more remote, well hidden baits may be worth the extra effort involved.

Baiting is a waiting game and comfort is essential whether a bowhunter chooses a ground blind or tree stand. Some sort of seat is a good idea and the hunter should practice shooting while sitting to be fully prepared. Some hunters prefer to stand, arrow nocked, during the final hour of daylight when the bear is most likely to visit the bait.

Soft, quiet camo clothing is essential since most shots will be taken at very close ranges, often 10 to 15 yards. Tree stands must be solid and not shift or squeak under the hunter's weight. Carpeting on the stand's floor is an excellent idea. Many bear hunters wear rubber boots to cut down on human scent leading to and from the stand. Some use masking scents to help hide their presence.

Note: Many bears **know** the bowhunter is at the bait site. Some walk to the base of the tree, sniffing loudly. Others may even stand on their hind legs to get a better look at the stand and its occupant (this can unnerve some novice bear hunters who don't expect such curiosity). It is not uncommon for the bear to simply stand nearby and peer up at the hunter. The hunter's presence may spook the bear or he may walk to the bait and begin to feed, casting occasional sidelong glances at the bowhunter. It goes without saying that a hunter should never move when the bear is staring at him.

The unpredictability of the black bear is one facet that adds to the animal's overall appeal. Combined with the animal's innate cunning, remarkable intelligence and amazing adapatability, it creates a worthy adversary for any bowhunter.

Trophy Recognition

Skull size is the sole determining factor in judging trophy-class bears for entry in the records and, quite naturally, estimating the size of a live animal's skull is difficult if not impossible.

To obtain an official measurement, a Pope and Young Club scorer measures the length and width of the cleaned skull to the nearest sixteenth of an inch. The combined total gives the official score.

A skull must score a minimum of 18 total inches.

The minimum score for grizzlies is 19 inches while brown bears and polar bears must score at least 20 inches. The Pope and Young Club is no longer accepting polar bear entries.

Certainly the weight of the bear and size of its hide are other considerations for the bowhunter. Some very large bears have relatively small heads and, conversely, a few little bears have exceptionally large skulls. Consequently, it may sound more impressive for a bowhunter to claim a 400-lb. bear than to say it had an 18-inch skull.

Big bears, examined in detail in the chapter on brown and grizzly bears, are often judged by the "square" of the hide. The measurement is made by taping the animal from nose to tail and then adding the width of the front paw to paw spread. The total is divided by two to obtain the "squared" size of the hide. Naturally, the coloration and condition of the hide are also important. Pelts with long, glossy hair free of rubbed spots are highly prized trophies, even when they do not qualify as record book animals. Such subjective considerations and comparative evaluations make for interesting discussions wherever bear hunters gather.

The largest Pope and Young black bear on record was killed in Colorado in 1978 by bowhunter Ray Cox. The huge boar's skull measured 13-7/16 inches long and 8-13/16 inches wide for a total score of 22-4/16.

In the grizzly bear category, a big boar arrowed in 1972 by Harley Tison ranks as the biggest ever claimed by a bowhunter. The grizzly was shot along the Anzac River in British Columbia. Its skull length is an even 16 inches and the width is 9-6/16 inches. The official score is 25-6/16.

Fred Bear's Alaska brown bear tops all entries in this category. Shot near Wide Bay on the Alaskan peninsula in 1960, the bruin's skull measures 17-15/16 inches long and 10-1/16 inches wide. The official score is a truly impressive 28 inches.

For the record, Richard McIntyre has the best of only four polar bears ever entered in the Pope and Young listings. McIntyre arrowed the bear near Cape Lisburne, Alaska in 1958. The bear's skull is

16-4/16 inches long and 10-2/16 inches wide for a combined score of 26-6/16.

Note: The Pope and Young Club is observing a moratorium on the hunting of polar bears. While these animals may be legally hunted today, the Club does not accept entries in this big game category.

Bowhunters wanting a record book bear must take the largest animal they can locate and hope the skull size exceeds qualifying minimums. But since almost any bear encountered in the wild may **look** big, what are some guidelines that can help the hunter judge his trophy? Following are some generalities any bear hunter should keep in mind:

* Big bears often have massive bodies but heads that may appear small by comparison to the rest of them. They often appear to lumber ponderously from place to place and may actually grunt softly as they walk as if movements are an effort.

* Older bears have the biggest skulls. Bears that look and act old probably are. In grizzly, brown and cinnamon-phase black bears, the older animals frequently have darker pelage.

* Bears traveling together are likely to be a sow with cubs or yearlings. Boars prefer a solitary life, frequently in remote and desolate areas.

* Younger bears are gangly-looking animals with pointed noses and ears that appear outsized. Some have a dog-like appearance.

* A fall bear will be larger than a bear fresh from his winter den. Some big bears will add perhaps 150 to 200 pounds of body weight in a matter of a few months.

* Tracks give a fairly reliable clue to body size. If a hunter measures the width of a bear's front paw track, adds one inch and converts the total to feet, he'll have the approximate size of the squared hide.

* Females have narrower skulls than males. Bears with wide, massive-looking heads are usually big boars.

* Grizzly and brown bears have obvious shoulder humps and big males—usually found alone—walk with a heavy, rolling stride.

* A spring bear wears a prime coat of thick, luxuriant hair for the first month or so. Bears shot in the summer or early fall may have rubbed spots on their hips or sides. By September the glossy winter pelage is forming.

Again, there are many factors—beyond skull size—in determining a trophy-class bear. Adult bears of any species make beautiful bowhunting trophies if taken legally under the rules of Fair Chase. Without question the bears are a fascinating, challenging big game animal worthy of any bowhunter's consideration and respect.

Grizzly/Brown Bears . . . Big Trouble

11

The grizzly and his big brother, the Alaska brown bear, are awesomely powerful animals that few modern bowhunters consider seriously when planning their future trips afield. The danger is great and even the promise of taking such a regal trophy is not enough to tempt the average bow and arrow hunter. Bowhunting these big bears is no idle undertaking because without a doubt two lives—the bear's and the hunter's—are always on the line.

Grizzlies (*Ursus arctos horribilis*) were once found through much of Western North America where they reigned as undisputed monarchs of the animal kingdom until the coming of the white man. Fearless and formidable, they faced guns with disdain—and perished. Today they are true wilderness animals found in huntable numbers below the Canadian border only in remote sections of Montana. In Alaska and British Columbia, however, there is a healthy population of the hump-shouldered bruins. The same is true in parts of the Yukon, Northwest Territories and Alberta.

Larger than most black bears, the grizzly is smaller than many hunters may imagine. Average boar grizzlies weigh 350 to 450 pounds with occasional specimens running upwards of 700 pounds; females are generally smaller by one-third. Adults stand between three and four feet at the muscular hump and are six to seven feet in length.

Coloration varies from creamy blond to dark brown with white or silver-tipped guard hairs along the shoulders. Long, curving claws are apparent on the forefeet. Body hair is long and thick, rippling as the bear moves. It is well-suited for ensuring the animal's survival in cold north country habitat.

Grizzlies have concave or "dished" faces, large ears and broad heads. Eyes are small and eyesight is regarded as fair to poor. Hearing is acute but the bears' sense of smell is exceptional. Grizzlies primarily use their noses to locate food and detect danger.

The bears love meat—freshly killed or carrion—but they spend considerable time eating grass, sedges and berries. Grizzlies commonly gather along streams during annual salmon runs and gorge themselves with fish. They've also been seen on open slopes, digging out ground squirrels and small rodents that hardly seem worth the effort.

Grizzlies seek—and require—the solitude of remote wilderness country and seem to prefer the higher elevations. Each has a home range varying in size from as little as five to perhaps 20 square miles. Boars were once thought to mark their territories by leaving claw marks on "bear trees" located at the boundaries of their range; however, some researchers now believe the trees are simply convenient scratching posts which the bears visit to relieve themselves by rubbing itches and clawing at the bark.

Boars roam almost constantly and have surprising speed for such big animals. They can attain speeds of 30 to 35 miles per hour in a bounding, ground-gaining gallop. When alarmed they may rapidly retreat or they may charge. At times these charges are bluffing rushes toward the intruder which end with the bear sliding to a stop, huffing indignantly, growling and popping its teeth and eventually moving away. At other times the charges are for real and heaven help the hunter who cannot escape or stop the deadly determined animal before it reaches him.

The breeding season is in May and June of each year and the cubs are born in January while the sow is in her den. Twins and triplets are not uncommon and the newborns are less than a foot long and under a pound at birth. They begin nursing immediately and grow quickly. Cubs taste their first solid food after they leave the den with their mother in late April or May although they may continue to nurse throughout their first year. It is common for the cubs to den with their mother during their first winter. Most sows breed only every other year.

Grizzly dens are often dug-out depressions among boulders on craggy, north-facing slopes. Another favorite site is beneath the tangled roots of large trees. Branches and leaves are carried into the dens but the bears wait for the first heavy snowfall-which obliterates tracks and covers the den's entrance—before retiring for the winter. The bears do not hibernate; rather, they begin a period of dormancy which lasts until the following spring.

Tracks are the most recognizable grizzly sign and may be confused with large black bears except the claw marks are usually more obvious. Along favorite fishing areas "bear highways" are actually worn in the earth. The result is two ruts with a grassy area between them often marked with piles of droppings. Bear scat frequently contains evidence of whatever the animals have been feeding on with berry seeds, hair tufts, fish scales or grass shoots apparent in the droppings.

Wild grizzlies have a life expectancy of 15 to 20 years although some bears may live twice this norm. Although on the brink of extinction in the lower 48 states, the grizzly continues to reign over the high, wild places of Alaska and western Canada. Population estimates vary but it is believed that 15,000 to 20,000 of the big grizzly/brown bears remain in Alaska with another 5,000 to 10,000 grizzlies in British Columbia. Lesser numbers are found throughout the balance of the bear's range.

Although their ranges may overlap, grizzlies are generally inland animals while the Alaska brown bear (Ursus arctos middendorffi) are animals of the coastal regions and adjacent offshore Alaskan islands. Except for the larger size of the browns, there is absolutely no difference in the two species. Brown bears are the largest—perhaps the most potentially dangerous—meat-eater on earth. Certainly no bowhunter can find a more formidable quarry.

Brown bears—also called Kodiak bears—stand between four and five feet at the withers and measure between nine and 10 feet from nose to stunted tail. The biggest, oldest boars may weigh upwards of 1,500 pounds but "average" brownies tip the scales at 800 to 1,200 pounds. The females weigh considerably less with big sows running between 700 and 800 pounds.

Like the grizzly, brown bears come in various shadings ranging from blond to almost black; rich brown is the typical hue. Additionally, they have the same shoulder hump and dished face. And like the other bears, they use their noses to locate food and to warn them of approaching danger. Eyesight is poor, especially when it comes to identifying stationary objects, but they do detect motion and may stand erect on their hind legs, mouth agape, to get a better view and scent of the intruder. Hearing is good but along rushing salmon streams the sense is frequently negated.

The bears' denning sites are high on mountainsides which overlook the coastal regions where they spend the summer months. Most large-scale movements occur between these two locations. A few brown bears do develop wanderlust and may move inland; most remain along the seacoasts and stay within a relatively small home range unless food shortages or hunting pressure forces them to move.

Brown bears emerge from their dens in late April or early May and graze on grass shoots to get their digestive systems functioning again. Grass, winter-killed game and small rodents comprise the bulk of their diet until the first salmon runs begin in June. Berries and fish are favorite fall foods and most bears become gluttons shortly before returning to the dens. Some animals actually gain hundreds of pounds during the time they emerge from and return to their winter's sleep.

Breeding takes place in June or July and the cubs are born during the sow's period of winter domancy. As with other bears, browns frequently give birth to twins and triplets which weigh perhaps one pound or less. By the time the denning period ends the cubs are able to follow and keep up with their mother and learn the lessons of survival. Big boars constitute the biggest threat to the young bears since the old males kill and eat the youngsters whenever they can. Cubs frequently remain with their mother until their second year of life. Bears that survive their own kind and hunters often live past their mid-teens into their twenties.

Brown bears are normally less aggressive and slower to anger than the quick-tempered grizzlies; however, an enraged brownie is a terrifying sight. Their roar is a blood-chilling scream often punctuated with growls and angry teeth-popping. A charging brown bear can reach 30 miles per hour and easily run down any man alive.

Bear paths or trails and tracks are the most obvious brown bear sign. Generations of bruins use the same pathways, especially near feeding areas, and wear deep, well-defined trails through the grass and brush ground cover. The tracks themselves are usually huge, unmistakable. Tidal flats and the soft earth along salmon streams are often pocked with bear tracks. Brown bear scat is much like that of a grizzly or black but deposits are usually larger.

The dark, coarse meat of both grizzly and brown bears is edible although many hunters do not salvage much beyond choice cuts. Native Americans and more than one early-day or contemporary woodsman have welcomed a supply of bear meat to his cache.

Effective Bowhunting Techniques

Generally speaking, the bowhunting of grizzly and brown bears is an expensive, time-consuming

venture which requires the use of an outfitter or guide who not only helps locate the big animals but who serves as a back-up with a large caliber rifle. Considerable patience—and common sense caution—must be employed as well. While a hunting bow and well-placed arrow will put down the biggest bears on earth, a rushed shot or bad hit could be the beginning of a nightmare situation because either animal can turn on and kill a hunter.

A number of grizzlies have been taken by bowhunters in elevated stands hunting over bait. If it's legal, this is undoubtedly the best—and safest—method of collecting a silvertip. Several Pope and Young grizzlies in the record book were collected by this fashion in British Columbia before a change in game regulations ended the practice.

Where baiting is illegal, this leaves still-hunting and stalking as the only practical means of taking a grizzly. Some bowhunters locate bears feeding on ripe berries, low sedges or digging for rodents and manage to slip within range while the bruin is busily occupied.

Note: It's always best to approach a bear from uphill or at least the same level. Wounded bears tend to run downhill and head for the nearest cover.

Working close to a huge bear is seldom easy because of the animal's exceptional olfactory abilities. And what escapes the bear's nose is likely to be detected by his ears. Regardless, it can be done if the hunter is patient—and lucky.

During the salmon runs when bears are fishing in the streams and rivers, stalking the shorelines can pay off; however, this is no undertaking for the faint-hearted. Visibility is almost always limited by dense stands of willows, alder thickets or other screening cover. The only way to move quietly is to follow the well-worn bear trails or, wearing hip boots or waders, to ease into shallow water and move slowly upstream.

The trick is for the hunter to spot the fishing or feeding bear first. Most bears sighted will be spotted at close range and the danger of surprising and provoking a feeding bear always exists. Bears jealously guard their prey and their prime fishing areas; few hesitate to tangle with any intruder. Such thoughts are anything but comforting as the bowman eases through heavy cover where visibility is cut to a few yards in any direction.

A few hunters on combination fall bowhunts in prime grizzly country will keep close tabs on the kill sites of moose, caribou or other big game animals. Gut piles, bones, hides and other such offal may attract keen-nosed bears who quickly claim the feeding rights. A bowhunter with a grizzly tag may watch through binoculars from a safe distance or slip in quietly from time to time to check on the kill site. Grizzlies commonly rake leaves, dirt and brush over the carcass or offal and bed nearby. They are quick to defend any food they've claimed so extreme caution is advised when approaching the area.

Note: Food in hunting camps can attract bears and should be cached in trees above the bears' reach whenever possible.

Grizzly bears are hunted in both the spring and fall. Some hunters prefer the springtime because the bears may be easier to locate. After emerging from their dens they wander about in search of food, grazing on open hillsides like cattle and digging rodents from their burrows. Also, the improving weather is often more pleasant and pelts of spring bears are of prime quality. Perhaps the biggest advantage to a fall hunt is found in the fact other game may be hunted on the same trip. An added bonus is the aesthetic appeal of a fall hunt in wilderness valleys and high basins where the riot of alpine colors prints an indelible image on the hunter's mind.

Brown bears may be hunted in either the spring or fall as well; however, most hunts for the huge coastal bears take place in the spring. Typically the hunter is flown or boated to the hunting camp where daily hikes into bear country are made. A brown bear hunter can expect to do a considerable amount of walking although long periods of sitting and glassing from high vantage points are common.

Bears on the move are very difficult to intercept. A feeding or bedded bear is ideal for the stalking hunter; however, getting close without being detected by the bruin is usually difficult. Early morning and evening hours are prime hunting times.

Often bear hunters may be based on a fishing boat which cruises the coastlines, anchoring offshore at the mouth of shallow streams. Daily forays are made by dinghy to likely looking spots where inland stalks are made when bears are sighted on the open slopes above the beach. Generally it's best to climb and circle above the bears and stalk downhill. Not only is it safer to remain uphill from a bear but the animals seem to pay more attention to the lower hillsides than the higher slopes.

Another effective method during the salmon runs is following streams inland, staying in the shallow riffles or easing along the shore. Bears may be located feeding in the streams and successfully stalked or intercepted after the bowhunter and his guide determine the route of travel.

Brown and grizzly bears are big, muscular animals with heavy coats. Bows of heavier poundages are recommended providing the hunter can shoot them accurately. Sixty to sixty-five pounds should be the absolute minimum bow weight for big bears.

Finally, the nagging and inevitable questions of risk and danger are worth additional consideration. The fact that many guides and outfitters will not book bowhunters for big bears—especially brownies—should be noted. Bowhunting for browns and grizzlies is tough, time-demanding work. The need to get close—thirty yards or less—introduces an element of risk that is missing when firearms are used. Also, since arrows kill by hemorrhage and have minimal shocking power, even a mortally wounded bear is capable of attacking and mauling a bowhunter.

The chances of this happening are probably remote if caution is used; however, it **could** happen. Each hunter going after the big bears must realize this sobering fact and decide for himself if it's worth the danger involved.

Bison . . . A Glimpse of the Past

Bison 103

INSTRUCTIONS

All measurements must be made with a flexible steel tape to the nearest one-eighth of an inch. To simplify addition, please enter fractional figures in eighths.

Official measurements cannot be taken for at least sixty days after the animal was killed. Please submit photographs.

Supplementary Data measurements indicate conformation of the trophy. None of the figures in Lines A and B are to be included in the score. Evaluation of conformation is a matter of personal preference.

A. **Greatest Spread** measured between perpendiculars at right angles to the center line of the skull.

B. **Tip to Tip Spread** measured between tips of horns.

C. **Length of Horn** measured from lowest point on under side over outer curve to a point in line with tip.

D-1. **Circumference of Base** measured at right angles to axis of horn. DO NOT follow irregular edge of horn.

D-2-3-4. **Divide** measurement C of LONGER horn by four; mark BOTH horns at these quarters even though the other horn is shorter, and measure circumference at these marks.

Bison: In order to be acceptable the bison must be taken from a free ranging herd on state or federal lands. It must be classed as a game animal in the state or province where taken and a photo copy of the hunting permit must be submitted with the trophy form.

Drying Period: To be eligible for entry in the Pope & Young Records, a trophy must first have been stored under normal room temperature and humidity for at least 60 consecutive days prior to measurement. No trophy will be considered which has in any way been altered from its natural state.

Photographs: All entries must include photographs of the trophy. A right side, left side and front view photograph will be required for all antlers, horns and skulls. A photograph of the entire animal is requested if at all possible.

THIS SCORING FORM MUST BE ACCOMPANIED BY A SIGNED POPE & YOUNG FAIR CHASE AFFIDAVIT AND A RECORDING FEE OF $10.00.

animals—especially on open range—is easy and there is little need to check for sign. Good binoculars can help evaluate trophy animals. Buffalo tracks are quite similar to cattle but generally larger. The dung of the two species is likewise similar.

Buffalo breed each summer with bulls gathering harems and frequently battling rivals for breeding rights. The rutting bulls should be considered dangerous and battles are a sight to behold. Bellowing and pawing up clouds of prairie dust, rivals engage in head-butting contests which literally shake the ground. The bulls continually charge each other until one has had enough and is chased away. The victor then gathers the cows and yearlings, guarding them with a jealous fervor throughout the breeding season.

Cows remain in heat for a period of about 24 hours. If not serviced and impregnated by a bull, they'll come into estrous 28 days later. Typically, single calves are generally born in May of the following year and will be considered adults at four or five years of age. Bison enjoy a fairly long lifespan, frequently living into their twenties and longer. There are cases of some buffalo living for more than 40 years.

Effective Bowhunting Techniques

There are very few locations where wild buffalo live in free-ranging herds. The Pope and Young Club recognizes animals taken only in the Henry Mountains of Utah, the Wrangell Mountains of Alaska and areas of Alberta and the Northwest Territories. Hunting is limited and permits—if and when they're drawn—are often expensive.

Most bowhunters wanting to add a buffalo mount to their collections turn to private ranches with surplus animals for sale. Even this is generally expensive with the "hunt" costing in the thousands of dollars.

These ranch-raised animals seldom offer much in the way of a challenging hunt, yet a massive bison mount is impressive. Many bowhunters wanting the experience of shooting a buffalo—and perhaps seeking to recapture the romance of an age when

Indian hunters stalked the ponderous beasts with hand-fashioned bows and arrows—book dates and pay the going rate for the right to shoot a buffalo.

Stalking is undoubtedly the most common way to ease within good arrow range. Some adventurous bowhunters have hunted from horseback Indian-fashion, shooting from a galloping pony at a fleeing target. This method, obviously, is not recommended. Staking out trails or wallows are possibilities; however, buffalo commonly wander over large areas of real estate and waits may prove long and uneventful.

A bowhunter should use fairly heavy tackle on buffalo. Bows of 60 to 65 pounds are minimum requirements for the big animals. The ideal shot is at a broadside or quartering away animal. Placing the shaving-sharp broadhead in the heart/lung area is vital for a quick kill. Wounded buffalo possess tremendous endurance and can be extremely dangerous if they decide to vent their anger on the nearest tormentor.

Note: Bowhunters should remember to hold below the mid-line of the animal's body. The hump creates an illusion of chest cavity depth which causes high hits—and potential trouble.

Perhaps the biggest danger to the bowhunter is the open terrain where most buffalo are found. With no cover for concealment and no trees available for climbing, a person could find himself face to face with a ton or so of enraged animal. Outrunning the animal is out of the question since a lumbering buffalo can reach speeds of 30 to 35 miles per hour. And for a ponderous, massive animal, a buffalo has amazing agility and is capable of quick, spinning turns. Some bowhunters flatly refuse an open prairie stalk unless backed by a suitable firearm.

One other possible danger lies in the herd itself. Unless one of the lone, solitary-seeking bulls is the target, generally there are a number of other buffalo nearby. Once the arrow hits and the scent of blood is in the air, there is no predicting the reaction of the other animals. While they may show total indifference or immediate alarm, they have been known to become enraged to the point of attacking the stricken animal. A hunter caught in the middle would likely come out second best in any confrontation with the belligerent beasts.

Nonetheless, a well-placed arrow can put down the biggest bull in a matter of seconds. The secret lies in getting close, keeping a cool head and steady hand and putting the shaft in the vitals. Most successful hunters agree that the buffalo mount, skull and robe make the experience worthwile.

Trophy Recognition

As mentioned, few bison qualify for entry in the Pope and Young records. At the time of this writing, the biggest bull taken by a modern day bowhunter was killed in 1972 by George Moerlein on a hunt in the Farewell Lake area of Alaska. It scored a total of 112 2/8 points. The right horn is 18 4/8 inches long with a circumference at the base of 14 1/8 inches. The left horn measures 18 inches even. The greatest spread between the horns is 29 6/8 inches.

The biggest buffalo on record was killed in Yellowstone Park in 1925 by a hunter named Woodring. This World Record animal had a score of 136 4/8. To qualify for the Pope and Young listings, a bison must score at least 80.

Since most buffalo will be ineligible for the official Pope and Young records, the judgment of what constitutes a trophy will be left to the individual bowhunter. As with all trophy-class game, outstanding specimens of any species appear huge, often dwarfing other herd members. Consequently, a patient, selective hunter can collect an exceptional trophy, especially if he has the money to pay for it.

Caribou . . . Northland Nomads

13

The caribou is to the northland what the elk is to the Rocky Mountains. Big, handsome and heavy-antlered, the white-maned bulls are impressive and prized big game trophies.

Once widely distributed along the northern tier of states abutting the Canadian border, caribou could not tolerate harrassment by man. Civilization pushed the herds further and further north. Today only a handful of animals may be found roaming south of Canada and the only state presently harboring a huntable population is Alaska.

Bowhunters focus attention on four separate classifications of caribou (*Rangifer tarandus*)—the Quebec/Labrador caribou of those Canadian provinces, numbering upwards of 100,000 animals; the woodland caribou of the northeast and Newfoundland (the island's herd numbers under 30,000; the mountain caribou of British Columbia and Alberta, with the former province harboring the most animals; and the barren ground caribou of Alaska and the Yukon tundras, the most populous type numbering perhaps one million animals. Although woodland caribou are generally smaller in body size and antler growth, all four varieties share certain characteristics.

Cousins of the European reindeer, caribou are the only members of the deer family with antlered males and females; however, they do not have the metarsal gland common to deer. They also are the most nomadic and migratory big game species on the North American continent.

Size and coloration varies widely among the four subspecies. Big bulls stand four to five feet tall at the shoulder and stretch perhaps six to eight feet in length. On the hoof, trophy males may weigh as much as 500 to 600 pounds; females, wearing stunted spindly antlers, are notably smaller than the bulls.

Trophy caribou carry high, sweptback, gracefully curved antlers with numerous points and often have palmated brow tines known as "shovels." Their racks may reach five feet in length. Each bull normally drops his headgear by January every winter.

Caribou change color with the seasons and their pelage varies from a rich chocolate to mousy gray with several intermediate hues. Generally speaking, the northernmost herds are lighter in color, their coats bleached by nearly continuous tundra sunshine. Caribou of the Canadian mountains and forests are typically darker. Hair is hollow, providing excellent buoyancy and insulation.

All species of the cattle-faced animals sport long-haired throat and chest manes—some startlingly white—and proportionally short ears. Faces are dark except for white-ringed eyes and muzzles. Traces of white are evident above each hoof and on the small rump patch.

The "Bigfoot" of the deer clan, caribou have hooves as big as a bull moose. Nearly perfectly round, each hoof is hollowed to help the animal negotiate deep snow and the spongy tundras. Dewclaws are quite apparent and when caribou run their hooves are widely splayed. As caribou walk, their ankles make a distinctive clicking sound that can easily be heard.

Lichens—commonly called "caribou moss"—is the caribou's principal food source. The animals also feed on berries, grasses, fungi, and willows. They feed on the move during daylight hours, frequently circling as they graze, and seldom stay long in one place. Once full, they may pause, laying themselves down to rest and chew their cuds before moving on.

Caribou are not vocal animals. Aside from an occasional cough or grunt, they remain silent and use body postures to communicate. It's reported that alarmed bulls emit a musk-like scent from the interdigital gland betwen their toes. This odor lingers and alerts other passing caribou.

Caribou have good eyesight but rely on their noses more than any other sense. Bulls may be quick to notice a crouching hunter but seldom show apparent concern unless they catch the scent of the intruder. Even when alarmed, they often demonstrate indecision and appear confused about exactly what to do. Some bowhunters have walked slowly toward herds—holding their bows horizontally over their heads like antlers—and approached within bow range of the staring animals. Such curiosity—or gullibility—has led some to label the caribou as "stupid."

This tag is probably unfair. Caribou normally have little contact with man; wolves are their primary enemy. It's not surprising that curiosity might get the best of them when confronted with some strange-looking tundra apparition.

Healthy caribou can easily outdistance pursuers, including wolf packs. Walking, heads down, they appear ungainly. But when caribou spring into a long-striding trot, they are pictures of grace. Heads and small, whitish tails held erect and still, massive antlers laid back over their bodies, they seem to float across the open ground with an unusually high leg-lifting motion. If pushed, caribou can gallop for short stretches at speeds upwards of 30 miles per hour before reverting to the familiar ground-eating trot they can maintain for hours.

Much of the bulls' summer is spent eating and putting on weight. Antler development is complete by September when the velvet is stripped off. By October the neck-swollen bulls become increasingly aggressive and begin to collect cows. Fights among rivals are common and serious injuries may result as the bulls clash antlers in a test of strength and will. Should the antlers accidentally lock together, certain death awaits the luckless combatants.

During the rut the bulls seemingly go crazy, jumping about, swapping ends and racing off for no apparent reason. Their antics border on the insane. Food is forgotten. Mounting and servicing cows as they come into heat is each bull's obsession throughout the month-long breeding season. Finally, gaunt and exhausted by rut's end, they regain some semblance of reason and begin gorging themselves to replenish used body fat.

Calves are born the following spring, usually in May or June. Unspotted and brown at birth, each calf weighs an average of 15 pounds. Within a few hours it is following its mother and keeping up with her. In less than a week it is able to run with her as weight and strength blossom. Woodland caribou frequently have twin calves while single births are common among mountain, Quebec/Labrador and barren ground cows. In the wild, caribou often live a dozen years or so.

Caribou are extremely visible animals, especially when the great herds are migrating. Timing a hunt to coincide with these annual movements is often more important than learning to recognize caribou tracks or droppings. The best caribou tracks to look for are ones with a big bull standing in them.

Bow season is generally early in the fall or late in the summer—August and September, typically—when bulls are in prime physical condition. Good binoculars or a lightweight spotting scope are important in locating distant animals and studying potential trophy heads.

Effective Bowhunting Techniques

Glassing and stalking are generally the most important elements of any caribou bowhunt. Finding a high point with a good view of the remote terrain, many bowhunters first invest time locating the animals. Next they plan how to close the distance. Mornings and evenings are prime feeding times but all the daylight hours are good for locating either grazing or bedded, cud-chewing bulls.

Note: As previously indicated, caribou seem reluctant to move at night and animals located too late in the day to be stalked may well be in the same general area come first light.

Caribou commonly feed into the wind, if any, and in one direction. Many successful bowhunters have used this trait to their advantage, working ahead but staying to one side and downwind of the moving animals. Finding suitable concealment—a small boulder or bush will do—they allow the caribou to come to them and take shots as they pass.

Bulls seemingly prefer to bed on open points or rises where they can keep a wary eye on their surroundings. Stalking resting animals is sometimes difficult but possible, especially in broken or rolling terrain. A few bowhunters have crawled within range, keeping the bull's location in view by watching his antlers above the ridgeline.

Caribou are sound sleepers. Catch a bull dozing and it's possible to literally walk up to him. But often there's more than one animal to consider and chances are slim a hunter will find all of the caribou asleep.

Sit-and-wait tactics may work if a hunter is on hand during peak periods of migration. Caribou trails are well-defined and the animals follow these paths year after year. Patient hunters without much faith in their stalking abilities often have plenty of action by choosing an ambush site along the migration route. During the migration it is not uncommon to have caribou within sight continuously. One blown chance seldom spoils the hunt since more animals are on the way.

All caribou seem to have short memories. Some bowhunters, who spook bulls with missed shots or who have blown stalks, report they've followed the boogered animals and found them peacefully grazing just over the next hill. In some cases this trait has spelled success for a persistent hunter who followed a bull until he got a second chance.

Because of the desolate, isolated areas favored by caribou, bowhunters must expect to spend time getting "back in" where the action is. Bush planes often ferry hunters to and from base camps although horses, boats and—in certain parts of Alaska—4WD vehicles may serve the same purpose.

Hunting barren ground and mountain caribou in their high, open summer ranges can be a test of patience and skill. Often it's best accomplished by putting lots of miles on shank's mare or saddle horses. In good caribou country, it's often only a matter of time until the animals are found.

Where rivers cut through prime caribou country, a hunter may opt to hunt by boat, drifting with the current until game is sighted or beaching occasionally to glass the countryside near the waterway. Rivers pose little threat for the buoyant, strong-swimming animals although unusually high, fast-flowing water can claim weaker animals. Tragedies such as occurred in Quebec in 1984—where perhaps 2,000 animals drowned while fording the rampaging George River—are rare indeed.

Some weak-willed hunters have yielded to the temptation of arrowing swimming animals or shooting from boats as the bulls emerged from the water. Such tactics are not condoned by the Pope and Young Club and bulls killed in this manner are not considered eligible for the records.

Is it permissible—and ethical—to locate, stalk or intercept a bull and shoot it from the beach as it emerges from the water? This same question was the subject of considerable discussion among Regular and Senior members of the Pope and Young Club at that organization's 1983 meeting in Milwaukee, Wisconsin. Pressed for some kind of direction as to what's acceptable and what isn't, then-President Jim Dougherty agreed that under certain conditions a hunter could stalk and arrow a bull as it clambered from a lake or river. "Just don't sink 'em," he stated succinctly.

Common sense will tell any responsible bowhunter whether the bull is shot under the rules of Fair Chase. Swimming animals are considered helpless and therefore are off limits. Also it is highly

POPE & YOUNG CLUB
NORTH AMERICAN BIG GAME TROPHY SCORING FORM
BOWHUNTING

P & Y Records Office
Rt. 1, Box 147
Salmon, Id. 83467

CARIBOU

BIG GAME RECORDS

KIND OF CARIBOU _____

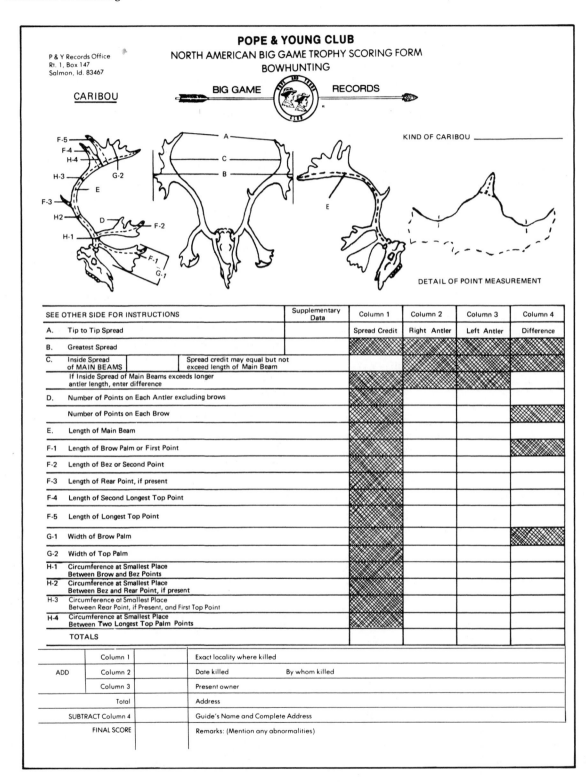

DETAIL OF POINT MEASUREMENT

SEE OTHER SIDE FOR INSTRUCTIONS		Supplementary Data	Column 1	Column 2	Column 3	Column 4
			Spread Credit	Right Antler	Left Antler	Difference
A.	Tip to Tip Spread					
B.	Greatest Spread					
C.	Inside Spread of MAIN BEAMS — Spread credit may equal but not exceed length of Main Beam					
	If Inside Spread of Main Beams exceeds longer antler length, enter difference					
D.	Number of Points on Each Antler excluding brows					
	Number of Points on Each Brow					
E.	Length of Main Beam					
F-1	Length of Brow Palm or First Point					
F-2	Length of Bez or Second Point					
F-3	Length of Rear Point, if present					
F-4	Length of Second Longest Top Point					
F-5	Length of Longest Top Point					
G-1	Width of Brow Palm					
G-2	Width of Top Palm					
H-1	Circumference at Smallest Place Between Brow and Bez Points					
H-2	Circumference at Smallest Place Between Bez and Rear Point, if present					
H-3	Circumference at Smallest Place Between Rear Point, if Present, and First Top Point					
H-4	Circumference at Smallest Place Between Two Longest Top Palm Points					
	TOTALS					

ADD	Column 1		Exact locality where killed
	Column 2		Date killed By whom killed
	Column 3		Present owner
Total			Address
SUBTRACT Column 4			Guide's Name and Complete Address
FINAL SCORE			Remarks: (Mention any abnormalities)

I certify that I have measured the above trophy on _____ 19_____
at (address) _____ City _____
State _____ Zip Code _____ and that these measurements and data are, to the best of my knowledge and belief, made in accordance with the instructions given.

Witness:_____ Signature _____

Pope & Young Club Official Measurer

_____
MEASURER (Print)

_____
ADDRESS

_____
CITY　　　　　**STATE**　　　　　**ZIP**

INSTRUCTIONS

All measurements must be made with a flexible steel tape to the nearest one-eighth of an inch. Wherever it is necessary to change direction of measurement, mark a control point and swing tape at that point. To simplify addition, enter fractional figures in eighths.

Official measurements cannot be taken for at least sixty days after the animal was killed. Photos of left side, right side, and front of antlers are required.

Supplementary Data measurements indicate conformation of the trophy. None of the figures in line A and line B are to be included in the score. Evaluation of conformation is a matter of personal preference.

A. Tip to Tip Spread is measured between tips of Main Beams.

B. Greatest Spread is measured between perpendiculars, at right angles to the center line of the skull, at the widest part whether across main beams or points.

C. Inside Spread of Main Beams is measured, at right angles to the center line of the skull, at the widest place between main beams. Enter this measurement again in "Spread Credit" column if it is less than or equal to the length of the longer main beam.

D. Number of Points on each antler. A projection is to be classified as a point if at some location, at least one-half inch from the tip of the antler projection, the length of this point exceeds the width of this point at that location. Beam tip is counted as a point but not measured as a point. There are no "abnormal" points in Caribou.

E. Length of Main Beam is measured from the lowest outside edge of the burr over the outer curve to the most distant point of what is, or appears to be, the main beam. The point of beginning is that point on the burr where the center line, along the outer curve of the beam, intersects the burr.

F-1-2-3. Length of Points are measured from the center of the point's base line over the outer curve to the tip. To determine the base line, lay the tape along the outer curve of the beam so that the top edge of the tape coincides with the nearest edge of the beam on both sides of the point. Draw the base line along the top edge of the tape. For F-1 and F-2 measurements the tip that gives the longest measurement is used.

F-4-5. Length of Points are measured from the point's tip to the center of the point's base line, then at a right angle to the main beam, to the midpoint of the lower edge of the main beam. No point which branches off the longest point is ever to be considered as "second longest."

G-1. Width of Brow is measured in a straight line from the top edge to the lower edge, with measurement line at a right angle to the main axis of the brow. If the brow point is an unbranched spike a credit of one-eighth inch is awarded to the spike.

G-2. Width of Top Palm is measured from midpoint of the lower edge of the main beam to the midpoint of the upper edge of the palm, at the narrowest part of a dip between points, at the widest part of the palm.

H-1-2-3-4. Circumferences. If rear point is missing, take H-2 and H-3 measurements at the smallest place between the bez and the first top point.

Photographs: All entries must include photographs of the trophy. A right side, left side and front view photograph will be required for all antlers, horns and skulls. A photograph of the entire animal is requested if at all possible.

Drying Period: To be eligible for entry in the Pope & Young Records, a trophy must first have been stored under normal room temperature and humidity for at least 60 consecutive days. No trophy will be considered which has in any way been altered from its natural state.

THIS SCORING FORM MUST BE ACCOMPANIED BY A SIGNED POPE & YOUNG FAIR CHASE AFFIDAVIT, 3 PHOTOS AND A RECORDING FEE OF $25.00.

unethical and unsporting to drive or course animals toward waiting hunters by the use of a motorized vehicle or boat. Such actions are definite no-nos.

Caribou bulls are prized for two basic reasons. First, they are impressive, beautiful big game animals. Second, fairly hunted, they represent a true one-on-one test between man and animal. The open country they favor is a challenge for any stalker and the close-up sight of a bull's massive headgear has unnerved more than one bowhunter. Most caribou are well-earned trophies.

Woodland caribou are hunted in much the same fashion as their cousins with stalking and shooting from ambush the two most effective hunting methods. It is possible to drive caribou at times. Guides sometimes will post a hunter along a trail or near some natural pass between two ridges. They then attempt to work the caribou past the waiting bowhunter. Although not an easy feat to accomplish, this method has proved successful on some occasions.

Arrowed caribou tend to run until they drop. Keeping a hit animal in sight may not prove too difficult in much caribou country; however, in the boggy, wooded areas of Newfoundland, for example, and in some tag alder thickets common to Alaska, locating a downed bull might prove difficult. Wet, swampy terrain is not good for blood trailing and the heavy coats of the animals themselves tend to soak up much of the blood. It's best to keep any wounded bull in sight until he goes down for keeps.

As already noted, caribou are good sized members of the deer family and hunting bows beginning in the 60-pound range should be considered minimum. All shots should be taken at one target—the animals' heart-lung-liver areas. Shots at running caribou are risky and should not be attempted under normal circumstances.

The meat of caribou is excellent table fare and should be attended to promptly. Field dressing is the first order of business, especially early in the season when the weather is warm. Another reason for prompt attention is some caribou country is shared by black bears and grizzlies. These bears

have been known to stake a claim to a downed caribou and to fight for rights to ownership. Few bowhunters win such disputes.

Because of their size, caribou are too much for one man to pack out whole. Quartering or boning out the carcass is likely to be necessary unless pack horses are available or unless the animal is killed near water where a power boat could tow it to camp intact for more leisurely processing.

Caribou antlers themselves may pose a problem for the trophy hunter, especially on fly-in trips where baggage/storage space is at a premium. Splitting the skull makes for easier transport; however, it also makes the trophy ineligible for the records. And some passenger airlines have been known to charge not just by the pound—but by the square inch!—for excess baggage. A wise hunter checks out such details in advance of his trip and makes necessary shipping arrangements. Guides or game officials, along with airline personnel, can answer questions and assist bowhunters in preparing to ship their caribou meat and antlers.

Trophy Recognition

Judging caribou antlers is sometimes difficult because they'll still be in the velvet during most open seasons. The velvet always gives antlers additional bulk and makes them appear slightly larger than they are.

Note: At this writing the Pope and Young Club will not accept antlered game unless the velvet is stripped from each beam and tine prior to official scoring.

Regardless, trophy caribou carry racks that appear huge in proportion to body size. Any bull whose antlers, if placed on the ground beside him, would approach the animal's height at the shoulder should be considered an exceptional trophy. Antler thickness, points and symmetry are additional plusses.

Many caribou bulls have single brow tines which extend vertically over the animal's face. These palmated, many-pointed tines are called "shovels" and the bulls carrying "double shovels" are considered to make the best trophies.

The World's Record barren ground caribou was shot in 1984 by bowhunter Dennis Burdick on a hunt along the Lake Clark region of Alaska. The antlers scored 448 6/8 points. The right beam tapes 48 4/8 inches and sports 17 points. The left beam has 20 points and is 48 5/8 inches long. The inside spread is 40 3/8 inches. The minimum score for barren ground caribou is 300.

Thomas Frye shot the *numero uno* mountain caribou in 1978 while hunting in British Columbia's Cassiar Mountains. Mountain caribou must score at least 265 to qualify for the record listings; Frye's bull measured 410 2/8. The bull's antlers have an inside spread of 46 inches. Its right beam is 54 inches long and sprouts 15 points. The left beam is 55 6/8 inches in length and has a dozen points.

Dempsey Cape's huge Newfoundland bull, arrowed along the Victoria River on a 1966 bowhunt, still stands as a World Record at the time of this writing. It has a score of 345 2/8. The right beam is 46 6/8 inches long with 11 points while the left beam is 46 4/8 inches and boasts 12 points. The inside spread is 27 3/8 inches. To qualify for the records, a woodland caribou must score at least 220 points.

Finally, the World Record Quebec/Labrador caribou was taken in 1977 by Richard S. Neely. The bull was shot in Quebec's Ungava Region and has an overall score of 411 4/8. Its right beam has 16 points and is 56 4/8 inches long; the left beam is an even 52 inches and has 14 points. The inside spread is 52 inches. To make the Pope and Young listings, a Quebec/Labrador bull must exceed the minimum of 300 points.

Cougar . . . King of America's Cats

14

Cougars operate under more aliases than a team of forgers on a check-writing spree. Their scientific name, *Felis concolor,* means "cat of a single color" which refers to the fact they are unspotted except as kittens. Adult lions generally have surprisingly soft, tawny coats although the coloration may be gray or red or brown with dark faces and off-white to gray underparts. Rarely, an all-black specimen is reported.

Although cougars were once found throughout much of North America, the coming of the white man and relentless advance of his civilization pushed the cats—more commonly known today as mountain lions—further and further into rugged, wildly inaccessible areas of the continent. Often considered to be a threat to humans and livestock, cougars were branded as predators or varmints and often shot on sight or hunted relentlessly. Today the big cats are justifiably recognized as big game animals and thrive in much of the western United States thanks to closed areas and strict hunting controls. Regionally known as "painters" (panthers), pumas and catamounts, cougars are still found in southern swamplands and the Ozark Foothills; lion sightings are occasionally reported and confirmed in various states across the continent. Cougars are also native to western Canada and Mexico as well as Central and South America. Although an accurate count of lions is impossible, lion experts place the present North American population at between 15,000 and 20,000 animals.

Adults may be seven to nine feet in length, including the tail, and weigh from 125 to 175 pounds. Some cats will grow to a slightly larger size; however, most reports of those 10-foot, 200-pound cougars are based on campfire bull sessions and complementary bottles of chill-chaser. While there are exceptions, an average cougar stands only two to two and one-half feet at the shoulder. Incidentally, the largest cougar ever weighed checked in at a scale-straining 276 pounds—field dressed!

For the most part, cougars are solitary, nocturnal hunters. Their large yellow eyes are well suited for seeing in poor light and their white, conspicuous whiskers are believed to help the lion "feel" his way through cover and dark places. A lion's hearing is especially acute. Each cat is equipped with five claws on the forepaws and four on the hind feet. The claws are retractable and do not normally show in tracks.

The big cats' favorite prey is deer and lions typically kill one or two every week of the year. When venison is in short supply, cougars satisfy their hunger by catching and eating rodents, birds or, on occasion, domesticated poultry and stock. More on stock-killing cats later.

When on the prowl, cougars still-hunt alertly and slowly, moving silently. Once game is scented or seen, the big cats slink as close as possible, keeping to cover and bellying to the point where a sudden rush may catch their unsuspecting targets in a slashing surprise attack.

Lions have surprisingly little lung capacity and are quickly winded. Deer and other animals which escape the initial rush of a hunting lion frequently live to see another sunrise. But those unlucky animals caught in a cougar's powerful grip usually die quickly of a single bite which crushes the spinal column.

Once their prey is dead, lions typically drag the carcass to nearby cover and gorge themselves. Entrails and organs such as the heart and liver are favorites and single meals of six to eight pounds are common. Once their hunger is sated, lions cover the carcass with sticks, grasses or leaves and commonly remain in the area, returning until the animal is eaten or the meat turns sour.

Cougars cover considerable ground within the boundaries of their natural habitat, often ranging 10 to 20 miles in a single night. Their home territory may include a wide, circuitous route of perhaps 50 to 60 or more miles. Females with kittens or yearlings are not as far-ranging as the solitary toms. Frequently, all lions follow the seasonal wanderings of deer herds and stay on the periphery of large game concentrations.

Although females may come into heat at any time of the year and accept the advances of an amorous tom, most kittens are born in the spring following a gestation period of about three months. Two to four kittens are common in most litters and at birth the lions weigh less than a pound. Blind and helpless for the first few weeks of life, the spotted kittens nurse without leaving the den, normally a shallow cave or fissure in the rocks of some remote mountain canyon. By one month of age the kittens are accepting bits of meat and by two months are following their mother to nearby kills. Six-month old kittens are hunting on their own although the youngsters usually stay with their mother for a full year or more. By this time they are approaching adult size and soon leave to establish their own territories. Young females seldom breed before their second or third season.

Folklore is replete with tales of lions pouncing from ledges or trees onto unsuspecting victims; however, as already noted, most cougar attacks are staged from ground level following a successful stalk. Another popular misconception is centered around the cougar's scream. While it makes good reading to have a marauding lion's scream in the night send shivers down the spines of campers or individuals lost in the wilds, much of this is more fantasy than fact. Cougars do scream, especially during the mating season, but for the most part the big cats are quiet, stealthy hunters who rarely announce their presence.

Kittens communicate with cat-like mewing sounds. Adult lions growl and hiss when treed or cornered. They also grunt, purr and on rare occasions reportedly make a shrill, whistling sound some liken to the call of a bird. A cougar's scream, mentioned in the previous paragraph, is unforgettable. Those who have heard it describe it as a eerie drawn out scream that sounds shockingly like a woman in mortal fear of her life.

Because of their nocturnal nature and the rugged country they call home, cougars are seldom heard or seen in the wild. More likely man finds evidence of their presence in the form of lion kills, scratches or tracks. Scratches are piles of loose dirt raked up by male cats who then urinate on the mounds before moving on. Other toms in the same territory are believed to share the scratches, marking the piles with their own scent. The four-toed tracks, especially those left in snow or soft earth, are easily recognized by lion hunters who seek out the staggered line of telltale pad marks for their hounds to follow. On occasion scat piles may be found. The same is true of marks on trees where cougars pause to sharpen their claws by raking at the tree bark.

In the wild, cougars have few natural enemies besides man. Adult lions—especially toms—may kill and eat unprotected kittens or engage in occasional battles with rivals which result in serious injury. But for the most part they prowl their domain without fear, avoiding other large carnivores like bears or jaguars. Some staged fights between these species have shown lions quite capable of holding their own, thanks mainly to lightning reflexes and surprising strength.

There is, of course, some danger inherent in the business of killing other animals in order to survive. There are reports in game department files of lions being kicked or gored to death by deer. And in some states there are authenticated cases of lions coming out second best in meeting with that relentless killer of all wildlife, the automobile. Lions which avoid such accidental or ignominious fates typically live six to eight years and, in some cases, on into their teens.

Finally, no discussion of mountain lions would be complete without answering the question, "Just how dangerous are cougars to man?" Cougars can kill. Make no mistake about it. Records show some two dozen authenticated cases where mountain lions have attacked and killed humans. Yet lion attacks—provoked or unprovoked—are rare. True, woodsmen have found evidence of cougars following and watching them and such occurances naturally lead to the claim that the lions were stalking them. Most experts discount that idea, pointing to the cats' natural curiosity as the reason for following human intruders in their home territory.

Lion hunters typically have little to fear if they treat cougars with the respect they deserve. The big cats have a morbid fear of dogs and although a few lions "jump tree" despite a pack of yammering hounds, escape—not attack—is the primary objective.

Willis Butolph, the former government hunter and Utah houndsman, has been credited with over 1,000 cougar captures and kills. Late in his life, Butolph specialized in guiding bear and lion hunters. He once said of lions: "Those cats could come down out of that tree, chew up the dogs and take on hunters too. They just don't know it. We'd all better pray to heaven they never find out. I for one ain't about to tell 'em!"

Effective Bowhunting Techniques

The only truly effective way to hunt lion is behind a pack of specially trained hounds. And as is the case with any kind of hunting involving dogs, the thrill of the hunt is in the chase, in watching the hounds working to unravel a cold trail, and in hearing their bawling cries echoing off rocky canyon walls. Such is the essence of lion hunting. Once the chase is over and the cougar is treed or otherwise brought to bay, the kill is often anticlimatic.

A bowhunter who sets out to add a mountain lion trophy to his collection of game frequently has his work cut out for him. Proper conditioning is important because of the rugged and desolate terrain favored by the cougar. Proper clothing and footwear are equally vital since most lion hunting is a winter pastime when snow and cold quickly discourages or defeats an ill-prepared hunter. Finally, a proper attitude and plenty of patience are likewise essential. Lion hunting is many things; easy isn't one of them.

Since few hunters own their own dogs or have friends who do, most begin by locating a good guide with a kennel of top-flight cougar hounds. Colorado, Utah and Idaho are three of the most popular lion hunting states.

Note: Lion hunting is most often a time-consuming and costly venture. The price of the hunt itself may well run several thousand dollars. Tack on the license fees and travel expenses and the total tab rises quickly. A bowhunter seeking a cougar must be prepared for the financial outlays.

While it is possible to book cougar hunts for specific calendar dates, many guides prefer to place their clients "on call." Simply put, this means making a deposit to confirm the hunt. Next the guide waits for ideal weather conditions—especially a fresh tracking snow—and searches for lion sign. When a recent kill is located or fresh tracks cut, the guide telephones and has his hunter catch the next plane out. Within twenty-four hours or so they're together in lion country and the chase is on.

Weather, of course, is a big factor. A sudden, prolonged storm can obliterate all old sign and make hunting impossible for days on end. Also a stretch of unseasonably mild weather could work against a hunter. For these reasons it's wise to allow lots of time to make a cougar hunt and, perhaps, to agree to an "on call" arrangement to time arrival when the chances for success are, in the opinion of the guide, best for success.

POPE AND YOUNG CLUB
NORTH AMERICAN BIG GAME TROPHY SCORING FORM
BOWHUNTING

BIG GAME   RECORDS

To:

P & Y Records Office
1804 Borah
Moscow, ID 83843

COUGAR and JAGUAR   KIND OF ANIMAL _____

SEX _____

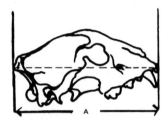 

SEE OTHER SIDE FOR INSTRUCTIONS		Measurements
A. Greatest Length Without Lower Jaw (Measured in Sixteenths)		
B Greatest Width (Measured in Sixteenths)		
TOTAL AND FINAL SCORE		

Exact locality where killed	(County)	(State)
Date killed	By whom killed	
Present owner		
Address		
Guide's Name and Address		
Remarks: (Mention any abnormalities)		

I certify that I have measured the above trophy on _____ 19 _____

at (address) _____ City _____

State _____ Zip Code _____ and that these measurements and data are, to the best

of my knowledge and belief, made in accordance with the instructions given.

Witness: _____   Signature _____

(To Measurer's Signature)

Pope & Young Club Official Measurer

_____

MEASURER (Print)

_____

ADDRESS

CITY   STATE   ZIP

INSTRUCTIONS

All measurements must be made with a flexible steel tape to the nearest one-sixteenth of an inch.

Official measurements cannot be taken for at least sixty days after the animal was killed. Photographs of right side, left side, and front of skull are required.

A. Greatest Length measured between perpendiculars to the long axis of the skull WITHOUT the lower jaw and EXCLUDING malformations. (Normal teeth included)

B. Greatest Width measured between perpendiculars at right angles to the long axis.

These measurements are best taken with calipers.

All adhering flesh, membrane and cartilage must be completely removed before official measurements are taken.

Photographs: All entries **must** include photographs of the trophy. A right side, left side and front view photograph is required for all skulls. A photograph of the entire animal is requested if at all possible. The photograph should clearly show the cheek bones (zygomatic arches), front and rear portions of the skull.

Drying Period: To be eligible for entry in the Pope & Young Records, a trophy must first have been stored under normal room temperature and humidity for at least 60 consecutive days. No trophy will be considered which has in any way been altered from its natural state.

All flesh and membrane must be completely removed from skull prior to measuring.

THIS SCORING FORM MUST BE ACCOMPANIED BY A SIGNED
POPE & YOUNG FAIR CHASE AFFIDAVIT, 3 PHOTOS OF SKULL, AND A
RECORDING FEE OF $25.00

Lion hunting, so far as the guide and his client are concerned, consists mainly of searching for fresh spoor. Typically, this means traversing the back country on foot, horseback, by 4WD vehicle or snow machine. Tracks are the primary objective although the knowledgeable lion hunter keeps an eye peeled for scavenger birds such as ravens, magpies or jays. Such birds often congregrate at a kill site and lead hunters to an ideal starting point to begin the chase, especially if the kill is fresh.

If there is no tracking snow, guides routinely check out high ridges and natural saddles leading from one creek drainage to another. Here a good strike dog is the key to success since cougars leave next to no noticeable sign—except for kills and scratch piles—as they move through the brushy, rocky terrain so typical of good lion country. The hound, generally still on a leash, ranges along seeking a trace of lion scent. Good strike dogs will open on tracks up to several days old. Once the dog begins to bay, it's up to the guide to check the freshness of the sign and direction of travel before setting the pack on the lion's trail. If conditions are judged right for a chase and the sign indicates an adult lion, the dogs are set free and it's up to the guide and hunter to stay within hearing distance of the pack. Realistically, unless the tracks are less than twenty-four hours old, the chances of treeing the lion are not considered good.

Perhaps the best starting point for a lion chase is a kill where the lion has just fed. Chances are that the big cat is still nearby, resting with a full belly. If the dogs quickly jump the cougar, the chase may be short-lived. Quite often the cats stick tight until jumped by the trailing hounds. But often the old, hunt-wise lions are on the move at the first distant sounds of the dogs on his trail. And generally the jumped lion heads for steep, rimrock country where hounds and hunters will have a difficult time following. A favorite trick is working higher and higher, following narrow ledges along faces of sheer cliffs. Frequently the less agile dogs follow and find themselves "ledged," unable to pursue the lion any further.

Keeping up with the dogs is next to impossible.

Staying within hearing distance is difficult enough, especially in crotch-deep drifts or mostly vertical canyon country. Because of this, some guides have resorted to radio-controlled collars which emit radio signals and help in locating lost dogs. Others have someone whose responsibility it is to stay within hearing by following on horseback or snowmobile. The guide and his hunter follow at a more reasonable pace, keeping in contact by CB radio. Some purists have questioned the ethics of using such devices; however, proponents argue that most critics are individuals with little or no concept of the vastness of lion country or the difficulty of such hunting. Of course, each hunter must make up his own mind in deciding whether he wishes to take a trophy in this fashion. Such decisions should be made well in advance of booking the hunt and discussed thoroughly with the guide beforehand.

Note: In 1985 the Pope and Young Club amended its Fair Chase affadavit to read: "The term 'Fair Chase' shall not include..use of electronics for attracting, locating, or pursuing game, or guiding the hunter to such game." Dr. Randall Byers, Pope and Young Records Chairman, says the intent of this change is to preclude the use of electronic calls, walkie talkies and other forms of electronic game locating devices. The amendment is not designed to abolish radio-collars which help guides locate and recover their high-priced hounds.

Once a full-bellied lion is jumped by the dogs, it frequently trees within a relatively short distance. And when the trailing hunters hear the chopping barks that signal a cat is cornered or treed, it's up to them to get to the dogs as quickly as possible. Quite often they'll arrive at the scene to find a cougar staring disdainfully down at the frantically baying dogs ringing the tree where it's taken refuge. And although cougars sometimes "jump tree" as the hunters approach, they generally quickly tree again and often accept their fate with a stoic cat-like indifference.

A bowhunter frequently has plenty of time to mentally and physically prepare himself once he's reached the tree. Some photograph the lion while the guide and his assistants catch and tie the hounds.

A wounded cougar can kill or maim valuable dogs in less time than it takes to mention the possibility and few guides are willing to run that risk. Consequently, expect the hounds to be leashed nearby before the word is given for the shot to be made.

A sharp broadhead through the animal's chest will quickly kill any lion alive. Quite often the cat is stone dead when it drops from the tree. Even when it bails out following the shot, it seldom runs far before giving up the ghost if the arrow is well-placed. No hunter should be bashful about making a follow-up shot in the event of a marginal or poor hit. The key, however, is taking your time and putting the first shot in the lion's chest.

Once the cat is dead and the guide makes sure the arrowhead poses no threat to his hounds, he'll likely turn the dogs loose to worry the carcass. Hunters needn't be concerned that the chewing and shaking by the dogs will ruin the hide. It's the dogs' reward for a job well done and quite often pieces of lion meat are fed to the hounds during the skinning process. Regardless, hunters should be aware that mountain lion meat is widely viewed as excellent table fare—not unlike veal—and should be saved for processing.

Some guides keep tabs on problem lions—those with a taste for livestock such as sheep, cattle, horses or hogs. Each year a few cougars will prey on ranch and farm animals, raising havoc and the ire of stockmen who welcome houndsmen and hunters as possible solutions to their problem. While cougars generally kill for food, a few kill for fun, slaughtering stock and leaving it where it falls. This is not typical lion behavior, but there are cases of a single lion practically decimating a flock of sheep in one raid. There are many reports of sheep-killing cats leaving dozens of dead or dying animals behind. One lion is credited with killing 192 sheep in a single attack!

Some unscrupulous guides illegally offer "canned hunts" for cougars that are previously caught or perhaps purchased from zoos, game farms or private sources. Once the client arrives for his cougar hunt, the lion is released (often without knowledge of the unsuspecting hunter) into a tree where the hounds hold him at bay. The hunter arrives, shoots the cat and returns home singing the praises of the "guide" who got him his cat within hours of arrival. The guide laughs all the way to the bank, having made perhaps double what he paid for the lion...all for a few hours' work. True, some lion hunts last only a matter of hours and are first class, fair chase hunts; however, generally a bowhunter can count on lots of riding or walking, looking and listening before he's looking up at his treed trophy. In these cases the guide truly earns his fee and the hunter earns his lion.

Other unethical guides offer to find and tree a cat before calling the client to come on the "hunt." Any hunter who could consider such an arrangement is no hunter—simply an executioner—and unworthy of the name. As for the lion, he is an outstanding game animal and deserves a better fate. Under normal conditions he's hard to come by and therein lies his appeal.

Any hunting bow of 50 pounds or more will prove to be potent lion medicine and more often than not the shot will be made at close range. The main problems likely to be confronted are finding a suitable opening among the branches and taking a shot at an overhead target. Hard-hit lions tend to die quickly.

Bowhunters should understand that their equipment can take a real beating on a lion chase. It's a good idea to check the bow for problems and to spine-check arrows for straightness before taking the shot. Give the nocks a quick inspection, too. Some stick bow shooters favor take-down recurves for lion hunts, carrying their weapons in packs until the cat is treed and assembling the bow just prior to taking the shot.

Despite the fact that most lions are taken in high, rocky country during wintertime hunts, year 'round lion hunts are possible. In Arizona, for example, some lion hunts involve chases through hot, arid terrain. Also problem cats—stock-killers or other troublemakers—may be pursued by predator control teams in all cougar country at any time of the year. Such hunts are extremely difficult on man and dogs alike. Wind and a scorching sun can wipe out a fresh cat trail in no time at all. Often water must be packed for the thirsty hounds. It's hot, sweaty work that may make hunters wish for a fresh tracking snow and icy temperatures.

Chance encounters with lions are rare but they do occur. At this writing only four bowhunters—Jim Jordan and William Holt of Texas, Ted Grover of Colorado and Chester Stevenson of Oregon—have been publicly credited with legally taking lions without the use of dogs. Several other bowhunters have reported opportunities but were not licensed to hunt lion at the time.

And more than one predator caller has reported being startled to have a lion respond to his rabbit-in-distress cries. Still, such sightings are uncommon and a poor way for a bowhunter to set about collecting a lion skin rug or mount for his den. Any callers serious about trying for lion should work in pairs with one slated to do the calling and a buddy posted nearby to shoot when the ideal time presents itself.

A final but extremely remote possibility is staking out a fresh kill in hopes of intercepting the lion as it returns to feed. Considering the general nocturnal nature of the big cats and their stealth afoot, chances of success in such an undertaking are probably a million to one—or more!

Trophy Recognition

Judging the trophy cougar as future record book material is difficult, since the final score is based on measurements totaling the length and width of the fleshed out skull after a minimum drying period of 60 days. This fact, combined with the visual impression that big-bodied lions have comparatively small heads, creates some problems for the trophy hunter.

But most adult male cougars will qualify for the Pope and Young bowhunting records (the current minimum score is 13 inches). Truly outstanding cats, those with skulls large enough to surpass the Boone and Crockett minimum score of 15 inches, will—or should be—immediately recognized as exceptional

trophies by even a novice lion hunter. Big lions are...well, **big**! And even the greenhorn who loses his cool at the sight of a bayed cougar and wrongly believes the medium-sized cat is the King Kong of cougars, still has his guide's judgment to count on.

Note: Most bowhunters consider a lion hunt as a once-in-a-lifetime venture. Consequently they should regard any adult cougar legally taken under the rules of Fair Chase as a true **trophy** animal. Any record book recognition is simply icing on the cake.

The world record cougar was shot in Idaho in 1982 by bowhunter Jerry James. The skull measures a whopping 15 11/16 inches. Its length is 9 2/16 and its width 6 9/16 inches.

Mule Deer ... Big Ears & Antlers

15

The long-eared mule deer is as much a part of the Western prairies and mountains as sagebrush and quaking aspen. Largest of the three primary species of North American deer, the muley is a blockier, less graceful animal than the whitetail; however, its bounding, pogo-stick gait and the high, branched antlers of mature bucks make this deer a unique trophy. There are some bowhunters who are convinced that the trophy-class mule deer buck is the most challenging big game animal on this continent.

Mule deer *(Odocoileus hemionus hemionus)* range from southern Alaska to Mexico and from the Pacific coast occasionally eastward as far as states like Minnesota and Iowa. Although part of the same family, mule deer and blacktail deer are divided into three separate categories by the Pope and Young Club. Columbian blacktail deer *(Odocoileus hemionus columbianus)* are animals of the coastal ranges of British Columbia, Washington, Oregon and northern California. Sitka blacktail deer *(Odocoileus hemionus sitkensis)* live in Alaska's coastal ranges and the Queen Charlotte Islands. All other members of the *Odocoileus hemionus* family found outside of these areas are known simply as mule deer.

In fact, blacktails are somewhat smaller versions of mule deer. The Columbian blacktail bucks sport similar but more diminutive muley antlers; however, the Sitkas wear racks that often are mistaken for whitetails since the distinctive branched antlers are lacking. They typically are more brush-loving animals than their larger cousins

and are quite at home in the thick coastal forests along the northwestern edge of the continent. These deer typically stand slightly over three feet at the shoulder and are up to five feet in length. Bucks average perhaps 150 pounds.

Mule deer average three and one-half feet at the shoulder and measure between six and seven feet in length. Average bucks weigh between 180 and 200 pounds with some documented cases of 400-plus pound animals on record. The biggest blacktails reported have flirted with the 300-pound mark.

Named for their prominent mule-like ears, mule deer have a distinct U-shaped patch of dark hair on their foreheads and two white throat patches. Body hair ranges from a reddish-brown in summer months to a light gray in the wintertime. Underbellies and rumps are white. The animals' tails are narrow and tipped with tufts of black hair. Unlike the whitetail, mule deer keep their tail down when running.

The muley's metarsal glands are conspicuous patches of hair growing on the outside of each hind leg. These glands are the largest of any deer species. The tarsal or musk glands are conspicuous swirls of hair found on the inside of each rear leg. Also notable are the lachrynal glands located just in front of each eye. These glands are deeper and more obvious than those of the whitetail.

Tracks and droppings are the most common mule deer sign. Tracks are similar to a whitetail's but slightly larger and more rounded. Also, a muley's dewclaws seldom show, even in tracks made when the animal is running. The peculiar bounding gait of mule deer—with all four feet leaving and striking the ground together—accounts for this, although the impressions left by dewclaws may be readily apparent in snow or on soft ground. The scat is normally found in groupings of hard pellets although soft masses may be found where the deer have been grazing on grasses.

The headgear of trophy bucks is a real attention getter with high, wide, heavy racks the norm. Unlike the whitetail, a mule deer's antler points do not originate off a single main beam; the beams separate and branch into Y-shaped forks. Mature bucks commonly carry at least four points on each antler not counting the brow tine. The term four-point or four-by-four is used by most mule deer hunters referring to deer that an Eastern whitetail hunter would call an eight-pointer or 10-pointer. Western hunters typically count points only on one side of the antlers and ignore shorter points like the eyeguards. The number of points is no indication of any deer's age. A mule deer buck with spikes or forked horns one year may well be a four-point buck the following year if he is healthy and feeds in mineral-rich country.

Mule deer are not picky eaters. Grasses are an important part of their diet each spring and summer; however, they commonly browse on brush and small trees—whatever is available—in the fall and winter months. Nuts, berries and mushrooms are considered delicacies and are eagerly eaten. Feeding generally takes place during early morning and late evening hours. Deer commonly remain in feeding areas throughout the night and return to secluded bedding spots to rest and chew their cuds during daylight hours.

A mule deer's senses of sight, hearing and smell are all well-developed and which is most important depends on the type of terrain the deer choose to call home. On the open prairies and in the semi-arid deserts, a moving hunter will attract attention long before he moves within range to be scented or heard. But in the brushy canyons and thickly forested mountain country where vision is limited, a careless sound or errant breeze can foil any

bowhunter's best made plans. In all likelihood, mule deer typically rely on their noses to warn of imminent danger more than any other sense. Noisy, gusty days with strong or swirling winds will make deer nervous and jumpy since two basic defenses—smell and hearing—are affected.

Deer beds are often found on high shady points where the animals have a good view of the surroundings and where rising or descending thermals will warn of approaching danger. In areas where encounters with humans are common, mule deer have adopted a common whitetail ploy of bedding in dense cover where it would be impossible for an enemy to approach quietly and undetected.

Mule deer tend to be more gregarious and more far-ranging than whitetails. Although segregation by sexes is common—except during the winter months—older bucks tend to hang together in bachelor bands unless the rut is imminent or underway; does, fawns, yearlings and young bucks often congregate and share each other's company. Movements within a home range are common. Generally speaking, mule deer spend the summer months in the higher elevations—8,000 to 10,000 feet—and begin a seasonal drift into lower, more sheltered canyons and foothills when the first snows cover high country forage. In years past mule deer migrations of perhaps 100 miles or more were noted; however, in most cases today the annual movements between summer and winter ranges could not be classified as true migrations.

Most bowhunting seasons begin during the summer months—as early as July in California—when the deer are high in their summer haunts and the bucks are sporting velvet-covered antlers. By late August or early September the antlers are fully developed beneath the drying velvet, which soon begins to peel. Bucks frequently hasten the process by rubbing their racks on brush and small trees.

The rut in most mule deer country does not begin until October. At this time the bucks begin a search for receptive does. Their testicles lower into the scrotal sac and their necks swell. Fights between rivals are most often shoving matches with few injuries resulting; however, when antlers interlock the result is usually a death sentence for both animals.

Mule deer bucks, unlike bull elk, do not collect or jealously guard true harems. Instead it is more common for a buck to hang with a group of does, breeding each as she comes into estrous. Does in heat are fertile for a period of slightly more than 24 hours and if not bred will become receptive again 28 days later. This cycle may recur several times but in most instances the does will be impregnated soon after the onset of rut. Young does commonly have single births while twins are the norm for does after their first breeding season.

Fawns are generally born in June or July and weigh five or six pounds at birth. The spotted, russet-coated youngsters spend their early days hidden in some grassy, shaded area which their mother visits on a regular schedule to nurse and check on her fawns. The fawns are virtually odorless at birth and does keep their distance for fear of attracting the attention of some lurking predator. Regardless, numerous fawns are caught and eaten by cougars, bobcats, coyotes, bears and, on occasion, an eagle. Even in the open spaces of the West, autos and trucks also account for many deer deaths.

The youngsters that survive develop quickly and within a period of weeks are following their mothers about, nibbling on vegetation but continuing to nurse until September, when they lose their spotted coats to the growth of greyish winter coats. Fawns usually remain with their mothers until birthing time the following year.

Cougars are the mule deer's greatest threat for each cat makes one or two kills per week. Disease and the starvation which results during severe winters also may take a heavy toll. While blacktail populations are up, overall numbers of mule deer have declined slightly in recent years and numerous reasons—severe winter losses, poor fawn survival, disease, predation, habitat deterioration, overharvest and low reproduction—are suggested.

Nonetheless, the mule deer is found in huntable numbers throughout much of its original and current range. Estimates of mule deer/blacktail populations indicate several million animals roam North America in the mid-1980s.

Effective Bowhunting Techniques

Mule deer, despite their reputation for being less wily than the whitetail, are not pushovers. Bowhunters after a bragging-size buck will find this to be especially true.

Unlike their seemingly invisible eastern cousins, however, muleys are visible animals. Locating them by sight rather than sign is easier and consequently still-hunting and stalking are popular hunting methods. In mountainous terrain, a favorite method is working high ridges—staying off the skyline—and moving downslope early in the day. The rising thermals will carry a hunter's scent away from deer feeding or bedded below. Also, the higher ground offers a good vantage point where glassing may detect moving game in the lower canyons.

Easy-does-it is a good rule of thumb for the still-hunter. The idea is for the bowhunter to locate the deer before any animals are aware of his presence. This means lots of standing and looking between steps. And care must always be taken to avoid careless noise. A branch cracking under a bootsole may not immediately spook a deer, but it may alert him. Combine such noise with movement and it's safe to bet the hunter will never get close enough to release an arrow.

Still-hunting hunters must learn to look for parts of deer rather than the entire animals. Horizontal shapes, especially, are worth a second look. Patches of reddish-brown among white-trunked aspens or the green of late summer foliage are noteworthy. A flicker of movement might be a jay flitting its wings in the oakbrush—or it could be a muley's ear. And that forked branch jutting above the sage may be just that—but it could be a bedded buck's antler tines.

Once a deer is spotted, the still-hunt becomes a stalk as the bowhunter attempts to work within range. Mule deer are not particularly difficult

POPE & YOUNG CLUB
NORTH AMERICAN BIG GAME TROPHY SCORING FORM
BOWHUNTING

To:

P & Y Records Office
1804 Borah
Moscow, ID 83843

BIG GAME   RECORDS

KIND OF DEER_____

TYPICAL MULE - BLACKTAIL and SITKA DEER

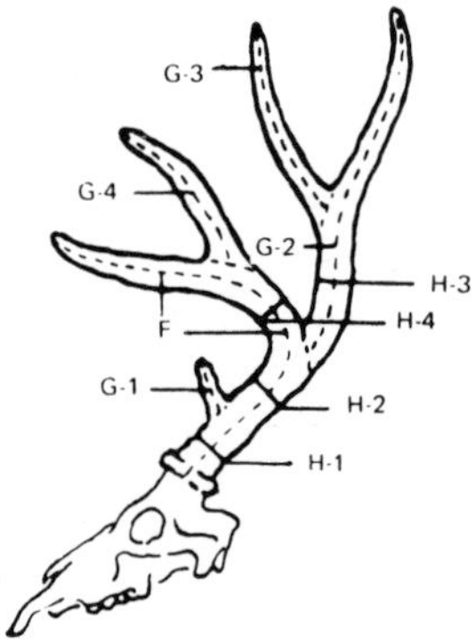

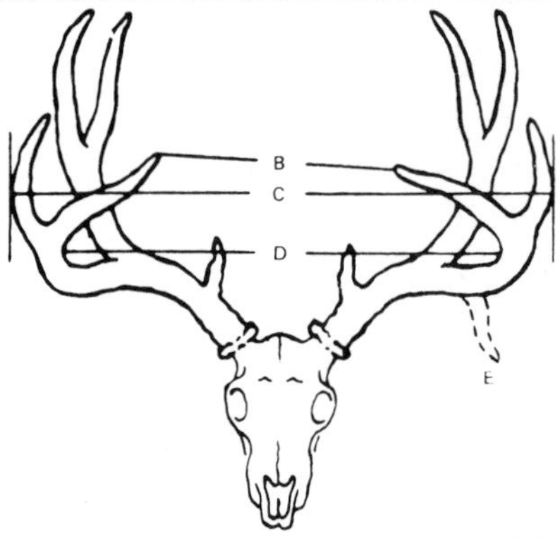

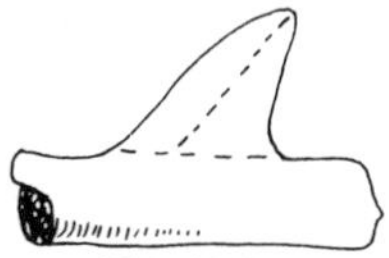

DETAIL OF POINT
MEASUREMENT

Abnormal Points	
Right	Left
Total To E	

SEE OTHER SIDE FOR INSTRUCTIONS		Supplementary Data		Column 1	Column 2	Column 3	Column 4
		R	L	Spread Credit	Right Antler	Left Antler	Difference
A.	Number of Points on Each Antler						
B.	Tip to Tip Spread						
C.	Greatest Spread						
D.	Inside Spread of MAIN BEAMS	Spread credit may equal but not exceed length of longer antler					
	If Inside Spread of Main Beams exceeds longer antler length, enter difference						
E.	Total of Lengths of all Abnormal Points						
F.	Length of Main Beam						
G-1	Length of First Point, if present						
G-2	Length of Second Point						
G-3	Length of Third Point						
G-4	Length of Fourth Point, if present						
H-1	Circumference at Smallest Place Between Burr and First Point						
H-2	Circumference at Smallest Place Between First and Second Points						
H-3	Circumference at Smallest Place Between Main Beam and Third Points						
H-4	Circumference at Smallest Place between Second and Fourth Points or half way between Second Point and Beam tip if Fourth Point is missing						
TOTALS							

	Column 1		Exact locality where killed		(County)	(State)
ADD	Column 2		Date killed	By whom killed		
	Column 3		Present owner			
	Total		Address			
SUBTRACT Column 4			Guide's Name and Complete Address			
FINAL SCORE			Remarks: (Mention any abnormalities)			

I certify that I have measured the above trophy on _____ 19 _____

at (address) _____ City _____

State _____ Zip Code _____ and that these measurements and data are, to the best

of my knowledge and belief, made in accordance with the instructions given.

Witness: _____ Signature _____

(To Measurer's Signature)

Pope & Young Club Official Measurer

_____

MEASURER (Print)

_____

ADDRESS

_____

CITY   STATE   ZIP

All measurements must be made with a flexible steel tape or measuring cable to the nearest one-eighth of an inch. Wherever it is necessary to change direction of measurement, mark a control point and swing tape at this point. To simplify addition, please enter fractional figures in eighths. Official measurements cannot be take for at least sixty days after the animal was killed. **Photos of left side, right side, and front of antlers are required.**

Supplementary Data measurements indicate conformation of the trophy, and none of the figures in Lines A, B and C are to be included in the score. Evaluation of conformation is a matter of personal preference. Excellent, but nontypical Mule Deer heads with many points shall be placed and judged in a separate class.

A. Number of Points on Each Antler. To be counted a point, a projection must be at least one inch long AND its length must exceed the length of its base. All points are measured from tip of point to nearest edge of beam as illustrated. **Beam tip is counted as a point but not measured as a point.**

B. Tip to Tip Spread measured between tips of main beams.

C. Greatest Spread measured between perpendiculars at right angles to the center line of the skull at widest part whether across main beams or points.

D. Inside Spread of Main Beams measured at right angles to the center line of the skull at widest point between main beams. Enter this measurement again in "Spread Credit" column if it is less than or equal to the length of longer antler.

E. Total of Lengths of all Abnormal Points. Abnormal points are generally considered to be those nontypical in shape or location.

F. Length of Main Beam measured from lowest outside edge of burr over outer curve to the tip of the main beam. The point of beginning is that point on the burr where the center line along the outer curve of the beam intersects the burr.

G-1-2-3-4. Length of Normal Points. Normal points are the brow (or first) and the upper and lower forks as shown in illustration. They are measured from nearest edge of beam over outer curve to tip. To determine nearest edge (top edge) of beam, lay the tape along the outer curve of the beam so that the top edge of the tape coincides with the top edge of the beam on both sides of the point. Draw line along top of tape. This line will be base line from which point is measured.

H-1-2-3-4. Circumferences - If first point is missing, take H-1 and H-2 at smallest place between burr and second point. If third point is missing, take H-3 half way between the base and tip of second point. If the fourth is missing, take H-4 half way between the second point and tip of main beam. Circumference measurements must be taken with a steel tape.

Photographs: All entries must include photographs of the trophy. A right side, left side and front view photograph will be required for all antlers, horns and skulls. A photograph of the entire animal is requested if at all possible.

Drying Period: To be eligible for entry in the Pope & Young Records, a trophy must first have been stored under normal room temperature and humidity for at least 60 consecutive days. No trophy will be considered which has in any way been altered from its natural state.

THIS SCORING FORM MUST BE ACCOMPANIED BY A SIGNED
**POPE & YOUNG FAIR CHASE AFFIDAVITT, 3 PHOTOS OF ANTLERS, AND A
RECORDING FEE OF $25.00**
Copyright 1965 by Boone and Crockett Club
(Written request for privilege of complete reproduction is required)

animals to stalk but a hunter must never allow himself to get in a hurry. Movement must be slow, deliberate and silent. A step is taken only when the deer's head is down or obscured by brush. Any time a hunter can see a deer's eyes, the deer can see him. And while deer commonly ignore motionless objects—even those in plain view—a stalker caught moving will attract immediate, careful attention.

The gregarious nature of mule deer poses a problem at times and even when only one animal is sighted a bowhunter should assume there are others nearby. More than one careful stalk has been ruined by a second unnoticed deer that spooked when the approaching hunter was sighted.

Feeding deer can be frustrating to stalk because it's easy for them to maintain some distance between them and the bowhunter. The stalker takes one quiet, careful step—the browsing deer nibbles at some browse and takes a step—or two—searching for tasty morsels. But feeding deer, especially those with their heads down, are concentrating on filling their rumen. And unless alerted they can be approached by a patient, determined hunter.

Another possibility for stalking exists by determining the animals' direction of travel and attempting to work into position ahead of them. This method is risky since the deer may change direction or decide to bed down before reaching the ambush spot. But if things go as planned and the hunter remains undetected, the deer may feed into easy bow range and offer a good shot.

In the lower elevations of the prairies and deserts a stalking hunter must adhere to the same rules. Some of this country seems barren and far too open to contain either deer or adequate cover for a stalk. First appearances are often deceptive. Often there are shallow draws and cuts among the gently rolling terrain. And in the rugged badlands country where grasses and brush are at a premium the bowhunter must take advantage of undulations in the broken land for concealment.

Mule deer often bed at the base of cliffs or rocky overhangs where they have a good view of the surroundings. With the natural protection at their backs, they rely on their eyes and noses to warn them of danger approaching from the front or sides. Such deer are difficult but not impossible to stalk; however, the hunter must keep out of sight and stalk a spot rather than the animal itself. Special attention should be paid to the area immediately surrounding the deer's bed, and the bowhunter must remember that once he is in a different position the terrain will appear to change. Landmarks must be noted because the stalking hunter won't see the animal again until he is within bow range.

Alarmed mule deer often spring from their beds and bound away in high gear. Some stand and stare stupidly at the intruder, allowing ample time for a shot. Generally speaking, the ideal shot is taken while the animal is still bedded or when he finally stands of his own accord. If the hunter can approach from above and behind the deer, he can drive the arrow down into the chest cavity much the same way he'd take a shot from an elevated stand. If he is on the same level with a bedded deer, he must remember the resting animal's shoulders and hams will cover much of the vital area and place the shot accordingly.

Tree stand hunting can be effective for mule deer bowhunters who are not comfortable stalking their game. Many Eastern whitetail hunters on their initial hunts for muleys have quickly discovered that the same methods used in their backyards work well west of the Mississippi. Tree stands located over natural mineral licks and salt blocks left for range cattle definitely work. The same is true where water is scarce and the animals must visit springs, seeps or stock tanks to drink. Another excellent location for tree stands is along well-tracked trails leading to feeding areas. Ranch crops such as alfalfa and some grains may act as a magnet, pulling deer from surrounding hills to those green oases each evening. Does, fawns and yearlings typically visit the fields first but patient hunters may be rewarded with a good shot at a hungry buck entering the feeding area just before nightfall. Haystacks and windmill platforms are other possibilities. Trail watching is often chancy because of the vastness of much mule deer range. Animals may be on one ridge today and two mountains away the next.

Ground blinds are often equally effective where trails pass natural cover such as deadfalls, rockpiles and brushy clumps. Some bowhunters use native materials—limbs, brush, vegetation boulders and the like—to construct crude blinds. Others opt to use lightweight camo netting which is carried in a pocket or pack and strung between limbs, rocks or whatever. The ideal ground blind has adequate cover behind the hunter to break his silhouette and enough cover in front to conceal him and allow cautious movements as the bow is being drawn. Several shooting lanes should be cleared in natural blinds and at least two shooting windows should be cut into cloth blinds.

Mule deer learn quickly. Where hunted from trees, they quickly learn to look up for danger just as whitetails do. And muleys are especially alert for danger from ground level. As already mentioned in the chapter on mountain lions, despite what fiction writers would have you believe, cougars rarely pounce on their prey from overhanging limbs or rocks. They much prefer to slip within a short distance and bring their victim down with a surprising rush. So feeding deer commonly keep their eyes open for approaching danger. While they do not appear to notice stationary hunters, they are quick to pick up ground level movements. In addition, a hunter on the ground must be especially conscious of his scent and ideally keep the prevailing breeze in his face.

Note: On a calm, still day a hunter's scent will pool and spread slowly outward. It's much like the ripples created when a rock is dropped into a pond only with the scent it's more of a slow motion effect. Regardless, any deer entering the hunter's scent pool will be immediately alerted. While the same thing happens to tree stand hunters, the scent is higher off the ground and less likely to be as concentrated.

Some bowhunters use masking scents to dilute or camouflage their natural body odor. Arguments abound concerning the effectiveness of such scents, but it only makes sense that an unwashed hunter wearing sweaty, soiled clothing is not going to fool the keen-nosed deer no matter how much masking

scent he uses. Personal cleanliness is a consideration which should not be overlooked by any serious hunter.

Whether hunting from a tree stand or ground blind, a hunter should remember that deer are quick to pick up on obvious changes in their surroundings. Tree stands should be erected accordingly and located against a background where the hunter does not stand out against the sky. Whenever possible, it's wise to use a natural stand—a blowdown, snag or boulder—and disturb the surroundings as little as possible. If time permits, ground blinds should be established in advance of the hunt; they are most effective if they blend in naturally or are constructed far enough in advance of the season or hunt to allow the game to grow accustomed to them. Any necessary trimming to clear shooting lanes should be kept to a minimum and clippings gathered up. The white stubs of small limbs or branches which show plainly after trimming need attention; dabbing them with dirt, mud—even camo face paint—hides the evidence of human activity from sharp-eyed deer.

Stands are especially effective when used patiently and intelligently. Location, of course, is a primary concern and depends on knowledge of the terrain and game movements. Some guides offer tree stand hunting from time-tested sites season after season. And no one can question the results of this type of hunting.

In areas where stands are located in shelterbelts, along river bottoms or in natural saddles between rimrocks or high ridges, driving deer can result in shots. This method works best if the animals are not spooked but merely disturbed to the point they move out slowly ahead of drivers. Running deer are risky targets for bowhunters and frightened animals, with adrenaline pumping, are much harder to put down—gun or bow. But a slowly moving deer passing beneath a hunter stationed above an escape route can offer an excellent shot.

Some Western hunting camps offer tree stand hunting early and late in the day when deer are leaving or returning to feeding areas and organized drives for muleys during the mid-day hours when

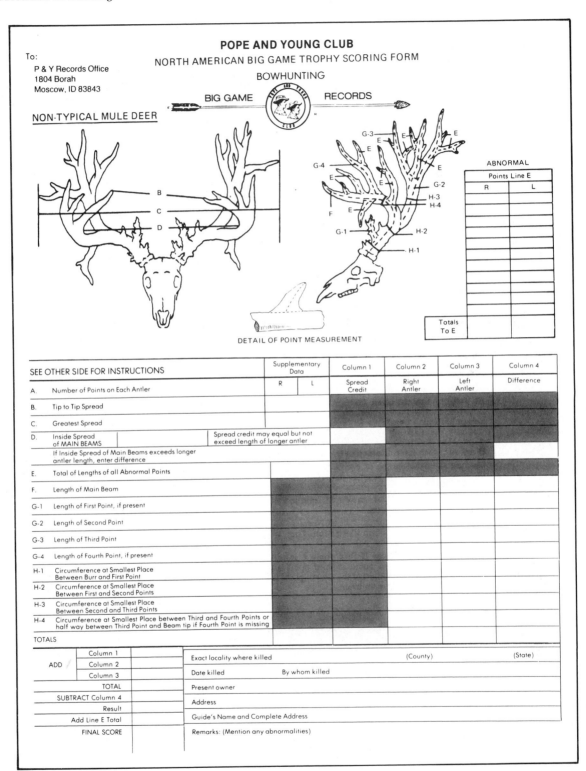

POPE AND YOUNG CLUB
NORTH AMERICAN BIG GAME TROPHY SCORING FORM
BOWHUNTING
BIG GAME   RECORDS

To:
P & Y Records Office
1804 Borah
Moscow, ID 83843

NON-TYPICAL MULE DEER

ABNORMAL
Points Line E

	R	L

Totals
To E

DETAIL OF POINT MEASUREMENT

SEE OTHER SIDE FOR INSTRUCTIONS		Supplementary Data		Column 1	Column 2	Column 3	Column 4
		R	L	Spread Credit	Right Antler	Left Antler	Difference
A.	Number of Points on Each Antler						
B.	Tip to Tip Spread						
C.	Greatest Spread						
D.	Inside Spread of MAIN BEAMS	Spread credit may equal but not exceed length of longer antler					
	If Inside Spread of Main Beams exceeds longer antler length, enter difference						
E.	Total of Lengths of all Abnormal Points						
F.	Length of Main Beam						
G-1	Length of First Point, if present						
G-2	Length of Second Point						
G-3	Length of Third Point						
G-4	Length of Fourth Point, if present						
H-1	Circumference at Smallest Place Between Burr and First Point						
H-2	Circumference at Smallest Place Between First and Second Points						
H-3	Circumference at Smallest Place Between Second and Third Points						
H-4	Circumference at Smallest Place between Third and Fourth Points or half way between Third Point and Beam tip if Fourth Point is missing						
TOTALS							

ADD	Column 1	
	Column 2	
	Column 3	
	TOTAL	
SUBTRACT Column 4		
	Result	
Add Line E Total		
FINAL SCORE		

Exact locality where killed _____ (County) _____ (State)

Date killed _____ By whom killed _____

Present owner _____

Address _____

Guide's Name and Complete Address _____

Remarks: (Mention any abnormalities) _____

I certify that I have measured the above trophy on _____ 19 _____
at (address)_____ City _____
State _____ Zip Code_____ and that these measurements and data are, to the
best of my knowledge and belief, made in accordance with the instructions given.

Witness: _____ Signature _____
                                                    Pope & Young Club Official Measurer

_____
MEASURER (Print)
_____
ADDRESS
_____
CITY   STATE   ZIP

INSTRUCTIONS

All measurements must be made with a flexible steel tape to the nearest one-eighth of an inch. To simplify addition, please enter fractional figures in eighths.

Official measurements cannot be taken for at least sixty days after the animal was killed. Please submit photographs.

Supplementary Data measurements indicate conformation of the trophy, and none of the figures in Lines A, B and C are to be included in the score. Evaluation of conformation is a matter of personal preference.

A. Number of Points on Each Antler. To be counted a point, a projection must be at least one inch long AND its length must exceed the length of its base. All points are measured from tip to point to nearest edge of beam as illustrated. Beam tip is counted as a point but not measured as a point.

B. Tip to Tip Spread measured between tips of antlers.

C. Greatest Spread measured between perpendiculars at right angles to the center line of the skull at widest part whether across main beams or points.

D. Inside Spread of Main Beams measured at right angles to the center line of the skull at widest point between main beams. Enter this measurement again in "Spread Credit" column if it is less than or equal to the length of longer antler.

E. Total of Lengths of all Abnormal Points. Abnormal points are considered to be those nontypical in shape or location. It is very important, in scoring nontypical heads, to determine which points are to be classed as normal and which are not. To do this, study carefully the markings G-1, G-2, G-3 and G-4 on the diagram, which indicate the normal points. On the trophy to be scored, select the points which most closely correspond to these. All others over one inch in length (See A, above) are considered abnormal.

Measure the exact length of each abnormal point, over the outer curve, from the tip to the nearest edge of the beam or point from which it projects. Then add these lengths and enter the total in the space provided.

F. Length of Main Beams measured from lowest outside edge of burr over outer curve to the tip of the main beam.

G-1-2-3-4. Length of Normal Points. Normal points are the brow (or first) and the upper and lower forks as shown in illustration. They are measured from nearest edge of beam over outer curve to tip.

H-1-2-3-4. Circumferences If first point is missing, take H-1 and H-2 at smallest place between burr and second point. If third point is missing, take H-3 half way between the base and tip of second point. If the fourth point is missing take H-4 half way between the second point and tip of main beam.

Photographs: All entries must include photographs of the trophy. A right side, left side and front view photograph will be required for all antlers, horns and skulls. A photograph of the entire animal is requested if at all possible.

Drying Period: To be eligible for entry in the the Pope & Young Records, a trophy must first have been stored under normal room temperature and humidity for at least 60 consecutive days. No trophy will be considered which has in any way been altered from its natural state.

THIS SCORING FORM MUST BE ACCOMPANIED BY A SIGNED POPE & YOUNG FAIR CHASE AFFIDAVIT, 3 PHOTOS AND A RECORDING FEE OF $25.00.

the animals are bedded. Often the term "organized drive" is a misnomer; often there's lots of confusion as a band of bowhunters surrounds an aspen pocket and proceeds to sweep through it. The result may be spooked mule deer bouncing in every direction, breaking through the lines of advancing hunters and disappearing over the skyline. These animals generally make for very poor targets. Another negative against such "organized" deer drives is found in the fact that muleys don't like to be disturbed. Unlike whitetails with established home territories, mule deer are much more nomadic and if pressured in one part of their range simply move on to less hectic surroundings.

A few hunters have been successful in luring mule deer into good bow range by calling them with homemade or specially manufactured deer calls. Some veteran bowhunters believe that blacktails answer deer calls far more readily than their cousins; however, given the proper conditions—and effective calling techniques—muleys can be duped by this method.

The same may be said of horn rattling, although much less experimentation has been done on mule deer than whitetails. Mule deer bucks can be rattled up on occasion, especially during the rut when actual fighting is occurring. However, as previously noted, most bow seasons occur in the late summer or early fall months, ahead of the rutting season. Horn rattling at this time of year is undoubtedly a waste of time and best left to the bowhunters living in or near mule deer country or those non-residents who may take advantage of late seasons to try their hand with rattling horns.

Early seasons also preclude the possibility of employing scrape hunting techniques to arrow a buck. There is some disagreement among hunters as to the effectiveness of scrape hunting for wide-ranging mule deer during the rut. Mule deer do make rubs and scrapes, but the animals' nomadic nature makes scrape-watching a chancy business.

Weather affects mule deer movements. Sensing an approaching storm, the deer may begin to feed at mid-day and continue until bad weather arrives. Light mist or rain doesn't appear to bother the deer but mountain storms and heavy rain sends them to cover. Heavy snowfalls commonly put deer on the move, most often from higher elevations down into the more sheltered canyons where browse remains readily available. Does, fawns and yearlings are generally the first to go, with the bigger, trophy-class bucks bringing up the rear. Some knowledgeable bowhunters watch the peaks and listen to weather forecasts for evidence of high country storms, spending considerable time afield after heavy snowfalls. A few trophy hunters actually wait until late in the season to begin serious hunting. By then the wall-hanger muleys are driven into lower elevations ahead of the advancing snow line.

A white-clad hunter, dressed in total winter camouflage, may have good success still-hunting deer when the snow is wet or powdery. Later, when crusted snow makes walking noisy and difficult, stalking into bow range is next to impossible. The animals will hear even the most careful stalker and be gone long before a good shot is possible. Where muleys are found competing with domestic livestock for winter forage, good ambush sites are haystacks or cottonwoods overlooking feeding areas.

A handful of bowhunters report taking bucks from horseback. A general rule is mule deer are not as alarmed by a horse and rider as by a man on foot. Some bowhunters have ridden close enough to deer to take a good shot without dismounting. For obvious reasons, the horse must understand what's going on and be gentle enough to allow a bow to be shot by his rider. Never under any circumstances should a novice horseman try this method on an untested mount. A bow may be quiet but the movement of drawing and shooting—plus the slight but sudden noise of release—can spook a horse. The end result may be a one-animal rodeo and a bowhunter finding out firsthand how a bronc buster feels when the chute is opened.

Some hopeful, imaginative bowhunters have tried baiting deer—where legal—into shooting range. Some whitetail hunters have actually packed apples, corn and other tasty baits cross country while others have relied on the artifical scents of favorite deer foods to attract muleys. Reports vary on the degree of success but the concensus seems to be that such attractant scents do more harm than good if the odor is alien to the deer. Regardless, setting out baits for deer is a controversial and often illegal practice. Game laws must be carefully checked to avoid potential legal problems.

Because of the open terrain commonly inhabited by mule deer, bowhunters have a tendency to take longer shots at these animals. This can create recovery problems as the result of bad hits. Many veteran hunters claim that muleys simply do not bleed as profusely as whitetails (their diet is rumored to promote clotting and result in skimpy bloodtrails). Whether this is fact or an old wives' tale, the advice stands: "Never attempt any shot beyond your effective shooting range."

Mule deer bucks are solid, stocky animals with considerable endurance. Certainly bows of 50 pounds and up are effective for mule deer, but razor sharp heads and well-placed shots are the keys to success.

Trophy Recognition

Immature mule deer bucks have spindly antlers that barely reach their ear tips. Average bucks carry at least four points on each side (discounting the brow tines) and have antlers that extend beyond their ears. Monster muleys have thick-beamed, massive racks that overhang their ears and bodies.

Talk about "30-inchers" refers to antler width or "spread," and some trophy hunters generalize with the statement that no buck with less than a 30-inch spread is a real trophy. That's nonsense, of course. While spread is impressive (some mule deer racks top 40 inches), mass and symmetry are keys to high record book scores. The unusually wide racks may be penalized in the scoring process since points are deducted if the inside spread of the main beams exceeds the antler length.

A small-bodied mule deer with an average rack may fool the novice; however, any mule deer wearing outsized antlers is worthy of consideration. Trophy racks are high and approach or exceed the

thickness of the deer's body. When the buck is facing away, the antlers of trophy-class bucks jut beyond the body by one-third to one-half.

Note: The velvet-covered antlers encountered on early season hunts generally makes the rack appear thicker than it actually is. The Pope and Young Club presently requires that the velvet be stripped from the antlers before the measuring is done.

Usually blacktail deer are porportionally smaller in both antler and body size. These miniature mule deer seldom carry antlers that "jump out" at the hunter; however, big bucks have balanced thick-beamed antlers that approach or exceed the ear tips.

Although non-typical antlers may be found in all deer species only the whitetail, Coues and mule deer have record book categories for trophy bucks with unusual, freakish antler growths.

The top typical mule deer was shot in 1979 by Colorado bowhunter Bill Barcus. Hunting the White River National Forest, Barcus shot a seven-by-seven buck with an inside spread of 30 2/8 inches. The right beam is 28 5/8 inches long and the left measures 27 6/8 inches. The total score is 201 4/8 inches.

Another Colorado buck claims the top spot in the non-typical category with a score of 258 2/8. The record muley has an inside spread of 24 0/8 inches. Its right beam has 13 points and is 26 6/8 inches long. The left beam has 11 points and measures 26 7/8 inches. The buck was arrowed in Mesa County during the 1976 bow season by David Glick.

The world record Columbian blacktail deer was shot near Silverton, Oregon in 1969 by bowhunter B. G. Shurtleff. The buck has seven points on each antler and the rack's inside spread is 20-4/8 inches. The right beam measures 26-3/8 inches and the left is 25-7/8 inches. The total score is 172-2/8.

Hunter Gene Coughlin took the top Sitka blacktail during the 1984 bow season while hunting Alaska's Kodiak Island. The five-by-five buck has a 17 inch inside spread. The right beam tapes 19 0/8 inches and the left beam is also 19 inches even. The buck's total score is 101 0/8.

To land in the Pope and Young listings, a mule deer must score a minimum of 145 (typical) and 160 (non-typical). A Columbian blacktail must score at least 90 and a Sitka blacktail 65 to qualify for the records.

Whitetails . . . Everyman's Deer

16

Whitetail bucks are the undisputed kings of North American big game. No other species is found in greater numbers over a wider area of the continent. Consequently, it's not surprising that whitetails are the most popular big game animal on earth.

Adaptable, durable, intelligent and unquestionably challenging, the whitetail *(Odocoileus virginianus)* lives in the shadows of city skylines and sprawling suburban development. But he's also found in remote mountain terrain and southern swamplands, in farmland shelterbelts and woodlots as well as along the fringes of unbroken tracts of north country timberlands, in semi-arid prairieland and on coastal islands. There are, in fact, very few areas of this continent where the whitetail is not found.

From no more than 500,000 animals in 1900 to a continental herd numbering perhaps 15 million or more today, the whitetail has staged a remarkable comeback. And when contemporary hunting pressure and habitat destruction are considered, the current status of the whitetail deer is nothing short of miraculous. Native North Americans, whitetail deer evolved from prehistoric ancestors into today's recognizable species perhaps a million years ago. Most modern whitetails are small, graceful, dainty animals standing about three feet at the shoulders. Big bucks may reach three and one-half feet in height and have a body length of between five and six feet. Does are slightly smaller. Weights vary greatly from region to region but 125 to 150 pounds is probably average. Many northern bucks top 200 pounds with an occasional 300

pounder reported. The biggest whitetail on record tipped the scales at over 500 pounds.

The whitetail's antlers, unlike those of a mule deer, consist of a single main beam and jutting, unforked tines. Most adult bucks have four to five points on each antler and Eastern whitetail hunters usually count all points, including the brow tines. As already noted, Western hunters typically count only one side of the rack and ignore the eyeguards, or they combine the points on each side by calling a 10-pointer a five-by-five. While the Pope and Young Club requires that each point be a minimum of one inch in length to qualify for measurement, the old rule that a point is "anything you can hang a ring on" is still the standard among many deer hunters.

The diminutive Coues deer of the dry southwest regions is an identical but scaled down version of the larger whitetail. A big Coues buck seldom exceeds 100 pounds and may stand only two and one-half feet at the shoulders. Antlers, likewise, are proportionally smaller. These deer are the only subspecies of whitetail recognized as a separate category by the Pope and Young Club.

Whitetails rely mainly on their extraordinary sense of smell to alert them to the presence of enemies. They also have above average hearing and good eyes which are quick to notice unusual movements. Time was when all deer were thought to be completely color blind; however, there is now evidence to support the theory that they do distinguish some colors. Regardless, it is probably safe to say that deer do not see the world in the same way man sees it and often look at stationary, camouflaged bowhunters without recognizing them for what they are.

No one who has ever watched a whitetail's bounding tail-waving departure has need to wonder how the animal acquired its name. The deer have snowy rumps and long tails—or flags—which are often held erect when they run. These tails have brilliantly white undersides and are visible at great distances even in the shadowy woodlands.

Most whitetails have reddish summer coats which are shed and replaced with brown or gray winter pelage as fall approaches. The hair is typically darker along the back and lighter along the sides. Underbellies and the insides of the upper legs are white. The deer have white throat patches, chins, nose bands and white circles around each eye. Deer hair is hollow and provides excellent insulation against bitter cold temperatures.

As already mentioned, whitetails are adaptable animals and are found thriving in all types of terrain. Generally speaking, they are brush-loving animals of the forest edges. Bucks and does live apart except during the fall rut and early winter. Does often lead groups of whitetails, even when bucks are present.

Like all deer, whitetails have several scent glands which play a major role in identification and communication within the herd. There is an interdigital gland between the toes on each hoof that gives off an identifying odor wherever they walk. On the outside of each hind leg just above the foot is a metarsal gland which reportedly gives off additional scent. The tarsal glands, tufts of hair on the inside of each hind leg hock, are also called "musk glands" and play an important role during the breeding season. Finally, deer have preorbital or lachrymal glands in front of each eye which emit a marking scent when rubbed on limbs and bushes.

Whitetails do not migrate and live out their lives within a relatively small area unless forced to move. During the rut bucks develop wanderlust and may roam widely in a consuming quest for willing does; however, whitetails have definite home territories and are generally found there season after season.

Unless pressured, deer typically follow the same daily routine. They move into feeding areas each evening and begin to fill their rumens with favorite foods including white oak acorns, willow, sumac, apples and other vegetation. In farmlands, alfalfa, corn and soybeans and similar crops attract considerable attention from hungry deer. Adult deer may consume as much as 10 pounds of forage each day.

After feeding, whitetails lay themselves down to rest and chew their cuds. Another feeding session occurs near dawn just before the animals return to their daytime bedding areas. Beds are typically found in thick cover, frequently along ridges where rising thermals will warn them of an enemy's approach.

Because of their daily routine, deer commonly create well-defined trails or runs between feeding and bedding areas. This can prove to be their undoing when a knowledgeable hunter selects an ambush site along these paths. Being creatures of habit, the deer follow the same daily routine unless hunting pressure, food scarcity or severe weather changes their patterns of movement.

When alarmed, a whitetail bounds away in graceful, ground-eating leaps that may cover 15 to 20 feet with each jump. Their top speed is said to be 35 to 40 miles per hour. Deer can easily clear barriers eight feet and slightly higher. Unlike the stiff-legged, bouncing gait of the fleeing mule deer, the whitetail's flight to safety is characterized by an agile, springy quality that makes the animals appear to glide over the ground in soaring, delicate jumps. These dashes are generally short-lived. Once cover is reached or suitable distance put between the deer and whatever boogered them, the animals often pause to check their backtrails and then move quickly away in a peculiar stiff-legged walk, often with their white rump and tail hairs flaring in alarm.

Across much of North America's whitetail range, the breeding season occurs in late October or early November. The furtive bucks abruptly forsake their solitary lives and begin to seek the company of receptive does. Necks of the rutting bucks swell and their testicles drop down into the scrotal sac. The animals develop a belligerent attitude and are quick to fight over breeding rights to a doe in estrous.

Fights between whitetail bucks are true tests of strength. The rivals clash, antlers first, and then push or shove their opponent off balance. Antler tines may inflict painful injuries or, on occasion, the antlers may become enmeshed and the combatants become unable to separate. Death by starvation is almost sure to result.

Once a lesser buck is defeated and driven off, the winner follows and claims his prize, mounting the willing doe. If breeding occurs during each doe's 30-hour fertile period, pregnancy results. If not bred, does will come into heat each 28 days until the rut is past. A single buck is capable—and eager—to service as many does as he can locate. During the rut a buck has little besides sex on his mind, losing his natural caution and frequently ignoring food, sleep and rest. Rutting bucks often become gaunt, foul-smelling, short-tempered animals. Some whitetail attacks on humans are reported each fall during the rut.

Most whitetail fawns are born in May or June. Does giving birth for the first time commonly have single births; older does typically have twins. The spotted fawns are wobbly, ungainly infants weighing four to five pounds. The does lick them dry and allow them to nurse almost immediately. Within a matter of minutes the fawns may take their first unsteady steps. In the first half hour of life the fawns are led to hiding places in suitable cover. Well-camouflaged and odorless, the baby deer spend most of their early lives resting and waiting for regular nursing visits from their mother. Within weeks the fawns are following their mothers and nibbling their first solid food. They usually remain with the doe through the first winter. Whitetail deer have a life expectancy of eight to 10 years although few bucks survive to reach half that age.

Deer tracks and droppings are the most common and easily recognizable evidence of animals in an area. Droppings are most often bunches of small brown or black pellets although the time of year and available diet may change the coloration and texture of excrement.

Some deer hunters claim they can tell the difference between the tracks of bucks and does; however, in truth, there is no sure way to differentiate unless they actually see the animal making the tracks. It's a common and erroneous notion that only a buck's dewclaws show in their tracks. It's also commonly believed that the biggest tracks belong to the biggest bucks. Quite often old does leave the biggest tracks, especially in heavily hunted areas where few bucks live long enough to reach a comparable age and size of some aging matriarch. Only when a light snow covers the ground can a tracker predict what sex deer made the sign. Does commonly lift their feet higher as they walk and leave well defined tracks. Bucks tend to drag their feet with each step and these drag marks show clearly in the snow behind each hoof print. In deeper snow both sexes leave tracks with drag marks.

Deer beds are also apparent to the knowledgeable hunter. Body-sized depressions in the grass or leaves show where a deer has rested to chew its cud. The vegetation will be packed by the animal's weight. In snow, beds are even more apparent and deer may paw away spots to reveal the leaves beneath the surface.

Bucks do leave very definite signs prior to and during the rut. These merit any hunter's attention. Buck rubs are markings on trees and brush where the buck has raked his antlers. This strips bark or bares limbs, leaving white, obvious rubbed marks which may be easily seen against the darker limbs and trees. Fresh rubs are sticky to the touch.

Scrapes are pawed areas in the leaves where bucks urinate and ejaculate to attract the attention of passing does. Most scrapes are circular and marked with a single, sharply defined track near the center of the pawed area. Typically there are overhanging limbs which the buck chews or marks with scent from the preorbital gland near the eyes. He may also slash at the limbs with his antlers, breaking or scarring them. Rubs are frequently found at or near scrapes.

Effective Bowhunting Techniques

There are three basic methods of bowhunting whitetails but many variations of each standard method. These three methods include stand hunting—or "posting"—from either a ground-level or elevated platform, still-hunting and stalking, and driving the deer.

Without question the most popular bowhunting method is to take a stand along a trail or near a feeding area. And far more bowhunters choose elevated stands than those who opt to remain on the ground. The reason should be obvious. Deer have no natural enemies which attack from above and seldom look up unless "educated" by hunting pressure from treeborne bowhunters.

Deer are constantly alert for danger and they know their home territory the way humans know the layouts of their own homes. Changes, even subtle ones, are immediately noted or sensed. An unfamiliar shape, a glint of light reflected from shiny equipment, an unusual noise or sudden movement will attract a deer's attention. When alerted, a deer often stamps its forefoot to warn nearby animals of possible danger. Whitetails commonly flare their rump hairs and tails as they adopt a stiff-legged walk and move away from or—at times—toward the object of their attention. If truly alarmed by a whiff of telltale man-smell, they blow, emitting a surprisingly loud blast of air through their nostrils. Blowing generally precedes and often follows a deer's bounding, tail-waving departure. It's one of the most frustrating sounds any whitetail hunter will ever hear.

Tree stands or other types of elevated platforms get the bowhunter above the deer's normal line of sight. They also keep human scent from reaching the deer as quickly as it does from ground-level stands.

Selecting the right tree can be a problem for some bowhunters who are not familiar with deer habits or movements. Also, some thought should be given to the size and shape of the tree itself. Unless it is big enough to break the hunter's outline and to support his weight comfortably, the tree probably won't do the job. Some veteran bowhunters disdain tree stands of any kind and prefer to locate suitable trees offering natural stands—limbs, crotches, etc.— for their ambush site. Others claim a portable stand is the best way to go since it gives the bowhunter the option of turning most any tree into a suitable site and, in effect, allows them to go where the action is.

There are many types of manufactured tree stands on the market today from lightweight but sturdy portable models to self-climbing stands to heavy, semi-permanent elevated platforms with built-in ladders. Some harness devices and folding wedges designed to fit in the forks of trees are small enough to fit in a hunter's pocket or pack. A few creative hunters who are handy with tools build their own tree stands.

Note: Permanent tree stands are looked on with disfavor by most responsible bowhunters. Boards and platforms left in trees the year 'round create eyesores and may quickly become unsafe after exposure to the elements. Also, nails and spikes damage—and sometimes kill—the trees. They also pose hazards long after the tree stands themselves have disappeared, ruining chainsaws and sawmill blades years later. Under no circumstances should a permanent tree stand be constructed on private land without the landowner's permission. And on public lands where the same area is shared by many outdoorsmen and women, common courtesy dictates that such structures—where legal—be removed at the end of the hunting season to avoid potential resentment and anti-hunting sentiment. If possible, the bowhunter should forget about constructing or using permanent stands altogether.

An ideal site for a tree stand is along well-used trails between bedding and feeding areas, preferably where two or more deer trails merge. Stands near natural mineral licks or watering holes may be effective at times. Also, stands near feed itself can pay off although hunting pressure may cause the deer to begin feeding only under the cover of darkness and make stands ringing farm fields, orchards and similar spots ineffective. Many knowledgeable bowhunters do not place their stands at the edge of feeding areas, preferring to locate nearer the bedding areas. A hunter should always be as quiet as possible when entering and leaving a stand.

When the rut is underway, scrape-watching is an excellent way to collect a whitetail buck. A portable tree stand should be located near a fresh scrape which attracts passing deer—does and bucks alike—for its maker is almost sure to return periodically to check and freshen it. When he does, a good shot is possible.

The bowhunter should understand that there are different types of scrapes made at different times of the rut. Bucks tend to mark their territories with scrapes and rubs bearing their scent. A single deer may make dozens of each before and during the annual breeding season. Bucks also create scrapes within the perimeters of their home ranges. These scrapes are advertisements for breeding services and are generally found in areas used year after year for rutting activities. It is not uncommon to find numerous scrapes along a well-used trail. Such scrape lines are visited by passing does and the bucks who made them during normal daily movements. Scrapes that are found alone in heavy cover or in secluded areas of the buck's range are probably the best bets for an ambush site. These primary rutting scrapes generally have a buck—perhaps a big one—hanging nearby. They are checked frequently and freshened regularly. If a bowhunter can find such a scrape and establish a stand without tipping off his presence to the buck, his chances of scoring are regarded as better than if he sits watching territorial scrapes or scrape lines.

Does determine whether scrapes are "hot" or not. As mentioned, scrapes are a buck's way of advertising for female companionship. And although it pays to advertise, unless a cooperative doe responds by leaving her scent in the scrape the buck is going to get frustrated and move on to repeat the process elsewhere. When a doe does respond, the buck trails and breeds her numerous times until the interest wanes. He then hotfoots it back to his scrape—or makes a new one—and waits anxiously for his next lady love. This continues until the rut peaks and both does and bucks forget what all the excitement was about and go about their daily lives.

Rutting bucks do some goofy things—and at times are downright stupid—but they're seldom pushovers. When they're traveling with does, the females remain alert and warn the bucks of danger. And even when the bucks appear to have a one-track mind, they seem to have automatic warning devices that alert them. Noise and scent must be kept to a minimum, even when the bowhunter is in a tree.

As the bowhunter prepares for a shot from an elevated stand, the motion and slight noises involved with raising the bow and drawing the arrow are minimal and not as likely to be detected as when the bowhunter is on the ground at eye-level. Nonetheless, a bowhunter in a tree cannot afford careless noises or sudden movements when a deer is beneath him. Deer do look up.

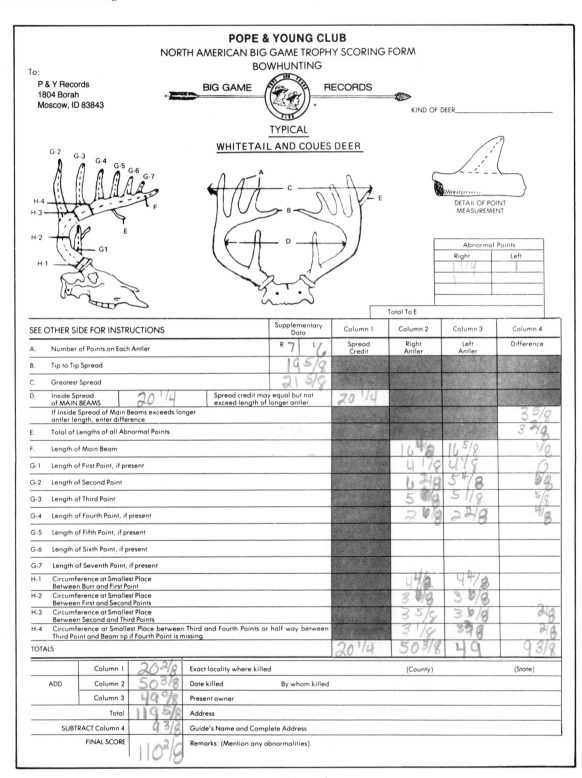

POPE & YOUNG CLUB

NORTH AMERICAN BIG GAME TROPHY SCORING FORM

BOWHUNTING

To:

P & Y Records
1804 Borah
Moscow, ID 83843

BIG GAME   RECORDS

KIND OF DEER_____

TYPICAL

WHITETAIL AND COUES DEER

DETAIL OF POINT
MEASUREMENT

Abnormal Points	
Right	Left
1 1/4	1

Total To E

	SEE OTHER SIDE FOR INSTRUCTIONS	Supplementary Data		Column 1	Column 2	Column 3	Column 4
		R	L	Spread Credit	Right Antler	Left Antler	Difference
A.	Number of Points on Each Antler	7	6				
B.	Tip to Tip Spread	19 5/8					
C.	Greatest Spread	21 5/8					
D.	Inside Spread of MAIN BEAMS 20 1/4 Spread credit may equal but not exceed length of longer antler			20 1/4			
	If Inside Spread of Main Beams exceeds longer antler length, enter difference						3 5/8
E.	Total of Lengths of all Abnormal Points						3 2/8
F.	Length of Main Beam				16 4/8	16 5/8	1/8
G-1	Length of First Point, if present				4 1/8	4 1/8	0
G-2	Length of Second Point				6 1/8	5 4/8	6/8
G-3	Length of Third Point				5 6/8	5 1/8	5/8
G-4	Length of Fourth Point, if present				2 0/8	2 2/8	4/8
G-5	Length of Fifth Point, if present						
G-6	Length of Sixth Point, if present						
G-7	Length of Seventh Point, if present						
H-1	Circumference at Smallest Place Between Burr and First Point				4 4/8	4 4/8	
H-2	Circumference at Smallest Place Between First and Second Points				3 6/8	3 6/8	
H-3	Circumference at Smallest Place Between Second and Third Points				3 5/8	3 6/8	2/8
H-4	Circumference at Smallest Place between Third and Fourth Points or half way between Third Point and Beam tip if Fourth Point is missing				3 1/8	3 3/8	2/8
	TOTALS			20 1/4	50 3/8	49	9 3/8

	Column 1	20 2/8	Exact locality where killed		(County)		(State)
ADD	Column 2	50 3/8	Date killed By whom killed				
	Column 3	49 0/8	Present owner				
	Total	119 5/8	Address				
	SUBTRACT Column 4	9 3/8	Guide's Name and Complete Address				
	FINAL SCORE	110 2/8	Remarks: (Mention any abnormalities)				

I certify that I have measured the above trophy on _____ 19 _____
at (address) _____ City _____
State _____ Zip Code _____ and that these measurements and data are, to the
best of my knowledge and belief, made in accordance with the instructions given.

Witness: _____ Signature _____
(To Measurer's Signature)

Pope & Young Club Official Measurer

_____
MEASURER (Print)

_____
ADDRESS

_____
CITY   STATE   ZIP

INSTRUCTIONS

All measurements must be made with a flexible steel tape to the nearest <u>one-eighth</u> of an inch. Wherever it is necessary to change direction of measurement, mark a control point and swing tape at this point. To simplify addition, please enter fractional figures in **eighths**. Official measurements cannot be taken for at least sixty days after the animal was killed. **Please submit photographs.** (see below).

Supplementary Data measurements indicate conformation of the trophy, and none of the figures in line A, B and C are to be included in the score. Evaluation of conformation is a matter of personal preference.

A. Number of Points on each antler. To be counted a point, a projection must be at least one inch long AND its length must exceed the length of its base. All points are measured from tip of point to nearest edge of beam as illustrated. **Beam tip is counted as a point but not measured as a point.**

B. Tip to Tip Spread measured between tips of Main Beams.

C. Greatest Spread measured between perpendiculars at right angles to the center line of the skull at widest part whether across main beams or points.

D. Inside Spread of Main Beams measured at right angles to the center line of the skull at widest point between main beams. Enter this measurement again in "Spread Credit" column if it is less than or equal to the length of longer antler.

E. Total of Lengths of all Abnormal Points. Abnormal points are generally considered to be those nontypical in shape or location. Sketch all abnormal points on antler illustration (front of form) showing location and approximate size.

F. Length of Main Beam measured from lowest outside edge of burr over outer curve to the most distant point of what is, or appears to be, the main beam. The point of beginning is that point on the burr where the center line along the outer curve of the beam intersects the burr.

G-1-2-3-4-5-6-7. Length of Normal Points. Normal points project from main beam. They are measured from nearest edge of main beam over outer curve to tip. To determine nearest edge (top edge) of beam, lay the tape along the outer curve of the beam so that the top edge of the tape coincides with the top edge of the beam on both sides of the point. Draw line along top edge of tape. This line will be base line from which point is measured.

H-1-2-3-4. Circumferences. If first point is missing, take H-1 and H-2 at smallest place between burr and second point.

Photographs: All entries must include photographs of the trophy. A right side, left side and front view photograph will be required for all antlers, horns and skulls. A photograph of the entire animal is requested if at all possible.

Drying Period: To be eligible for entry in the Pope & Young Records, a trophy must first have been stored under normal room temperature and humidity for at least 60 consecutive days after date of kill. No trophy will be considered which has in any way been altered from its natural state.

THIS SCORING FORM MUST BE ACCOMPANIED BY A SIGNED POPE & YOUNG FAIR CHASE AFFIDAVIT, 3 PHOTOS AND A RECORDING FEE OF $25.00.

One question which invariably arises is: "What's the proper height for a tree stand?" In truth, there is no single answer to that question; however, there are some general comments which should be made. While deer have been arrowed by bowhunters standing in trees barely six or seven feet off the ground, most stands should be placed higher—10 to 15 feet is an excellent average range—if there are screening limbs and suitable background to break the hunter's outline. Also, it's probably a good idea to avoid placing the stand **too** high since steep, downward shots are not ideal and in most cases there is no reason to hunt from "treetop stands." Regardless, the size, shape and location of the tree are always determining factors and a bowhunter should remain flexible in his choice.

Stands should always be located so the prevailing winds carry the bowhunter's scent away from the trail, scrape or feeding area. Portable stands should be camouflaged and quieted. Many hunters spray paint the stands with olive drab colors and tack carpeting or foam rubber to the floors of the stands. Since long waits are often required, tree stands with seats—or stands situated so limbs may be used as seats—are easier to take. No tree stand wait should be regarded as an endurance test; comfort must be considered.

Every bowhunter who hunts from a tree should use a safety belt or line to prevent what could be a nasty fall. Each year some falls result in broken bones and other serious injuries—including fractured necks and spines which leave the hunters paralyzed from the neck or waist down. Care must also be exercised when entering or leaving the stand, especially if the weather is wet, cold or icy. Under no circumstances should any bowhunter attempt to climb a tree while carrying his bow; the use of a light, strong cord to raise and lower bows, packs and similar gear is suggested.

If suitable limbs are available, they may be used as natural steps. Each should be capable of holding much more than the hunter's weight and no hunter should step or stand on a branch that could snap off beneath him. Where adequate limbs are not available, tree steps are the answer and either manufactured or homemade varieties work well. There are two basic types of tree steps, the screw-in and strap-on models. The latter are gaining in popularity due to their simplicity of design, ease of usage and the fact they do not damage the tree in any way. Screw-in steps are also easy to use but some object to the small holes they leave in trees. A bowhunter should check out the game laws and hunting regulations in his area before reaching a final decision. Also, it is important to obtain the landowner's permission before erecting stands and steps in any tree on private property.

Still-hunting for whitetails is a sometimes productive method of getting shots. Patience and slow, careful movements are keys to success.

The still-hunting bowhunter is, in fact, a mobile blind. He is most frequently camouflaged from cap to boots, including equipment. He moves slowly—very slowly—through prime deer country, easing into the wind one cautious, silent step at a time. He spends more time standing and looking than walking. He uses his eyes and ears constantly, knowing he must spot the deer before the deer sees him.

Most shots taken by still-hunters result when the deer moves close enough to allow the bowhunter to release an arrow. When the bowhunter must work close to the whitetail—by stalking—the results are seldom satisfactory.

Stalking within good bow range of whitetails is super-tough. While some individuals are capable of successful stalks, the plain truth is most bowhunters are not good enough to see a distant whitetail and ease to within 20 or 30 yards of the animal without being detected.

Most whitetails live in areas where contact with humans is common. They're constantly smelling, listening and looking for hints of man. Frequently when alerted they simply melt away into the brush. When surprised by a person at close range they generally explode into instant flight. The first instance leaves the bowhunter wondering where all the deer are. The second offers the poorest possible shot, a running shot at a spooked animal.

Still-hunting and stalking bowhunters do take whitetails each season. Deer hunters employing either or both methods should keep the following points in mind:

* Sudden movements must be avoided. A bowhunter should always do three to four times more standing and looking than walking.

* Steps should be short and quiet, allowing the hunter to keep his balance at all times.

* Clothing should be quiet, soft. A limb rasping across a pants leg can be heard by deer at surprising distances.

* Footwear should match the terrain and weather conditions but be pliable enough to allow the bowhunter to place each step by "feel" and avoid cracking dead limbs underfoot. Some successful still-hunters actually wear a pair of heavy wool socks **over** their boots or shoes to muffle noises.

* Knowledge of the hunting area is one investment which often pays dividends.

* Mornings and evenings following a rain or dewy mornings are good still-hunting days. The moisture dampens dry leaves and quiets walking. In the late season, after wet or powdery snowfalls, conditions are also good for soundless movements.

* When approaching a deer, the stalking hunter should try to keep a tree or screening brush between him and the animal. If the deer's head is up, the hunter should freeze in place until the animal resumes browsing or grazing. Any time a bowhunter can see a deer's eyes, he must realize the deer can see him.

* If the deer is bedded, a stalking hunter should approach from behind and watch the deer's ears or antlers to keep track of the animal's head position.

* When walking conditions are noisy, still-hunting for deer is generally a waste of time. The deer can hear a moving hunter long before he's close enough for an effective, killing shot. At times like these, a stand along a good run is apt to be more productive.

There is no doubt that ground-level stands or blinds can result in close shots at deer. Ideally, as with tree stands, blinds should be located downwind from game trails or feeding areas or active scrapes.

Because the bowhunter is on the same level as his quarry, he must avoid making sounds or movements which will call attention to his presence. Stands should be situated near natural blinds if possible. Windfalls, stumps, rockpiles, fencelines and brushpiles are good possibilities. The background must be adequate to disguise the bowhunter's telltale shape and the foreground should offer an adequate field of vision and shooting lanes.

Some hunters dig pit blinds to put them below ground level and camouflage the pits with natural materials or camo netting. In certain locations such stands can be especially effective.

Whenever possible, the bowhunter should construct his ground stand in advance of the season. Trimming of brush and limbs should be kept to a minimum. Deer are usually quick to notice changes in their surroundings. Regardless, shooting lanes must be carefully planned. Bowhunters in ground blinds usually do not have the same freedom of movement or shot options available to a hunter in a tree. They must plan their shots well in advance and take them immediately when offered.

As with any sit-and-wait method of hunting, there will be long periods of inactivity. Comfort must be considered. Kneeling and crouching are uncomfortable; muscles cramp, legs go to sleep. The hunter begins to fidget. The wait becomes an endurance test. This is **not** the way to bowhunt deer from a ground stand. A camp stool, cushioned log or rock offering a comfortable seat is ideal— providing the bowhunter has practiced shooting from a sitting position. Raising up to shoot seldom works.

Calling deer and horn rattling are two techniques which may work well when used by bowhunters in tree stands or ground blinds.

Whitetails are more vocal than most people realize. Does "talk" to their young and fawns and yearlings respond with a language of their own. Bucks, too, blat on occasion and often grunt while on the trail of a coquettish doe in heat. Commercially produced deer calls simulate deer

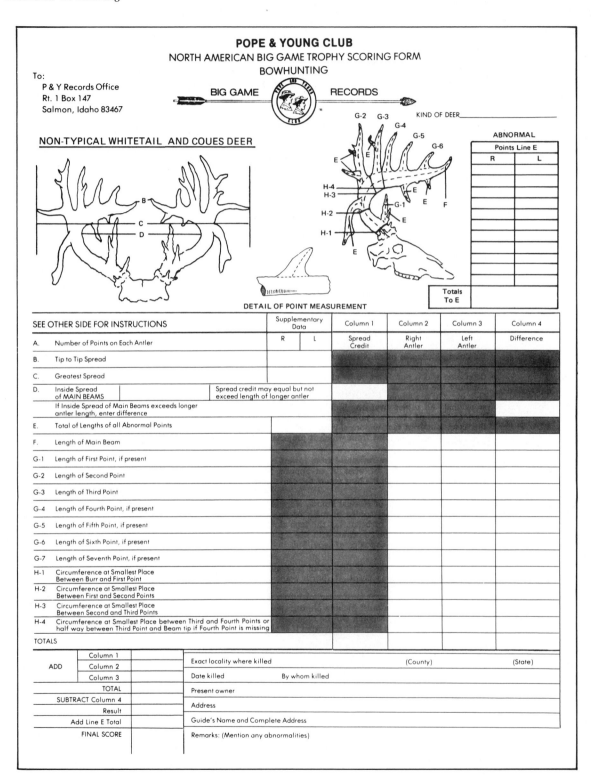

POPE & YOUNG CLUB
NORTH AMERICAN BIG GAME TROPHY SCORING FORM
BOWHUNTING

To:
P & Y Records Office
Rt. 1 Box 147
Salmon, Idaho 83467

BIG GAME   RECORDS

KIND OF DEER_____

NON-TYPICAL WHITETAIL AND COUES DEER

ABNORMAL	
Points Line E	
R	L
Totals To E	

DETAIL OF POINT MEASUREMENT

SEE OTHER SIDE FOR INSTRUCTIONS

		Supplementary Data R	Supplementary Data L	Column 1 Spread Credit	Column 2 Right Antler	Column 3 Left Antler	Column 4 Difference
A.	Number of Points on Each Antler						
B.	Tip to Tip Spread						
C.	Greatest Spread						
D.	Inside Spread of MAIN BEAMS	Spread credit may equal but not exceed length of longer antler					
	If Inside Spread of Main Beams exceeds longer antler length, enter difference						
E.	Total of Lengths of all Abnormal Points						
F.	Length of Main Beam						
G-1	Length of First Point, if present						
G-2	Length of Second Point						
G-3	Length of Third Point						
G-4	Length of Fourth Point, if present						
G-5	Length of Fifth Point, if present						
G-6	Length of Sixth Point, if present						
G-7	Length of Seventh Point, if present						
H-1	Circumference at Smallest Place Between Burr and First Point						
H-2	Circumference at Smallest Place Between First and Second Points						
H-3	Circumference at Smallest Place Between Second and Third Points						
H-4	Circumference at Smallest Place between Third and Fourth Points or half way between Third Point and Beam tip if Fourth Point is missing						
TOTALS							

ADD	Column 1		
	Column 2		
	Column 3		
	TOTAL		
	SUBTRACT Column 4		
	Result		
	Add Line E Total		
	FINAL SCORE		

Exact locality where killed _____ (County) _____ (State)

Date killed _____ By whom killed _____

Present owner _____

Address _____

Guide's Name and Complete Address _____

Remarks: (Mention any abnormalities) _____

I certify that I have measured the above trophy on _____ 19 _____
at (address)_____ City _____
State _____ Zip Code_____ and that these measurements and data are, to the
best of my knowledge and belief, made in accordance with the instructions given.

Witness: _____ Signature _____
(To Measurer's Signature)   Pope & Young Club Official Measurer

INSTRUCTIONS

All measurements must be made with a flexible steel tape to the nearest one-eighth of an inch. Wherever it is necessary to change direction of measurement, mark a control point and swing tape at this point. To simplify addition, please enter fractional figures in eighths. Official measurements cannot be taken for at least sixty days after the animal was killed. **Please submit photographs.**

Supplementary Data measurements indicate conformation of the trophy, and none of the figures in Lines A, B and C are to be included in the score. Evaluation of conformation is a matter of personal preference.

A. **Number of Points on each Antler.** To be counted a point, a projection must be at least one inch long AND its length must exceed the length of its base. All points are measured from tip of point to nearest edge of beam as illustrated. Beam tip is counted as a point but not measured as a point.

B. **Tip to Tip Spread** measured between tips of main beams.

C. **Greatest Spread** measured between perpendiculars at right angles to the center line of the skull at widest part whether across main beam or points.

D. **Inside Spread** of Main Beams measured at right angles to the center line of the skull at widest point between main beams. Enter this measurement again in "Spread Credit" column if it is less than or equal to the length of longer antler.

E. **Total of Lengths of all Abnormal Points.** Abnormal points are considered to be those nontypical in shape or location. It is very important, in scoring nontypical heads, to determine which points are to be classed as normal and which are not. To do this, study carefully the character of the normal points on the diagram, which are marked G-1, G-2, G-3, etc. On the trophy to be scored, the points which correspond to these are measured as normal. All others over one inch in length (See A, above) are considered abnormal. Various types of abnormal points are shown (marked with an E) on the diagram. Measure the exact length of each abnormal point, over the outer curve, from the tip to the nearest edge of the beam or point from which it projects. Then add these lengths and enter the total in the space provided.

F. **Length of Main Beam** measured from lowest outside edge of burr over outer curve to the most distant point of what is, or appears to be, the main beam. The point of beginning is the point on the burr where the center line along the outer curve of the beam intersects the burr.

G-1-2-3-4-5-6-7. **Length of Normal Points.** Normal points project from main beam They are measured from nearest edge of main beam over outer curve to tip. To determine nearest edge (top edge) of beam, lay the tape along the outer curve of the beam so that the top edge of the tape coincides with the top edge of the beam on both sides of the point. Draw line along top edge of tape. This line will be base line from which point is measured.

H-1-2-3-4. **Circumferences** - If first point is missing, take H-1 and H-2 at smallest place between burr and second point. If fourth point is missing, take H-4 half way between third point and beam tip.

Photographs: All entries must include photographs of the trophy. A right side, left side and front view photograph will be required for all antlers, horns and skulls. A photograph of the entire animal is requested if at all possible.

Drying Period: To be eligible for entry in the Pope & Young Records, a trophy must first have been stored under normal room temperature and humidity for at least 60 consecutive days. No trophy will be considered which has in any way been altered from its natural state.

THIS SCORING FORM MUST BE ACCOMPANIED BY A SIGNED **POPE & YOUNG FAIR CHASE AFFIDAVIT, 3 PHOTOS OF ANTLERS, AND A RECORDING FEE OF $25.00** vocalizations and are designed to attract the attention of real animals. Ideally, the curious whitetails come to investigate the sounds and walk under or past a waiting bowhunter.

While calls—or blatting by using human vocal chords—does work on occasion, the hunter must realize they are not a magic means of luring deer within easy range. They should be used in moderation, perhaps as a last resort when it is obvious a passing deer is not going to come close enough for an effective shot. But bowhunters need to understand that any deer responding to a call will be alert, looking for the source of the sound. Deer have an uncanny ability to pinpoint noises and a calling hunter should be totally camouflaged, motionless and well-hidden.

During the rut, bucks may be fooled by horn rattling. The bowhunter, using real antlers or commercially manufactured synthetic "rattling" products, simulates the sounds made by battling bucks banging their racks together. Popularized and perfected by hunters in the Texas brush country, the practice has spread to all parts of the country and can be quite effective at times. It seems the "fight" attracts the attention of bucks within earshot and can result in shots when the real deer come to size up their rivals—or steal does while the combatants are occupied.

Some bowhunters work in pairs while calling or rattling deer. One person does the work, vocalizing or clattering antlers together, while the second hunter—concealed nearby—does the shooting when deer come to investigate and their attention is diverted to the source of the sounds. There are many books, instruction manuals, tapes and videos now offered by companies and individuals willing to share secrets to calling and rattling success.

Deer scents also receive considerable attention from bowhunters who hope to fool or attract deer. Many use camouflaging or masking scents to help hide human odor. Such scents include skunk, fox or coyote, pine, sage and a host of other so-called natural scents. Others are directed at the animals themselves and contain deer musk or food scents; they appeal to the whitetails' sexual urge and the

need to eat.

Masking scents may help but a bowhunter should not place total confidence in them. Common sense dictates he keep as clean as possible and see that his hunting clothes are not contaminated with such odors as perspiration, tobacco smoke, cooking stoves or campfire smells and similar smells. Also scented deodorants, after shave, talc and hair oil or spray can work against a hunter hoping to remain undetected in the field. Many hunters bathe or wash frequently and change underwear and hunting clothes periodically. Some refuse to wear hunting clothes anywhere except in the field, hang them out to air after each hunt and commonly stow them in plastic bags filled with pine boughs, sage leaves or other trimmings from vegetation found in the hunting area.

There is also internal camouflage in the form of chlorophyll tablets. Such tablets are sold to be taken before and during the hunting season and reportedly neutralize human smell. External masking or camouflaging agents made for hunters include scentless soaps and rinses to be applied to the body after showers or baths. Common baking soda is widely recognized as an effective scent neutralizer when dusted on skin and clothing or sprinkled inside hunting boots.

Bowhunters must realize that human odor is as apparent to deer as a whiff of skunk scent is to us. They should also understand that it is very difficult—perhaps impossible—to completely fool a whitetail's highly developed olfactory organs. This is why the old hunter's advice to "always keep your nose in the wind" is worth remembering.

Just as it's erroneous to think that a few drops of masking scent completely covers human odor, it's foolish to believe that a splash or two of buck lure or food scent will bring deer on the run. These scents may draw a whitetail close enough to result in a good shot at point-blank range; however, misuse can alarm deer and actually drive them from an area or at least prompt them to change travel patterns.

Many veteran bowhunters have little faith in food

scents and experimentation tends to dispel the belief such "attractor scents" are truly effective. Scents having sex stimulants seem to work better than "food scents" but are best used in moderation and only at times of breeding activity. A few successful bowhunters report placing only a drop or two on brush, limbs or leaves along well-traveled trails. When a passing deer stops to nose the scent the waiting bowhunter has the opportunity to release an arrow at a stationary target. Most feel these scents do not bring sex-starved bucks on the run and any hunter hoping for such results will likely be disappointed.

One hunting method receiving some attention in recent years is the artifical or "mock scrape." It has been determined that manmade scrapes—created by clearing areas in fallen leaves and saturating the ground with buck scent—will attract deer. Bowhunters using this method advise taking pains to avoid leaving any evidence of human scent in the area. Some wear rubber boots and gloves. A few use urine they've collected from live bucks—or the bladder of previously killed deer—and some actually smear the overhanging limbs with scent swabbed from the lachrymal glands of whitetails. One obvious advantage of establishing a mock scrape is the site may be established near an ideal ambush spot.

Tree stands and ground blinds located near salt blocks and mineral licks can be productive; however, care must be taken to avoid violating any game laws in areas where baiting is illegal. In states where it is legal to bait deer—Michigan, for example—apples and grains soaked with molasses may be used effectively.

Driving deer is an effective means of putting game on the move. In most instances a deer drive involves a group of hunters divided into "drivers" and "standers." The standers take up positions along deer trails or open areas with a good view of the surroundings. Drivers then move through cover where deer normally bed, kicking animals from their beds and pushing them past the waiting hunters.

Deer driven in this method offer poor targets in most bowhunting situations. Shots at alarmed, running game are far from ideal and the chances of wounding and losing animals are great. Some guides use this method of hunting during the less productive mid-day hours when things are slow. Drives may stir things up and keep enthusiasm high if stand hunting is slow, but in truth deer drives are a poor way to bowhunt. Practice at moving targets is necessary before this method is attempted.

Far more effective are "drives" involving two or three people. In such cases a hunting buddy slowly eases through deer cover and hunts in the general direction of a companion in a tree stand or blind. Often deer slip out ahead of the approaching hunter and walk away into the wind or a quartering breeze. In some instances a whitetail eludes one hunter only to move into easy range of another. Bowhunters familiar with the terrain—especially likely escape routes—can turn this knowledge to their advantage through teamwork.

If hunting from canoes or other boats is legal and there are waterways cutting through prime deer country, drifting or floating may result in shots. Any hunter thinking about this method should be certain he has checked out game laws and has secured landowner permission if private land is involved. More common than drift hunting is the use of a boat to reach brushy islands located in rivers or coastal waters. Each year deer are arrowed by bowhunters who quietly paddle or motor to an island where they take a stand and wait for deer to pass. Whitetails are strong swimmers and often take up residence on islands to escape hunting pressure or to simply seek solitude.

Horseback and backpack hunting are worth consideration in some areas of the country, especially in the open areas of the Western and Southwestern United States. Coues deer haunt the remote, rugged, often broken terrain where finding a suitable tree stand site may be impossible. This means spending time on foot or horseback getting into country where time may be spent glassing for game. Once deer are sighted, stalks may be planned but getting up on these alert little animals is no easy trick. Regardless, stalking is one option worth considering. Another possibility is finding a water hole or mineral lick and establishing a ground stand nearby.

Decoys have been used to successfully lure whitetails into shooting range. Generally this involves a life-sized mount of a doe carried in and located near a trail or scrape area. Rutting bucks seeing the doe theoretically come to check out the attractive stranger and end up with an arrow in their ribs for their trouble. Considering the costs involved in obtaining a lifesize mount and the effort necessary to lug it to a good site, it may not be worth the effort. Then again, if a love-starved buck lowers his guard and tries to court the decoy, who can say it's too much trouble? Decoys are often used in combination with sex scents. Any bowhunter thinking about trying this method should clear the question of legality before investing money in a mount and venturing afield.

Bowhunting whitetails is the most popular outdoor pastime for those who choose to accept the challenge of trying to collect big game animals with the bow and arrow. These deer are the most common big game species and therefore more hunters are successful taking whitetails than any other animal. Regardless, wherever they are found and pursued by bowhunters, whatever hunting methods are employed, the advantage remains with the deer. Few bowhunters would have it any other way.

Trophy Recognition

Most mature whitetail bucks have at least four to five total points on each side. Trophy-class racks sport long, thick tines sprouting from heavy beams. Spreads of one and one-half to two feet are common. And as is the case with all antlered game, symmetry is the key to high scores in all but non-typical heads.

Generally, whitetail deer have smaller racks than their larger cousins, the mule deer. Estimating size is often a problem because of the brushy cover they inhabit and the fact it's often hard to get a clear look at a buck's headgear through ever-present limbs and foliage. But big antlers are unmistakable to experienced hunters in search of a real wall-hanger buck.

Any antlers which extend past the ears and exceed the width of the animal's body are above average. And when the height of the headgear approaches the depth of the deer's body from withers to brisket, the rack is likely to be trophy class.

Coues deer carry proportionally smaller racks. The inside spread seldom exceeds a foot and it takes an exceptional specimen to score over 100 total inches. The minimum qualifying score is 60 while a Pope and Young whitetail must have a minimum score of 125 (typical) points or 150 (non-typical) points to qualify for the record listings.

The Pope and Young World Record whitetail buck was shot in a soybean field just outside of Peoria, Illinois in 1965. Bowhunter Mel Johnson arrowed the huge 13-pointer as it walked past the spot where he crouched at the field's edge. Its official score of 204-4/8 places it among the top whitetail trophies of all time. The buck's inside spread is 23-5/8 inches. Its right beam measures 27-5/8 and the left beam is 26-6/8 inches. The circumference at the smallest place between the burr and the first point on each side exceeds six inches.

In the non-typical category, a Nebraska whitetail shot in 1962 continues to hold down the top spot. Hunting a brushy island in the shallow Platte River, bowhunter Del Austin shot a huge buck with a freak rack sporting 39 total points, 21 points on the right beam and 18 on the left. Its inside spread is 21-3/8 inches and the length of the right main beam is 27-7/8 inches while the left beam measures 28-1/8 inches. The buck, called "Mossyhorns," has an official Pope and Young score of 279-7/8.

The top Coues deer was killed in 1982 in Cochise County, Arizona by bowhunter Harlon Wilson. The 10-point buck has an inside spread of 14 3/8 inches. Its right beam is 17 5/8 inches long and the left beam is 18 5/8 inches. The official score is 106 5/8.

In 1985 the Pope and Young Club recognized and accepted the first non-typical Coues deer in the history of the competitions. The buck was shot in Arizona's Pima County by David Snyder. The 10-pointer's right beam is 18 4/8 inches long while the left beam is 18 6/8 inches. Its inside spread is 13 2/8 inches and the official score is 112 4/8. The minimum score for a non-typical Coues deer is 66.

Elk . . . Epitome of Wildness

17

Magnificent. That one word pretty well sums up the American elk (*Cervus canadensis*), the most regal member of North America's deer family. Huge and handsome, bull elk—with their heavy, sweptback antlers and eerie, piercing bugles—are the epitome of wildness. Not surprisingly, some bowhunters consider them the greatest trophy on this continent.

Once common throughout much of the United States, elk faced the same fate of the buffalo but ultimately fared better. Slaughtered to near extinction and forced from plains and lowland forests into the high, remote and inaccessible wilderness areas, elk nonetheless survived. Today herds are found in 16 states and several Canadian provinces. Game experts place the total number of animals at over one million.

Elk are large, leggy animals with big bulls standing five feet at the shoulders. Their overall body length is as much as 10 feet. Commonly the weight of elk is often overestimated by hunters who swear some bulls they've seen—or packed out of black timber hellholes—will go at least 1,200 pounds on the hoof. Some might—there are documented cases of bulls weighing over half a ton field dressed—but most bulls would weigh in the 700- to 800-pound range. Cows generally average about one-quarter less.

Two varieties of elk—the common Rocky Mountain or Yellowstone species and the slightly larger but scarcer Roosevelt or Olympic elk of the Pacific Northwest—offer modern bowhunters ample challenge. Antlers are high, branched and sweeping, spreading four to five feet or more and weighing

perhaps 50 pounds on the true trophy-class bulls. Undeniably, the headgear of a mature bull is awe inspiring.

Today the racks of adult bulls are sought by "horn-hunters" who sell deer and elk antlers by the pound. The antlers are ground to powder and sold abroad as potent medicine capable of curing ailments or improving sex lives. Some poachers take bull elk solely for their antlers disdaining the meat. Whether sold to illegal "horn-hunters" or as trophy room "decorations," elk antlers are valuable and impressive.

Both species of elk are greyish tan with dark faces and long, rich brown neck hair. The stubby tail and rump patch are yellowish to off-white. Cows are usually paler in color. Roosevelt elk have larger bodies than their Rocky Mountain cousins but the bulls grow smaller antlers.

Any bull's first line of defense is his nose. Frequently opting to bed in dense cover, often on elevated points, he relies on rising thermals or eddying mountain breezes to warn of approaching danger. Even if a stalking hunter or predator manages to baffle an elk's well developed sense of smell, silence is essential because the animals' auditory abilities are likewise exceptional. A stick cracking underfoot or a branch carelessly rasping on clothing fabric is sure to alert any bedded elk within hearing. Windy days which neutralize hearing make elk exceedingly nervous.

Like other members of the deer family, elk frequently overlook stationary objects but are quick to detect sudden or unusual movements. Still, their sense of sight comes in a poor third when compared to the senses of smell and hearing.

Elk will not tolerate human disturbance. Hunting pressure can move entire herds out of a territory and change their daily habits as well. During the lazy days of summer, elk commonly feed early in the morning and late in the evening. Daylight hours are spent resting and chewing cuds in shady areas. With the opening of bow season, when hunters first invade their domain, the herds often feed during the night and are in nearby bedding areas by first light where they await nightfall before venturing forth again. If itchy footed hunters force them from their beds, they may head over the mountain in search of more peaceful surroundings. They might move five to 10 miles after being disturbed and abandon an area entirely.

Spooked elk are known for noisy departures. They crash away, bowling through brush and lining out at speeds which may reach 30 to 35 miles per hour. And after an initial burst of speed, the big animals can fall into a steady, ground-eating gait that, if maintained, may put a dozen or more miles behind them in less than an hour. Running bulls are pictures of power and grace, noses up and antlers laid back over their blocky bodies. Cows also run with a characteristic heads-up gait. Deceptively agile, elk have been known to clear eight-foot barriers with ease.

Good elk country is most often a mixture of high, heavy timber dotted with alpine meadows—called "parks" by Westerners—or old logging sites or burns where ample grass is found. Elk are ruminants and graze on lush mountain grasses. Remote, mountainous terrain with good feed, springs, seeps and streams harbor scattered bands of elk. Throughout much of the year cows, calves and yearlings live apart from the older bulls, which show little interest in the herds until the rut which usually begins with the first frosty mornings in September.

The big bulls, after living alone or in small bachelor bands until the onset of the breeding season, begin searching out the cows and assembling jealously guarded harems. At times one bull may have as many as two or three dozen cows collected. These herd bulls are often the biggest, strongest animals and spend considerable time proving their superiority by bugling and chasing away lesser, outrider bulls lurking near the harem. Meanwhile they breed all of the cows as they come into heat.

Although intimidation through posturing is preferred, bulls do fight on occasion, clashing antlers, pushing and shoving in displays of strength. Severe injuries may result—broken necks and gashes from goring occur—and rarely the huge antlers lock, spelling almost certain death for the combatants. But most often the dominant bull sends his beaten challenger off in search of easier pickings and then quickly returns to his harem before smaller bulls can steal any cows for themselves.

This frenzied breeding period may last a month or more. During this time the herd bulls run themselves to the point of exhaustion, for the most part ignoring food and sleep while mounting each willing cow and answering each threat from lesser bulls. By the end of the rut the bulls frequently are gaunt, exhausted animals. Not surprisingly, a prolonged or unusually severe winter can spell the end for some weakened monarchs. Starvation, in fact, is a common problem in certain areas where large elk populations overbrowse available forage.

Calves are dropped the following May or June. At calving time, pregnant cows separate from the herd and find secluded spots—often in heavy cover—to give birth. Newborn elk are reddish brown with obvious white spots along their backs and sides. A calf will weigh 20 to 30 pounds at birth and within a week or so will follow its mother back to the herd. Single births are most common and cow elk typically begin to breed by their second season. The life expectancy of an elk is a dozen or more years with some animals living into their second decade.

Elk talk—besides the hauntingly familiar bugle of a rutting bull—consists mainly of squeals, bleats and grunts. And more than one hunter has had a stalk spoiled by the sharp bark of a keen-eyed cow. When feeding or on the move, elk make a considerable amount of non-vocal noise, breaking branches and rattling rocks as they walk.

Tracks and droppings are the most recognizable elk sign. Hoofprints are large, cow-like impressions. Scat is found either in masses—meaning the animals have been feeding on grasses—or elongated pellets, which means the current diet consists of browse including plants, leaves, buds and herbs.

Other sign is noteworthy. Rutting bulls commonly destroy bushes and saplings, raking them with their antlers and frequently stripping bark from young trees. Such rubs are generally higher and larger than those made by deer. Elk may use the same general breeding areas season after season so these rub hotspots should be checked and watched from year to year. Bulls also make scrapes, pawing holes in the soft earth near springs or seeps, ejaculating and urinating in the mud. They delight in wallowing in these smelly depressions, plastering their bodies with the odiferous mud. Some bowhunters take up stands near fresh wallows in hopes of intercepting the bull as he returns.

Elk migrations occur when high country snows cover the open meadows. Herds work their way down to lower elevations, preferring sheltered valleys with south-facing slopes which are generally free of snow. Migrations are commonly a nighttime activity and may cover a relatively short distance— or perhaps 100 miles or more. A similar reverse migration takes place each spring as snowmelt opens the steep, timbered slopes.

Elk are grazing animals and grass is the mainstay of an elk's diet although browse from trees, shrubs and brushes satisfies their appetites as well. The elk also favor bark and fresh bites or old scars in aspen trees near feeding grounds are obvious to any hunter who can recognize the gouges in the soft-barked trees. Willows, mountain maples and serviceberry bushes may receive considerable attention from browsing animals. Conifers are winter favorites and browse lines created by feeding elk may be apparent in stands of evergreens.

The sound of a bugling elk is like nothing else in nature. Heard across a conifer-studded canyon on a frosty morning, it has a clear, musical quality— not unlike a flutist gone berserk—starting low and rising several octaves. Bugles often conclude with coughing grunts. Heard close-up it's a spine-tingling, paralyzing scream challenging all comers to muster enough courage to show themselves. Writing O-o-o-ou-e-e-eeee-eeough! Ee-uhu! Ee-uhu! doesn't do justice to the high-pitched bugles which, once heard, are never forgotten.

Effective Bowhunting Techniques

There are several different ways to bowhunt elk but without question the most exciting—and challenging—is to bugle a bull within point-blank range.

Bugling a rutting bull can result in a number of happenings. The herd bull, if concerned about an intruder taking his harem, may shut up and quickly move the cows away from the sound of the challenger. Or he may simply move the harem away, bugling occasionally as if letting the interloper know he's not really afraid. But these frustrating possibilities aside, bull elk—especially lone bulls and eager young bulls—will respond at times by heading toward the source of the call to check out the rival—or to settle the matter once and for all. If it's a fight he's after, or if he's just curious and checking to determine if the rival has cows ripe for the stealing, he will come to the call. That's the important thing. Bugling does attract bulls. It also creates excitement aplenty.

Artificial bugles most often are created by specially manufactured tubes of wood or plastic which are sold as elk calls. Some buglers get good results with common conduit tubing, plastic PCV pipe or even rubber garden hose. Others opt to use mouth or diaphragm calls—developed by turkey hunters but adapted for elk calling since this leaves both hands free for shooting and reduces unnecessary hand movements as the bull approaches. Finally, a handful of talented elk hunters rely solely on their vocal chords to imitate a challenging bull. Any of these artificial calls—alone or used with an accompanying grunt tube specially designed to simulate the raspy, coughing or braying grunts many bulls add to the tail end of their bugles—can produce results. General instructional records and tapes are available and offered for sale by some call manufacturers. Tone and resonance are keys, along with a reasonable simulation of the bugle itself. Like people, bull elk have distinct yet individual voices and are not bothered by the false notes or middling imitations of their bugles.

The sound of an elk's bugle may carry a mile or more on calm, crisp mornings. As previously indicated, calling a bull to the hunter at such long distances is unlikely; however, a knowledgeable bugler can keep tabs on a bull by responding to his calls while closing the distance. At such times, if the bull believes he's being pushed into fight or a defense of his harem, he may aggressively meet his challenger. This gives the hunter the chance he needs to put an arrow in his vitals.

Perhaps the best time to bugle is shortly after sunrise. Calling from canyon rims and high ridges, a hunter may prompt a response from nearby bulls. At this point it's up to the hunter to move quickly toward the animal, assuming the role of an aggressor bull trying to provoke a confrontation. Sitting and calling may work on occasion—under ideal circumstances—but more often than not the bowhunter must go to the bull or at least meet him halfway.

Some very successful elk hunters practically run toward a bugling bull, making no effort to be quiet. They say the idea is to get as close as quickly as possible so a challenging response may just startle the elk into believing he's got a rival breathing down his mane. Of course, conditions must be right. Particular attention must always be paid to wind direction. A hunter with the wind at his back is wasting his energy sprinting noisily toward an elk. The bull will scent the hunter and spook long before he's in good arrow range. Nothing will booger elk faster than a whiff of human odor.

When a bull does come in response to a bugle, he's looking for trouble. More than one bowhunter has had second thoughts about confronting up to half a ton of enraged elk at point-blank range. Wild-eyed, slobbering, foul-smelling and angry, pausing to slash small trees to splintered kindling and bellow a ground-jarring challenge, a rutting bull on the prod is an unnerving sight.

Few elk hunting experts recommend getting too close in moving up on a bugling bull. Challenges issued from 100 yards or so commonly bring the bull to the waiting hunter. At close-up yardages, some buglers turn away from the bull and call, using their bodies to muffle the sound somewhat and appear to be further away. Seldom is there any doubt that the bull is on his way. Often it's as if a bull makes as much noise as possible in an attempt to intimidate his rival.

Noise can also benefit a bugler at times. Some hunters will thrash the brush with a tree limb, raking the ground and scraping tree trunks. These sounds simulate an angry bull venting his wrath on his surroundings and can be quite effective coaxing hesitant or call-shy bulls closer. Moderation is the key. Too much of a ruckus—or continuous noise for an extended period—seldom does more than arouse a bull's suspicion.

Timing of the bugles is vital to success and at least two separate schools of thought exist pertaining to the proper amount of calling. One group says keep calling to a minimum and let the bull take the lead. Others stress aggressiveness and try to infuriate the bull by constant intimidation. Both techniques work. Of course, each bugling encounter is different and often the hunter's common sense will dictate what method should be used.

Bowhunters should keep one thought in mind: An enraged bull is prone to making mistakes. And if the hunter is prepared, one mistake is all that is needed to put a bull on the ground.

As a final note on bugling, it should be mentioned that teamwork can pay off when this tactic is used. Two-man teams—with one person doing the bugling and the other crouching close at hand to take the shot—have fooled more than one elk. Bulls can often pinpoint locations of a bugle, especially at close range. Consequently, there is some advantage to having the animal's attention focused on the source of the bugle as long as the hunter is situated close enough to get the shot at an approaching bull zeroing in on the caller.

In recent seasons there has been special attention paid to calling bulls by cow talk including "lost calls" and "cohesion squeals." The idea here is to lure a rutting bull close by imitating a lost or receptive cow, rather than by bugling which is a challenge to fight. Several successful bowhunters report excellent results with this method and it is sure to be more popular in the seasons ahead, especially where bugle-shy bulls have been educated by over-zealous callers.

Still-hunting is a difficult but tremendously satisfying elk hunting method. As already noted, elk have excellent hearing and can detect unusual noises at considerable distances. Combine this with dense, nearly impenetrable bedding areas, and it's understandable why walking up on a resting elk and shooting it in its bed is no easy task. But it can be done.

As with any type of still-hunting, the key is to move as slowly and quietly as possible—and spot the game before it senses danger. When elk are spotted—feeding, walking or bedded—the stalk begins unless the herd's direction of travel will bring them within easy range.

Again, easy does it is the key. Ever mindful of the wind direction and careful not to make any telltale sound, the bowhunter must ease closer, one careful and quiet step at a time. Often there are many sets of eyes watching for danger and it seems one old cow is always standing guard. One slip and the entire herd is crashing down the canyon like a tan avalanche.

Still-hunting may be combined with bugling. Usually the bowhunter intends to cover a lot of ground during a day afield. Occasionally he'll pause and bugle in hopes of getting a response or to answer a bull he hears. Often this method is employed during slow times in the rut when most bulls are silent, as sometimes happens during a stretch of unseasonably warm weather. But instead of attempting to call the bull in, the hunter is simply trying to locate a bull's area. He then still-hunts it and hopes to catch sight of the bugling bull so a stalk can be made.

Good binoculars can assist a stalking hunter. Many compact, lightweight models are an important part of a serious elk hunter's field gear. He uses them to glass parks and sparsely timbered slopes where elk feed early and late in the day. He also scans bedding areas and the shady cover bordering the open parks, searching for something—the flick of an ear, the whiteness of an antler against a dark background of spruce or fir, a patch of tan that seems out of place—anything that will give away a bedded or stationary animal.

Note: A hunter must remember to look for **parts** of an elk, not the entire animal. And he must also keep in mind that any time **he** can see the animal's head or eyes, the elk can see **him**.

Snow is not uncommon in much of the northern elk country as the rut gets into gear and a fresh blanket of snow that muffles noise and leaves an untracked wilderness can benefit the still-hunter as he searches for sign. Any animals on the move following an overnight snow will leave unmistakable evidence of their passing. Under ideal conditions it's possible to follow and overtake moving bands of browsing elk, work close and get a shot. Perhaps the biggest problem is remaining undetected by so many pairs of eyes seemingly ever alert for impending danger. Also, a heavy high country snowfall can trigger the herd into immediately moving to lower terrain. Elk on the move are almost impossible to overtake by any hunter hoping to remain unnoticed.

Backpack bowhunting is a favorite technique of some wilderness veterans. They simply head into remote elk country packing enough food and gear for three, five or more days. Once the elk are located, the patient hunter follows and waits for his chance. At nightfall he makes a cold, quiet camp— with no fire or undue noise—wherever he happens to be. He resumes his hunt at first light. This method can be extremely effective; however, it's not for everybody and common sense dictates at least two people work together in a general hunting area. An injury involving a serious fall or broken leg could prove fatal to a lone hunter where bowhunters working in tandem have a definite advantage in an

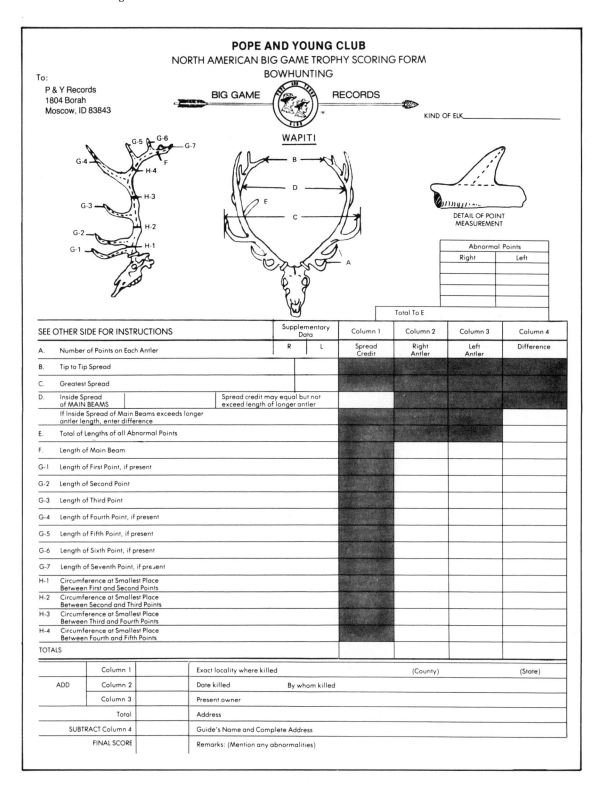

POPE AND YOUNG CLUB
NORTH AMERICAN BIG GAME TROPHY SCORING FORM
BOWHUNTING

To:
P & Y Records
1804 Borah
Moscow, ID 83843

BIG GAME   RECORDS

KIND OF ELK_____

WAPITI

DETAIL OF POINT MEASUREMENT

Abnormal Points	
Right	Left

Total To E

SEE OTHER SIDE FOR INSTRUCTIONS	Supplementary Data		Column 1	Column 2	Column 3	Column 4
	R	L	Spread Credit	Right Antler	Left Antler	Difference
A. Number of Points on Each Antler						
B. Tip to Tip Spread						
C. Greatest Spread						
D. Inside Spread of MAIN BEAMS	Spread credit may equal but not exceed length of longer antler					
If Inside Spread of Main Beams exceeds longer antler length, enter difference						
E. Total of Lengths of all Abnormal Points						
F. Length of Main Beam						
G-1 Length of First Point, if present						
G-2 Length of Second Point						
G-3 Length of Third Point						
G-4 Length of Fourth Point, if present						
G-5 Length of Fifth Point, if present						
G-6 Length of Sixth Point, if present						
G-7 Length of Seventh Point, if present						
H-1 Circumference at Smallest Place Between First and Second Points						
H-2 Circumference at Smallest Place Between Second and Third Points						
H-3 Circumference at Smallest Place Between Third and Fourth Points						
H-4 Circumference at Smallest Place Between Fourth and Fifth Points						
TOTALS						

ADD	Column 1		Exact locality where killed	(County)	(State)
	Column 2		Date killed By whom killed		
	Column 3		Present owner		
	Total		Address		
SUBTRACT Column 4			Guide's Name and Complete Address		
FINAL SCORE			Remarks: (Mention any abnormalities)		

I certify that I have measured the above trophy on _____ 19 _____
at (address) _____ City _____
State _____ Zip Code _____ and that these measurements and data are. to the
best of my knowledge and belief, made in accordance with the instructions given.

Witness: _____ Signature _____
(To Measurer's Signature)

Pope & Young Club Official Measurer

_____
MEASURER (Print)
_____
ADDRESS
_____
CITY   STATE   ZIP

INSTRUCTIONS

All measurements must be made with a flexible steel tape to the nearest one-eighth of an inch. Wherever it is necessary to change direction of measurement, mark a control point and swing tape at this point. To simplify addition, please enter fractional figures in **eighths.** Official measurements cannot be taken for at least sixty days after the animal was killed. **Please submit photographs. (see below).**

Supplementary Data measurements indicate conformation of the trophy, and none of the figures in line A, B and C are to be included in the score. Evaluation of conformation is a matter of personal preference.

A. Number of Points on each antler. To be counted a point, a projection must be at least one inch long AND its length must exceed the length of its base. All points are measured from tip of point to nearest edge of beam as illustrated. **Beam tip is counted as a point but not measured as a point.**

B. Tip to Tip Spread measured between tips of Main Beams.

C. Greatest Spread measured between perpendiculars at right angles to the center line of the skull at widest part whether across main beams or points.

D. Inside Spread of Main Beams measured at right angles to the center line of the skull at widest point between main beams. Enter this measurement again in "Spread Credit" column if it is less than or equal to the length of longer antler.

E. Total of Lengths of all Abnormal Points. Abnormal points are generally considered to be those nontypical in shape or location. Sketch all abnormal points on antler illustration (front of form) showing location and approximate size.

F. Length of Main Beam measured from lowest outside edge of burr over outer curve to the most distant point of what is, or appears to be, the main beam. The point of beginning is that point on the burr where the center line along the outer curve of the beam intersects the burr.

G-1-2-3-4-5-6-7. Length of Normal Points. Normal points project from main beam. They are measured from nearest edge of main beam over outer curve of the beam so that the top edge of the tape coincides with the top edge of the beam on both sides of the point. Draw line along top edge of tape. This line will be base line from which point is measured.

H-1-2-3-4. Circumferences. If first point is missing, take H-1 and H-2 at smallest place between burr and second point. IF G-5 is missing, take H-4 halfway between G-4 and beam tip.

Photographs: All entries must include photographs of the trophy. A right side, left side and front view photograph will be required for all antlers, horns and skulls. A photograph of the entire animal is requested if at all possible.

Drying Period: To be eligible for entry in the Pope & Young Records, a trophy must first have been stored under normal room temperature and humidity for at least 60 consecutive days after date of kill. No trophy will be considered which has in any way been altered from its natural state.

THIS SCORING FORM MUST BE ACCOMPANIED BY A SIGNED POPE & YOUNG FAIR CHASE AFFIDAVIT, 3 PHOTOS AND A RECORDING FEE OF $25.00.

emergency situation.

A similar technique involves hiking or riding horseback into prime elk country and establishing a base camp on the edge of a proven hotspot. Keeping a high ridge or wide valley between camp and the hunting area, the bowhunters use the base as a headquarters and head out well before dawn each day to try to locate elk. Most often they do not return 'til well after dark. This may be repeated day after day throughout the entire hunt. Obviously, conditioning is vital although some hunters use horses to ride to and from their hunting areas. Horses undeniably come in handy when an elk is down and the chore of packing out the meat lies ahead.

Elk hunting guides offer a wide range of services including those already noted. But there's one method that has become popular in some areas—tree stand hunting. Such stands are located near water holes, wallows, mineral licks, trails—any place frequented by elk. This is not elk hunting, per se. Elk waiting would be a more correct term but patient hunters used to tree stand techniques for whitetails or black bears find this method a viable option. The keys are patience and an area where the elk are not spooked by constant hunter harassment. Guides with leased or private land sometimes book a limited number of hunters and combine stand hunting with bugling or still-hunting, depending on the conditions and wishes of the hunters.

Some bowhunters who cut their teeth on tree stand hunting feel most comfortable sitting and waiting for the game to come to them. Others with physical disabilities or a lack of confidence in their stalking skills find this technique especially appealing. And every season many elk are tagged by hunters who shoot them from elevated perches.

A handful of elk hunters have attempted horn-rattling—using large mule deer antlers since elk antlers are much too large to be easily handled—and some swear it can work. Used from a stand with a bugle and grunt tube for added authenticity, it makes sense the technique could lure a rutting bull within bow range.

Driving elk is still another option; however, this method requires a team of hunters—one or two standers strategically positioned along escape routes and at least as many drivers who move slowly through cover in an attempt to push elk past the waiting hunters. Also, an alarmed elk is much harder to hit and put down than one that isn't boogered. It's generally agreed that bowhunters should not attempt any risky shot where the result may be a wounded animal. A shot at a running elk is among the riskiest of all.

Because of their size and stamina, elk are tough to kill—with guns or bows—and hard to recover if hit poorly. Most often a frontal shot is sheer folly and the heavy shoulders should be avoided at all costs. The ideal shot is the lung area when the target is broadside or slightly quartering away. Proper placement is the key to success.

Hunting bows should be a minimum of 60 pounds—more if the hunter can handle it comfortably and accurately—and large, well-honed broadheads are considered additional insurance against lost game. Big bulls can take an arrow through the vitals without so much as a flinch. Dead on their feet, they can cover considerable ground before going down. Heavy hunting tackle capable of punching through hide, ribs and organs make sense. Lighter hunting gear is best left to smaller, thin-skinned game.

Note: A heavy bow is perhaps even more important to the hunter shooting from a tree stand. Unless the arrow punches an exit hole low in the chest, blood will collect inside the wounded elk and make recovery doubly difficult without a blood trail to follow.

Wounded elk seem to head for dense cover and at times employ tactics—doubling back or circling—seemingly intended to throw a tracker off the trail. On rare occasions a wounded elk has proved dangerous and injured the bowhunter who shot him; however, common sense can keep a bowhunter out of any potentially dangerous situations. Only an idiot would walk up on a wounded bull without making certain he was down for keeps. An insurance arrow in the boiler room is seldom a bad idea.

Elk meat is excellent table fare, not unlike beef, but special pains must be taken to avoid losing it through spoilage. When bowhunters are commonly afield, in August and September, the weather fluctuates between nighttime cold and daytime hot. Consequently, immediate attention must be given to the carcass and perhaps the most important factor is locating the animal as quickly as possible.

Elk meat spoils unbelievably fast in warm weather. A hunter needs to locate his animal and field dress it on the spot, removing all internal organs quickly. Once the gutting is finished, it's necessary to cut out the windpipe and esophagus. Skinning is the next step, although some elk hunters believe the hide should remain on the carcass to prevent contamination of the meat during the packing out process. Under some conditions this may be all right, but commonly skinning is necessary to keep the meat from souring.

Elk hides are thick and hold in body heat. Many knowledgeable hunters not only remove the hide as quickly as possible but halve or quarter the carcass and even hang the sections—or at least prop them—so air can circulate and assist in the cooling process. Porous game bags come in handy in discouraging ever-present early season blowflies. Rope, a folding saw and a knife/sharpening stone are other elk skinning essentials.

Trophy-class bull elk make one of the most impressive of all big game mounts. Hunters wishing to save the antlers and cape for the taxidermist should follow this simple procedure:

Make a single cut up from a point between the bull's shoulders up the back of the neck to the base of the skull two or three inches behind the antlers. Next make an incision from the point between the shoulders down each side just behind and around each leg to a point on the chest well back of the brisket. Then begin carefully peeling the hide down using the knife and finger strength. When the hide is free all the way to the head, the exposed neck muscles are cut through to the spinal column. Twisting and cutting frees the head and cape. A

general, thorough application of salt will preserve most hides and heads long enough for the trip to the taxidermist. If the weather is exceptionally warm or the cape cannot be delivered for mounting for several days, the skull should be removed. This process involves turning the ears and cutting around the eyes, lachrymal glands at the corner of each eye, nose and teeth. This is not a difficult chore for a practiced hunter or guide but is best left to a taxidermist if the hunter is inexperienced at caping.

The elk's canine teeth—or ivories—are prized by some hunters. Indians once decorated their clothing with elk teeth and later members of the BPOE adopted elk ivory as a symbol of membership. Sadly, in the early days of market hunting, some elk were shot solely for their "trophy" teeth.

The antlers and cape of many bulls are one load for a lone hunter packing out his animal piece by piece. Quarters are ideal for horseback packing; however, they're too much for most men to handle. Proficient meat handlers often bone out their elk and pack out only the meat. Others enlist the aid of hunting companions to help tote the elk sections back to camp. Almost any way it's handled, it's hard work. One savvy Colorado guide summed it up well when he said, "Compared to packing out a big bull, finding and shooting him is a piece of cake!"

Trophy Recognition

Monarch...imperial...royal. These terms are bandied about by serious elk hunters and each has a special meaning concerning the number of points on each side of the bull's massive rack. Monarchs are the largest bulls with eight points to a side. Imperial bulls boast seven points while royals proudly wear six points on each antler beam.

Record book bulls generally carry antlers that approach body length, perhaps five feet or more. Hunting pressure has claimed many of the truly big bulls, especially in states like Colorado, and today a big six-point royal bull is regarded as an exceptional trophy. Some five-pointers may have the mass and length to qualify for the records but most Pope and Young Yellowstone bulls need at least six points or more to surpass the 260 qualifying score. The minimum score for Roosevelt elk is 210.

It may take five years for a bull to grow a true trophy class set of antlers. This fact, plus the theory that bulls are past their prime by age eight or nine—and frequently have antlers with declining scores—makes arrowing a monster bull with antlers to match a monumental chore.

Regardless, any elk with antlers approaching body length is an outstanding bull. Uniformity and mass will add to the overall score. Brow tines jut forward and up, reaching almost to the tip of the bull's nose. Thick ivory-tipped antler tines are another good indicator of a "keeper." As one veteran elk guide puts it, "The big bulls can tilt their heads back and use their horns to scratch an itch on their butts. If you see one doing that, shoot him. He's the one you're after."

The World Record Roosevelt elk was killed in Coos County, Oregon by Robert Dean Dunson on a 1982 bowhunt. The six-by-six bull has a 36 2/8-inch spread. The right beam is 51 1/8 inches long and the left beam 49 5/8 inches. The official score is 311 6/8.

David Snyder's huge Yellowstone elk, arrowed in Mercer County, Montana in 1981, is the best bull ever tagged by a bowhunter. The six-pointer's right beam is 53 4/8 inches long and the left beam tapes 54 6/8 inches. The bull's inside spread is 45 4/8 inches and the total score is 391 6/8.

Moose . . . America's Biggest Deer

18

Big and ugly. Those two words pretty well sum up the impression a person gets when looking at the largest of all North American deer for the first time. But the massive, palmated antlers of a true trophy-class bull moose more than offset the animal's homely appearance in the minds of many. His size and impressive headgear make him one of the most highly-prized big game species sought by contemporary bowhunters.

Modern bowhunters actually have three varieties of moose (*Alces alces*) to hunt—the huge Alaska-Yukon moose of the far northlands, the common Canadian or American moose of southern Canada and certain northern states, and the smaller Shiras or Wyoming moose of several Rocky Mountain states. Each is recognized as a separate classification by the Pope and Young Club.

As the first settlers pushed inland, moose were found roaming much of what would become northeastern America. In fact, remains of these big ruminants have been discovered as far south as Virginia. Despite being driven from much of their original range, moose have established ample home ranges throughout many forested areas—from high mountains to boggy lowlands—of the continent. Today's healthy moose population is estimated to be upwards of half a million animals.

As previously indicated, moose are not much to look at on the hoof, at least at first glance. Long-legged and ungainly, small-eyed, flop-eared, Roman-nosed and hump-shouldered, these north woods giants are truly unique (the French Canadian named them *l'original*) members of the animal world. But there is something awesome about the size and strength of moose which makes a person—especially a bowhunter—view these monarchs with respect and admiration.

Standing as much as seven feet at the shoulder and 10 feet at the antlers, bulls are imposing creatures. Many easily exceed half a ton in weight—a few may approach 2,000 pounds—and stretch perhaps 10 or more feet from snout to stubby tail. Cows average 600 to 800 pounds live weight.

From a distance, most moose appear black in color; however, close up inspection of some animals reveals dusky brown to russet bodies. Lower legs are often grayish or dirty white in color. Hair is coarse and hides are thick.

Moose have somewhat spindly-looking legs that are three to four feet from hoof to belly. Hooves are huge and the out-sized dewclaws assist moose in negotiating deep snow and the boggy, spongy haunts they favor. Excellent swimmers, moose are often located near water where they find food and relief from the summer heat and hordes of bothersome insects.

Moose bodies appear misproportioned with short necks above broad, muscular shoulders which taper to smaller, slender hindquarters. Noteworthy are the animals' neck manes—which stand erect when moose are angry—and the floppy "bells" dangling beneath their chins. These latter appendages are fleshy pouches of skin which serve no obvious purpose and do little to enhance their owners' appearance.

"Tremendous" would be a suitable adjective to describe the huge antlers of a trophy-class bull. Without any question moose carry more "horns" than any animal on earth! Antlers may span six or more feet and weigh upwards of 80 pounds! Numerous points are apparent along the outer palms.

Because they are browsers, moose favor a diet of twigs and leaves from trees such as alders, aspen, willow, fir, birch and ash (the Algonquins called them *musee*, the "woodeaters"). Bushes such as chokecherry and honeysuckle draw considerable attention and water grasses, as well as aquatic weeds and plants like water lillies, are devoured with enthusiasm. Where their home territory abuts croplands, raids into farmers' fields are not uncommon. An adult moose eats between 30 and 40 pounds of browse each day.

A moose relies mainly on well-developed senses of smell and hearing to avoid danger. Eyes are proportionally small; like most game, moose tend to overlook stationary objects. Regardless, a careless movement can quickly send a bull crashing away to safety.

Moose, like domestic cattle, have a wide range of vocal sounds. These range from the gutteral bellows of angry bulls to the high, quavering bleats of calves. Cows and bulls alike utter coughs and throaty grunts. During the rut the animals become especially vocal and a talented caller can lure lovesick bulls into bow range by grunting like an amorous cow.

For all their bulk and unseemly appearance, moose are deceptively agile animals. They have been clocked at speeds upwards of 40 miles per hour and can maintain a steady, ground-eating trot for long periods of time. If arrowed or alarmed, they can become runaway flesh and blood locomotives, plowing through dense brush and small trees as if the barriers didn't exist. On the other hand, if alerted to impending danger, a moose can ease off and vanish like some huge woodland apparition, silent and wraithlike.

Typically homebodies with well-defined ranges—sometimes living within a home area of one square mile or less—moose are often solitary animals. They spend much of their lives alternately eating and resting. Prime feeding times are early and late in the day although a hungry moose will browse at any time of the day or night.

By mid-September, when the breeding season gets into gear, the bulls are aggressive and may be found on the move in search of willing cows. At such times moose may leave their home territories, wandering about and perhaps covering many miles. Unlike elk or caribou, bull moose do not gather harems although they may "hang out" with several cows and breed each one as they come into heat. Bulls do create rubs, polishing newly hardened antlers on helpless saplings and brush. Bulls also paw shallow wallows, urinate in the mud and then roll in the foul-smelling mess to coat themselves with "love cologne."

A rutting bull—reeking and red-eyed—is nothing to mess with. More than one woodsman has been attacked by moose during the annual rut; there have been several cases of enraged bulls actually charging into cars, trucks and trains! Throughout the breeding season fights between bulls are common and sometimes savage. On occasion the combatants clash with such force their antlers lock, dooming both animals. At other times bulls have killed rivals and then continued to attack their fallen foe, goring the carcass and slashing it with their forefeet.

Bulls may stay with a receptive cow for several days—even a week or more—mounting her from time to time until his lust is eventually satisfied. He then heads off in search of another cow and repeats the mating process until the rut ends in October. At this point he quickly rediscovers his appetite and sets about to replenish dimished body fat. By year's end the bull sheds his antlers and continues to live a solitary, docile—even lethargic—existence until the following fall. Cows give birth to their calves in May and June, often dropping twins after their initial breeding season. Calves are usually 20 to 30 pounds at birth, possessing a face and leggy body only a mother could love. Their coats are unspotted and a brownish red in color. They develop quickly, quite capable of running and even swimming during their first weeks of life. Calves typically remain with their mother until she drives them off the following spring just before giving birth again. Mama moose are extremely protective of their young and will attack any man or beast she thinks poses a threat.

Moose mature in five to six years and a few may live to see their second decade. Starvation probably claims more moose than do hunters; wolves and bears both take an annual toll of calves and weaker animals.

Effective Bowhunting Techniques

Still-hunting, stalking, stand hunting and calling are all effective methods of arrowing a moose. Combine these tactics with a float trip bowhunt through prime moose country and a bowhunter has the makings of a first class wilderness adventure.

Some Alaskan outfitters and guides offer complete hunt packages—rafts, food, camping gear, calling instruction, etc.—along back country rivers cutting through prime moose habitat. The hunters seek to locate moose feeding on streambank willows and stalk them or, if the bulls are rutting, try to lure them within bow range by imitating the grunts of eager cows.

In certain spots—near well-tracked stream crossings, over wallows, mineral licks, or at the intersection of clearly defined game trails—tree stands or ground blinds can pay off for the patient hunter. Hunting early and late in the day is most productive except during the peak of the rut when stands could pay off at any time.

Stand hunting may appeal to the experienced sit-and-wait whitetail hunter who is used to spending long stationary hours on stand. It also is a natural for the individual who may be awed by the vast wilderness and hesitates to strike out on his own.

Others who take early morning and late evening stands may try their hand at still-hunting during other times of the day. Frequently they take to some high point and glass the forest edges or waterways for some telltale movement or glimpse of the animal

itself as it feeds or heads toward its bedding area. For their size, moose can be difficult to locate when stationary. This is especially true early in the season when foliage is still a cloaking on the trees and understory. Often the glint of sunlight on an antler tine or a suspicious horizontal shape among the vertical tree trunks is all a hunter sees. Then again moose may be quite apparent, standing in brushy lowland cover, and may be seen a mile or more away. In either case good binoculars are a plus.

Once the problem of locating a bull is overcome, the biggest difficulty is getting close enough to lace the big animal with a well-placed shaft. While moose are not the most difficult big game animal to stalk, closing within good bow range can present a challenge to even the best stalkers. Cover is generally thick and, as previously indicated, a moose has above average hearing.

A stalking bowhunter must always pay careful attention to wind direction and to where he places his feet. A whiff of man-scent will end any stalk in a hurry and a dead stick popping underfoot can alert any moose within earshot. The key is easing ahead, ever so slowly, approaching silently from downwind. This can be no small feat when wearing hip boots and traversing the spongy, mucky terrain common in prime moose country.

Where creeks, rivers and lakes dissect moose havens, hunting from rubber rafts or canoes can be deadly. Drifting silently with the current, often working in teams with a caller or guide in the lead raft, bowhunters may lure nearby bulls to the shoreline with appropriate coughs and grunts—just in time for the shooter in the second raft to get a good shot at a curious bull.

Drift hunting also allows bowhunters to surprise moose wading and feeding in the shallow water near shore or in streamside willows. The sudden appearance of a raft or canoe may send the moose splashing away to safety. But then again a bull may stand its ground, watching curiously as a bowhunter drifts within good range. As with caribou, shooting a swimming moose would be considered highly unethical.

POPE AND YOUNG CLUB

NORTH AMERICAN BIG GAME TROPHY SCORING FORM

BOWHUNTER COMPETITION

P & Y Records Office
1804 Borah
Moscow, ID 83843

MOOSE

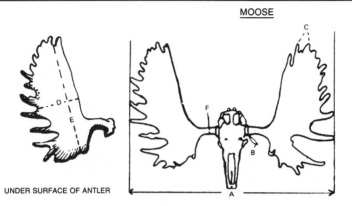

KIND OF MOOSE
_____

UNDER SURFACE OF ANTLER

DETAIL OF POINT MEASUREMENT

SEE OTHER SIDE FOR INSTRUCTIONS	Column 1 Greatest Spread	Column 2 Right Antler	Column 3 Left Antler	Column 4 Difference
A. Greatest Spread				
B. Number of Abnormal Points on Both Antlers				
C. Number of Normal Points				
D. Width of Palm				
E. Length of Palm including Brow Palm				
F. Circumference of Beam at Smallest Place				
TOTALS				

ADD	Column 1		Exact locality where killed	(County)		(State)
	Column 2		Date killed	By whom killed		
	Column 3		Present owner			
Total			Address			
SUBTRACT Column 4			Guide's Name and Address			
FINAL SCORE			Remarks: (Mention any abnormalities)			

I certify that I have measured the above trophy on _____ 19 _____

at (address) _____ City _____

State _____ Zip Code _____ and that these measurements and data are, to the best

of my knowledge and belief, made in accordance with the instructions given.

Witness: _____
(To Measurer's Signature)

Signature _____

Pope & Young Club Official Measurer

_____

MEASURER (Print)

_____

ADDRESS

CITY   STATE   ZIP

INSTRUCTIONS

All measurements must be made with a flexible steel tape or measuring cable to the nearest one-eight of an inch. Wherever it is necessary to change direction of measurement, mark a control point and swing tape at this point. To simplify addition, please enter fractional figures in eighths.

Official measurements cannot be taken for at least sixty days after the animal was killed. **Please submit photographs.**

A. Greatest Spreads - measured in a straight line at right angles to the center line of the skull.

B. Number of Abnormal Points on Both Antlers - Abnormal points are generally considered to be those nontypical in shape or location.

C. Number of Normal Points. Normal points are those which project from the outer edge of the antler. To be counted a point, a projection must be at least one inch long and the length must exceed the breadth of the point's base. The breadth need not be computed from the deepest adjacent dips in the palmation. The length may be measured to any location — at least one inch from the tip — at which the length of the point exceeds its breadth.

D. Width of Palm - taken in contact with the surface across the under side of the palm, at right angles to the inside edge of palm, to a dip between points at the greatest widge of palm.

E. Length of Palm including Brow Palm - taken in contact with the surface along the under side of the palm, parallel to the inner edge from dips between points at the greatest length of palm. If a deep bay is present in the palm, measure palm length across the open bay if the proper line of measurement crosses the bay.

F Circumference of Beam at Smallest Place - circumference measurements must be taken with a steel tape.

Photographs: All entries must include photographs of the trophy. A right side, left side and front view photograph will be required for all antlers, horns and skulls. A photograph of the entire animal is requested if at all possible.

Drying Period: To be eligible for entry in the Pope & Young Records, a trophy must first have been stored under normal room temperature and humidity for at least 60 consecutive days. No trophy will be considered which has in any way been altered from its natural state.

THIS SCORING FORM MUST BE ACCOMPANIED BY A FULLY COMPLETED AND SIGNED **POPE & YOUNG FAIR CHASE AFFIDAVIT PLUS A RECORDING FEE OF $25.00**

Because of their size, moose may appear to be much closer than they actually are. Combine this fact with the excitement of the moment and it's relatively easy for even a good shot to miss his target or—worse yet—the vitals. The only bowhunters who doubt they could miss a moose-sized animal are those who've never found themselves in a pulse-pounding confrontation with a trophy bull.

Note: Concentration is the key to placing the arrow where it'll do the most good. It's as vital to "pick a spot" while aiming at a moose standing broadside at 25 yards as it is a target one-tenth that size—perhaps even more important! Fail to remember this vital point and a bowhunter may find himself wondering how anyone could blow a shot at an animal seemingly the size of Old McDonald's dairy barn.

It goes without saying that heavy bowhunting tackle is almost mandatory for the moose hunter. Bows in the 65- to 75-pound range are adequate; lighter pulling weapons are best left in the bow rack. Large, well-honed broadheads are likewise necessary and many successful moose hunters favor the solid, fixed blade heads.

The aiming point should be the heart-lung area behind the front shoulder. The powerful shoulder itself is almost certain to stop any arrow; it should be avoided like a social disease. Neck shots are risky at best and should never be attempted. Shots at running animals—unless they're already hit—are foolish and most often futile.

For all his size, a moose laced by a well-placed arrow will likely go down fairly quickly. Hard-hit bulls may bed down when the first effects of the arrow begin to tell.

Trailing a wounded moose should be done with appropriate care and caution. A wounded bull could easily turn on a careless hunter and "do serious damage" in less time than it takes to tell. Any bedded bull capable of holding its head erect shouldn't be approached carelessly. This is where one or more follow-up arrows can keep the trophy anchored.

Getting back in, away from roads and people, is part of trophy hunting for moose. It's best accomplished on horseback, by boat or airplane. A few bowmen may even pack in on foot. This latter technique is foolish unless advance plans are made for getting back out with antlers, cape and meat.

Only when the moose is down does the hunter truly appreciate the size of these animals. Field dressing is often a two- or three-man job and as for the packing of the meat...well, a lone hunter is going to require assistance unless he dresses in red and blue, wears a cape and has a big "S" on his chest. While it is possible to bone out the meat at the kill site and pack it out—making dozens of backbreaking trips—such an undertaking may well sour the overall experience of the hunt.

Pack horses can make the job considerably easier. And even in states like Idaho, Wyoming and Montana, where camping or backpacking bowhunters successfully stalk and arrow Shiras moose each fall, most have made arrangements to have help when the hunt ends on a successful note. Horseflesh can be worth its weight in precious metals at such moments.

Moose meat, if properly attended, is delicious. Some Indians favor the tongue and nose although most modern bowhunters lean toward the tenderloins and backstraps. If the moose is taken early in the season, warm weather can pose a problem. Skinning and cooling the meat is essential.

Bears are an inherent problem in much moose country. Attracted to the gut pile or carcass by scent, bears have been known to stake a claim on what they consider to be a moosemeat bonanza. To avoid claim-jumping bruins some hunters urinate around the carcass or leave items of their clothing—ripe with man-scent—nearby. This can work; however, a prudent hunter always exercises some degree of caution each time he returns to the kill site. No moose that ever lived is worth a mauling—or worse—at the hands of an enraged bear.

Moose downed in or near water can prove easier to handle during the skinning and cutting process. A raft or boat can be moved close and easily loaded. Cool water also helps chase the body heat from the meat and keeps it free from hair, dirt and other contaminators that are often hard to avoid.

Time was when some moose guides flew their pontoon-equipped bush planes over prime habitat until a trophy bull was sighted. After touching down on a nearby lake, he'd then lead the client to the bull. Such tactics raised ethical questions and led Alaska to pass a law making it illegal for a hunter to shoot an animal the same day he has flown into a hunting area. Since moose have definite home territories—other than during the rut—it's likely a bull sighted from a plane will be in the same general area the following day, week or even year. Keeping this in mind, it's up to the hunter to determine the ethics of scouting from an airplane.

Undoubtedly, calling moose is the most exciting and challenging of any bowhunting method. Good callers can evoke immediate response in some bulls and literally bring them on the run to what they believe is a cow with romance on her mind. As an added inducement, a caller may spice things up by pouring water from his canteen to simulate a urinating cow moose.

As with elk bugling, bull moose can be tricked into believing a rival bull has entered his domain looking for a fight. A caller may break brush or scrape trees with a boat paddle—sounding like a bull polishing his antlers—to anger a real bull and make him show himself. The point to keep in mind here is that any bull responding to the challenge of an interloper is going to come looking for a fight. The sight of an angry bull, hackles raised and polished antlers gleaming like spear-tips, just may discourage some bowhunters from releasing an arrow.

Trophy Recognition

The truly outstanding record book moose will have heavy beams, huge palms with numerous points and an exceptional antler spread—approaching or exceeding six feet. A hunter who has to wonder about the size of the rack is probably going to be disappointed. There's no doubt when a true trophy-class bull steps out of the willows and turns his massive antlers in the direction of the waiting bowhunter.

The largest Alaska-Yukon moose was killed in 1973 by Dr. Michael Cusack. Its antlers have a 74-inch spread and each palm has 11 points. The right palm is 18 6/8 inches wide and the left is 19 2/8 inches wide. The bull, shot along Alaska's Bear Creek, has an official score of 248 0/8.

The record Canada moose scores 201 4/8. It was shot in the Mt. Lady Laurier area of British Columbia in 1968 by Peter Halbig. This bull has a spread of 55 2/8 inches. Its right palm is 12 4/8 inches in width and the left is 11 4/8 inches. Each palm has 12 points.

The top Shiras moose was arrowed by Kenneth Fordyce in 1983 in Idaho's Fremont County. This trophy bull boasts a spread of 48 1/8 inches. Its right palm has 10 points and is 10 4/8 inches wide. The other side is 11 0/8 inches wide and also has 10 points.

Minimum Pope and Young scores are 170 for Alaska/Yukon moose, 135 for Canada moose and 115 for Shiras/Wyoming moose.

Musk-Oxen . . . Arctic Cattle

19

These blocky, hardy cattle of the far northlands once ranged from the bleak polar regions south into the United States and parts of Asia. Shot for food by natives and explorers, they were driven from much of their original territory. Today the musk-oxen (*Ovibos moschatus*) number perhaps 30,000 animals in total and are found in North America, including parts of Alaska and the Canadian Arctic.

Both males and females have horns, humped shoulders and coats of long, flowing hair which all but obscures their bodies and legs. Bulls stand between four and five feet at the shoulder and are some seven feet from nose to short tail. Cows are proportionally smaller.

On Alaska's Nunivak Island, where most bowhunting for musk-oxen takes place, adult bulls average 500 to 600 pounds; cows weigh some 200 pounds less. In other parts of the Canadian north, musk-ox bulls commonly top 700 pounds. Some musk-oxen, captured for study or domestication, have weighed more than 1,000 pounds.

The animals' thick, rich coats make them appear to be larger and heavier than they actually are. Their dark brown to black guard hairs, some as much as two feet in length, drape the body and hide all but the white foot patches above each hoof. Beneath the outer hair is a soft undercoat called *qiviut* by Eskimos. This *qiviut* is collected and woven into highly prized, cold-resistant garments. It is what allows the animals themselves to survive some of the harshest terrain and weather on the continent.

Musk-oxen are herd animals and wander over their ranges in search of feed, frequently covering several miles each day. Their diet includes grasses, bushes and small trees such as dwarf willow and birches. Periods of feeding activity are typically followed by periods of rest with herd members bedding and chewing their cuds before rising again to repeat the cycle.

Each herd is dominated by a big bull and may include a dozen or more cows and their young. Young bulls are permitted to remain with the herd for as much as two years before being driven off. It is not uncommon for the smaller bulls to band together in bachelor groups. Older bulls, defeated by younger, stronger rivals for breeding rights to a harem of cows, may take up a solitary existence.

Much has been written about the musk-oxen's tendency to head for high ground and to form a protective circle when threatened. Adults may form a defensive ring with the calves and younger animals inside; however, if approached by a lone hunter instead of a wolf pack, musk-ox commonly stand their ground in a single defensive line. If the intruder gets too close, the herd bull or an old cow is apt to charge in an attempt to trample and gore their enemy.

The breeding season generally begins in August and runs into September. Fights for breeding rights are common and at times these confrontations between rutting bulls turn savage. Vicious head-butting clashes may last for an hour or more with the grunting rivals straining to knock their foes down and hook them with their flared horns. Death may result although many of these ground-jarring

HOW TO MEASURE AND SCORE BIG-GAME TROPHIES

POPE AND YOUNG CLUB
NORTH AMERICAN BIG GAME TROPHY SCORING FORM

BOWHUNTER COMPETITION

MUSKOX

Official Scoring
System of the Boone
and Crockett Club

KIND OF MUSKOX _____

SEX _____

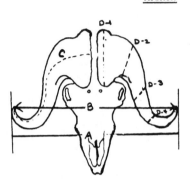

SEE OTHER SIDE FOR INSTRUCTIONS	Supplementary Data	Column 1	Column 2	Column 3
		Right Horn	Left Horn	Difference
A. Greatest Spread				
B. Tip to Tip Spread				
C. Length of Horn				
D-1. Width of Boss				
D-2. Width at First Quarter				
D-3. Circumference at Second Quarter				
D-4. Circumference at Third Quarter				
TOTALS				

ADD	Column 1		Exact locality where killed	
	Column 2		Date killed	By whom killed
	TOTAL		Present owner	
SUBTRACT Column 3			Address	
	FINAL SCORE		Guide's Name and Address	
			Remarks: (Mention any abnormalities)	

I certify that I have measured the above trophy on _____ 19 _____
at (address)_____City _____
State _____ Zip Code _____ and that these measurements and data are, to the
best of my knowledge and belief, made in accordance with the instructions given.

Witness: _____ Signature _____
Pope & Young Club Official Measurer

Muskox

INSTRUCTIONS

All measurements must be made with a flexible steel tape to the nearest one-eighth of an inch. Wherever it is necessary to change direction of measurement, mark a control point and swing tape at this point. To simplify addition, please enter fractional figures in eighths.

Official measurements cannot be taken for at least sixty days after the animal was killed.

Please submit photographs **of trophy front and sides.**

Supplementary Data measurements indicate conformation of the trophy. None of the figures in Lines A and B are to be included in the score. Evaluation of conformation is a matter of personal preference.

A. Greatest Spread measured between perpendiculars at right angles to the center line of the skull.

B. Tip to Tip Spread measured between tips of horns.

C. Length of Horn measured from inner edge at center of boss on outer curve to a point in line with tip.

D-1. Width of Boss — best measured with calipers at greatest width of base. If calipers are unavailable, use steel tape between perpendiculars.

D-2-3-4. Divide measurement C of LONGER horn by four, mark BOTH horns at these quarters even though other horn is shorter, measure width at D-2 and circumferences at D-3 and D-4.

Photographs: All entries must include photographs of the tropy. A right side, left side and front view photograph will be required for all antlers, horns and skulls. A photograph of the entire animal is requested if at all possible.

Drying Period: To be eligible for entry in the Pope & Young Records, a trophy must first have been stored under normal room temperature and humidity for at least 60 consecutive days. No trophy will be considered which has in any way been altered from its natural state.

THIS SCORING FORM MUST BE ACCOMPANIED BY A SIGNED **POPE & YOUNG** FAIR CHASE AFFIDAVIT AND A RECORDING FEE OF $10.00.

clashes end with the dominant bull simply chasing off his challenger.

Cows in heat are receptive for a period of about 24 hours and may be bred several times by the herd bull. If the initial servicing does not result in conception, the cows come into estrous several weeks later and the breeding ritual is repeated.

Calves are dropped the following May or June and most cows have single births. The newborns weigh about 30 pounds and are generally black in color. They can walk within a matter of hours and apparently have little trouble keeping up with their mother and the herd as they move about in search of food. Calves begin nursing immediately after birth and are grazing within a week or so. This diet of milk and solid food may continue throughout the calves' first year of life. Cows are quite tolerant of their young and quickly come to their defense in the event of any imminent danger.

Musk-oxen rely mainly on their keen sense of sight to warn of approaching enemies. On the flat, largely treeless terrain these animals favor, it is extremely difficult to get close to a herd without being detected. The animals' senses of hearing and smell are also reported to be well-developed. Musk-oxen are generally quiet animals, occasionally emitting cow-like sounds. Hunters in search of musk-oxen seldom bother looking for sign and concentrate on sighting the animals themselves. Tracks and droppings are quite similar to those left by domestic cattle; however, musk-oxen are visible animals and may be sighted at great distances across open tundras.

Wolf packs and an occasional bear are the musk-oxen's only natural enemies and adult animals may live into their second decade before succumbing to old age. Native hunters seeking a supply of winter meat and trophy hunters looking to add a unique trophy to their collection take a limited, closely regulated toll of musk-ox each year when the herds are culled to avoid habitat destruction and potential overbrowsing.

Effective Bowhunting Techniques

The most common modern bowhunting method

involves flying to some remote Eskimo camp and proceeding across frozen expanses of tundra by snow machine to areas known to contain herds of musk-oxen. Once the animals are sighted, the hunter and his guide approach, slipping within range or pressuring the animals until they form a defensive line or circle. When the herd bull is located it's usually a matter of getting close enough to make an effective shot without being charged and gored. For safety reasons, a rifle is usually carried by a guide to back up and protect the bowhunter.

The shooting of a musk-oxen is often somewhat tricky but rather anticlimatic. The animals typically face their enemies and present a less than ideal bow shot. Their dense coats and heavy bones can stop a broadhead short of the vitals. Consequently, care must be taken to ease into position for a killing shot, preferably at a stationary broadside animal. This may be accomplished when the guide can attract a bull's attention while the shooter moves off to one side to release his arrow.

Bulky clothing, sub-zero temperatures and milling musk-oxen in the herd—plus the natural excitement of the moment—can impede or adversely affect the bowhunter's performance. Regardless, a well-placed arrow will dispatch the biggest bulls within a brief period of time. No bowhunter should be bashful about shooting additional insurance arrows to facilitate a quick, humane kill.

Hunting musk-oxen with a bow and arrow is an expensive, time-consuming, physically demanding undertaking for most non-Alaskan, non-Canadian bowhunters. Licenses—often limited—and guide fees generally run high and are over and above transportation costs to and from the hunting camp. Such bowhunts often involve several thousand dollars. Not surprisingly, only 17 musk-oxen have been entered in the Pope and Young records through the Club's 14th recording period which ended December 31, 1984.

Trophy Recognition

As previously noted, both bulls and cows have horns; however, the musk-ox bull is easily recognizable by a solid boss or casque of horn across the frontal portion of the skull. The smaller horns of the females are generally divided by a clump of forehead hair.

The World Record musk-ox was shot by Ron Kolpin in 1981 on a hunt in Canada's Northwest Territories. The bull's right horn measures 26-3/8 inches and the left horn is 28-2/8 inches. The greatest spread is an even 27 inches. The top musk-ox has an official score of 108-4/8. To qualify for the records a musk-ox must score at least 65 inches.

Pronghorn . . . Prairie Survivor

20

The pronghorn antelope, *(Antilocapra americana)*, that handsome and graceful speedster of the western prairies, is a unique animal.

In the first place, it's the last survivor in a family of North American animals that began its long evolutionary process several million years ago. Second, it's partially misnamed inasmuch as it is not a true antelope; however, the official name "pronghorn" is both descriptive and acccurate since it reportedly is the only pronged horn, antelope-type animal in the world. Third, although nearly extinct early in this century, the species now thrives in desolate areas of the open country west of the Mississippi although fossils prove its prehistoric range once included certain areas of the Midwest. Fourth, it is undoubtedly the fastest animal in North America, quite capable of reaching—and exceeding—the 55 MPH speed limit posted on our nation's highways. Finally, it is a truly prized American big game trophy that is as much a part of the Western landscape as sagebrush and mountains.

Pronghorn bucks are deceptively small, sturdy animals, standing only about 36-40 inches at the shoulder and weighing perhaps slightly more than 100 pounds on the average. Does are somewhat smaller. Both sexes may have horns, although generally the does' headgear is short and unimpressive, while the trophy bucks have long, pronged horns that have been known to reach as much as 20 inches in length. Grown on permanent inner cores, the ebony-colored outer horn shells are shed annually.

Many people consider the pronghorn to be one of the most beautiful American big game species. The black-masked bucks have distinctive markings that include white underjaws and banded throats of buff and white bars. A short, black, neck mane is apparent on close examination. Rich brown upper bodies gradually fade to tan and then abruptly to white halfway down each side. Does are similarly colored except for the lighter faces. Both bucks and does have white rumps with erectile hairs that they use in communicating. If alarmed, pronghorns flare their rump hairs as a danger signal to herd members in the area. On a bright, sunny day this signal is visible for a mile or more when flashed and will alert any pronghorn within sight.

The pronghorns' eyesight is legendary, frequently compared to that of a man looking through 8X binoculars. Whether this comparison is valid or not, there is no doubt few animals can match them in the vision department. Their bulging eyes, strategically placed on the sides of their heads, can detect movement ahead, to either side and even **behind** them. Combine this highly developed sense of sight with sheer speed and a gregarious nature and you can understand why a hunter has his work cut out for him when he sets out to stalk within good bow range of antelope.

Certainly a pronghorn's senses of smell and hearing are also well-developed; however, they do not pose insurmountable problems to most hunters. The key is overcoming the sense of sight and letting everything else take care of itself. More about this later in the discussion of hunting techniques.

Today's antelope hunter may legally try for a trophy in a dozen or so Western states with Wyoming attracting the most attention since more pronghorns are found there than any other locale. The herds in Wyoming and elsewhere have made a remarkable comeback from the brink of extinction. Earlier this century it was estimated only 12,000 animals were left. By the 1980s, thanks to restocking programs, habitat restoration and closely regulated seasons and bag limits, the number of antelope had topped the 500,000 mark.

Pronghorns commonly feed on common prairie grasses and brush including sage, juniper, greasewood, rabbitbrush and bitterbrush. Despite what some ranchers believe, pronghorns do not directly compete with livestock for feed since antelope favor forage often ignored by sheep and cattle. But antelope can and do develop a taste for alfalfa and grain crops.

Predators—especially coyotes and bobcats—take a modest annual toll and a few young pronghorns fall prey to eagles each year. In some areas where major highways cut through pronghorn country motor vehicles pose a danger and road kills are not uncommon. But it is Mother Nature herself that stands as the biggest threat to antelope. When deep, heavy snows shroud the prairies, starvation often follows on the heels of the howling blizzards which pile deep drifts over life-sustaining forage. There is some evidence which suggests that hard winters claim a surprising number of mature, trophy-class bucks. The reason cited is the big bucks are generally the old animals and often are worn down by frenzied breeding activity the preceding fall. Regardless, pronghorns are short-lived animals, seldom living beyond eight or nine years of age.

The rut normally takes place in September and October, depending on the particular location of the herds. Bucks grow restless and display mood shifts which range from comical antics to open hostility. Some fights result, but most of these contests are horn-rattling shoving matches between rivals that do not result in serious injuries to the combatants.

At the onset of the rut, the bucks begin gathering harems of does. Some groups are small with only a handful of animals while others may have 12 to 15 females. Bucks become insanely jealous and constantly guard against rivals attempting to approach and lure does from the harem. Naturally, the larger the harem the more difficult it is to watch over the animals. Quite often a buck can run himself to the point of exhaustion protecting his does.

Some researchers say that unlike deer the female antelope have only a single receptive period each year when conception is possible. Does not bred at this time will have no fawns the following May or June. Like deer, however, young does generally give birth to a single fawn while older females frequently have twins. A few does have triple births.

Fawns are leggy, grayish versions of their parents, almost odorless at birth and weighing only a few pounds and standing about a foot and a half at the shoulder. Development is swift, however, and within a matter of days the gangly youngsters can be racing across the prairie at speeds of 20 to 25 miles per hour. By the end of the first two weeks of life the fawns' white rump patches are evident and used in signaling.

Antelope, like deer, will sometimes snort when boogered, emitting high, sharp blasts of air through their nostrils. Does and fawns may bleat on occasion and rutting bucks may grunt. Wounded bucks sometimes utter low, gutteral blatts.

Pronghorns are extremely visible animals when standing or moving on the open prairies. Consequently, locating sign is not so important as with some other species. There's seldom any need to spend time looking for fresh tracks, droppings, slides or scrapes when the same time spent with a good pair of binoculars would likely locate the distant animals themselves. Fresh sign, of course, can help the hunter locate an ambush site near water holes, fence crossings or scrapes.

Antelope tracks are slightly smaller but quite similar to those left by deer; however, pronghorns have no dewclaws and simply leave impressions made by the two halves of each hoof. Actually, it takes a good, experienced tracker to distinguish subtle differences in sign left by the two species. Droppings are likewise similar to deer pellets.

Knowledgeable hunters locate scrapes—pawed areas where the animals urinate and defecate—to insure the proper identification of antelope tracks and droppings. Some even establish blinds nearby since the animals making such scrapes frequently visit them. The only major problem with this tactic is found in the fact the antelope may range over wide areas of their territory and may have many such scrapes which they visit on a regular basis.

A few hunters position themselves in cover near "slides" along fencelines. Much has been written about the pronghorns' reluctance to jump fences. While they can and do leap these obstacles on occasion, they commonly try to go around or under. Favorite fence-crossing locations may be recognized by shallow depressions worn in the prairie beneath the stands of barbed wire and telltale back hairs snagged in the barbs. Such slide areas may produce shooting for the concealed hunter who has the patience to wait for herds or individual animals crossing from one section of their range to another.

Effective Bowhunting Techniques

There is no question the most effective antelope hunting method is to locate a stand near a stock tank or water hole. Much pronghorn country is arid with only handfuls of locations where life-sustaining water is found. Pronghorns, like other wildlife and livestock sharing their range, know these locations and make regular visits to drink. A waiting hunter can often get a short-range shot as the animals visit the site.

Since trees are often few and far apart in antelope country, bowhunters looking to hunt from elevated stands have a limited choice of options. Windmills and haystacks are two realistic possibilities and each can be quite effective since pronghorns don't expect danger from above. Sudden or undue movements may draw attention to a hunter on an elevated perch; however, pronghorns often ignore silhouetted bowhunters standing on windmill platforms or crossbeams. And some keen-eyed antelope are arrowed each season by bowhunters who have attached portable tree stands to the legs of windmills just above eye level!

Pit blinds are perhaps the most popular water hole ploy, but antelope nervously shy away from thick stands of natural cover which could conceal predators. Consequently, carefully dug pits or scooped out depressions—generally ringed by camo netting, sagebrush or another common prairie shrub—are ideal. Shooting lanes in the netting or brush allow the bowhunter to draw and release his arrow without standing. Toaster tactics—pop up and shoot—are futile under normal circumstances. Pits should be dug and blinds constructed well in advance of the season. This allows suspicious antelope to get used to the man-made structures.

Antelope are conscious of their vulnerability when approaching a watering site. They often stand nearby for long periods of time and carefully scan the surrounding area. When the animals finally approach, they commonly cover the last few yards alertly but quickly, often running to the water's edge where they'll take time for another brief look before lowering their heads to drink. Even then pronghorns frequently jerk back to attention as if trying to capture a lurking predator in the act of moving. Only when they're satisfied all's well will pronghorns drink their fill—usually taking only a matter of seconds—and then promptly depart the area.

It is when the buck has its muzzle in the water or lowered to feed that he is most vulnerable to a well-placed arrow. Relaxed, his full attention is briefly focused on drinking or eating. This is the ideal bowhunting shot. Hunters who have tried their luck shooting at approaching or departing antelope can sadly attest to the animals' lightning reflexes and uncanny arrow-dodging ability.

Much of a sit-and-wait hunter's time is spent doing just that, often from dawn to dusk; therefore, it is imperative that comfort be a major consideration. A foam cushion, full canteen and snacks, reading material—even plastic bags for human waste—are part of any successful pronghorn hunter's pack. Some wise bowhunters even include a sun screen.

Stalking antelope is quite difficult but possible and each season patient hunters are able to ease within bow range of feeding or bedded animals. Stalkers expect to spend considerable time on their stomachs or hands and knees (some serious stalkers wear elbow and knee pads on each trip afield). Durable yet lightweight and quiet clothing and footwear is preferred. Stalking tactics are most successful in more rugged or broken country where coulees, arroyos and rolling terrain help neutralize the pronghorns' amazing eyesight. Regardless, it takes a patient stalker—and more than a smidgen of luck—to fill an antelope tag by this method. Most stalks are almost sure to end in frustration with the hunter watching the white rumps of his intended targets disappearing into the far distance.But such is the challenge—and excitement—of stalking antelope.

Note: Much prime pronghorn country is also rattlesnake country. Any bowhunter crawling on his hands and knees through sage, avoiding prickly pear clumps while watching for snakes and attempting to remain unseen, truly has his work cut out for him. Combine this with a merciless late summer sun, rocky terrain that sprouts all sorts of sticky, spiny plant growth and a reader gets some idea of what stalking pronghorns is all about.

Antelope are naturally curious, nervous animals. Rifle hunters often relate tales of how animals are lured within range by "flagging"—waving a hat, handkerchief or bandanna above some hiding spot. Such tactics rarely pay off for the bowhunter since pronghorns seldom approach close enough for a good bow shot and those that do are already nervously alert. Additionally, it's much easier to fire a rifle from a prone position. A bowhunter who tries to shoot while prone—or one who jumps up from concealment in hopes of getting a shot—is almost certain to fail.

Regardless, one effective way to take advantage of an antelope's innate curiosity is by decoying. American Indians once donned hides and horned capes to lure animals or to ease within shooting range; the same methods can work today. While it would be foolhardy and dangerous to attempt such a gambit during the firearms season, some bowhunters create lifelike, full-size, three dimensional pronghorn decoys or silhouettes and take cover nearby. This ploy is especially effective during the rut and either a buck or doe decoy will work. Sex-hungry bucks are anxious to collect does for their harems and may come on the run to a doe decoy to add another mate. A buck decoy can attract a real-life rival who believes a stranger is attempting to horn in and take over his territory.

Driving antelope has been known to work under certain conditions. One or more standers may conceal themselves near a fenceline or near an opening in some natural barrier. Other hunters show themselves to the antelope and try to move the animals in the direction of their waiting companions. A big drawback to this tactic is that pronghorns have minds of their own and may not go where drivers want them to. Also, driven animals may be spooked or alert to danger. Shots at trotting or running game are far from ideal since the risk of wounding is great.

Whatever hunting method is chosen, care should be given to camouflaging face, hands, body and equipment. Good binoculars are considered essential by most pronghorn hunters, as is a well-honed skinning knife. All movements, even those made by a stalking bowhunter, must be kept to a minimum. Human odor, especially at close range, will disturb and alert antelope although few react as explosively as deer. Some bowhunters use cover-up or masking scents as an insurance policy against discovery. Others simply locate their stands where prevailing prairie winds blow away from water holes or ambush sites. Stalking hunters are advised to keep the wind in their faces.

Unlike deer, pronghorns are not nocturnal and antelope bands may be on the move at any time of the day and night. They can be counted on to make at least one visit to a favorite watering site during daylight hours unless passing rain storms make water available elsewhere. However, there is evidence that in heavily hunted arid areas where water holes and tanks may be practically ringed by hopeful hunters, pronghorns quickly learn to wait and water under the protective curtain of darkness.

Such adaptability is survival insurance.

Antelope are surprisingly durable animals despite their small stature and delicate appearance. A bad hit spells trouble since wounded pronghorns have amazing reserve and can keep on the go for miles. In most antelope country it's hard—if not impossible—to slip within range of a marginly hit animal to get in a clean, killing shot with a second arrow. Consequently, every effort possible must be made to make the first shot count.

A bowhunter should always try for a lung shot on antelope. Broadside or quartering away shots are best. As previously noted, the best time to release an arrow is when the animal is in a drinking or feeding position with its head down.

Any hunting bow pulling 50 pounds or more will be effective on pronghorns. Broadheads—if razor sharp—often drive an arrow completely through these small targets. Once the hit is made, it's important for the shooter to keep the animal in sight. Often a bowhunter will see the antelope drop or bed down and pinpointing this location is important in the recovery process. Pronghorn blood trails are frequently skimpy and tracks may be obliterated by other animals in the herd. A hunter who keeps an arrowed antelope in view has a head start at putting his tag on the animal. Surprisingly, knee-high sage, dry washes and even prairie grass can sometimes swallow up a downed trophy, making quick recovery difficult. In typical bowhunting weather, a hunter should make every effort to promptly recover his animal, field dress it and get the carcass out of the hot sun where cooling is possible. A sprinkling of pepper or a porous game bag can discourage the ever-present flies. The bag will also help to protect the meat from dust or dirt during the trip back to camp or to the nearest food processing locker.

Antelope meat is praised by some and panned by others. Proper field care goes a long way toward enhancing the meat's flavor and there is no question that the meat is quite edible. Like deer, it is lean and quite dry. Suet should be added to meat being ground into antelope patties.

Pronghorns make especially attractive mounts. In warm or hot weather immediate attention must be paid to the skinning and caping procedure to prevent hair slippage or spoilage. Bowhunters familiar with the caping procedure can do the job and preserve the skin with a liberal application of salt. Others may wish to have a food processor or taxidermist cape their trophy; they gladly pay the modest fee frequently charged for this service. Some guides or outfitters offer trophy care as part of the hunt package. Regardless, a well-mounted pronghorn is a welcome addition to any bowhunter's home or office and often serves as a lasting memento of a hard-earned trophy.

Note: Antelope hair is stiff and brittle. Animals bound for the taxidermist should be carried rather than dragged to avoid rubbed patches which may spoil a cape.

Bowhunters living in or near good antelope country often opt to try the do-it-yourself hunting method—and many enjoy fair to good success. The same may be said of out-of-staters who have the knowledge and time needed to hunt pronghorns. Others prefer to book a pronghorn hunt with an experienced guide or outfitter who will have an area scouted and a pit blind waiting. Either way, proper planning is a key to a successful trip.

Finding a good place to hunt is an increasingly difficult task for most people. Government-owned land such as that under the control of the Bureau of Land Management or National Grasslands where antelope hunting is permitted often is crowded with hopefuls who seek out prime areas, especially water holes. There's nothing more discouraging than having someone spoil a long stalk or arrive at the remote water hole found on a pre-season scouting trip to find some claim jumper in your carefully constructed blind. Such problems are not uncommon on public lands.

Consequently, many bowhunters seek out private ranchlands where they can obtain permission to hunt—or perhaps pay a modest trespass fee for the privilege. Hunting behind locked gates on private land certainly has some advantages, not the least of which is more privacy than most public land. The kicker is obtaining a landowner's permission to hunt

POPE & YOUNG CLUB
NORTH AMERICAN BIG GAME TROPHY SCORING FORM
BOWHUNTING

P & Y Records Office
1804 Borah
Moscow, ID 83843

BIG GAME   RECORDS

PRONGHORN

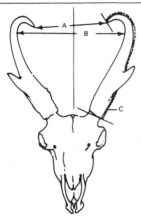

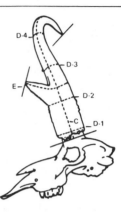

SEE OTHER SIDE FOR INSTRUCTIONS		Supplementary Data	Column 1	Column 2	Column 3
			Right Horn	Left Horn	Difference
A.	Tip to Tip Spread				
B.	Inside Spread of Main Beams		▨	▨	▨
	If Inside Spread of Main Beams exceeds longer horn length, enter difference.		▨	▨	
C.	Length of Horn				
D-1.	Circumference of Base				
D-2.	Circumference at First Quarter	(this measurement taken at _____ inches from base)			
D-3.	Circumference at Second Quarter	(this measurement taken at _____ inches from base)			
D-4.	Circumference at Third Quarter	(this measurement taken at _____ inches from base)			
E.	Length of Prong				
	TOTALS				

ADD	Column 1		Exact locality where killed	(County)	(State)
	Column 2		Date killed	By whom killed	
	Total		Present owner		
SUBTRACT Column 3			Address		
FINAL SCORE			Guide's Name and Address		

Remarks: (Mention any abnormalities)

I certify that I have measured the above trophy on _____ 19 _____
at (address) _____ City _____
State _____ Zip Code _____ and that these measurements and data are, to the best
of my knowledge and belief, made in accordance with the instructions given.

Witness: _____ Signature _____
(To Measurer's Signature)

Pope & Young Club Official Measurer

MEASURER (Print) _____

ADDRESS _____

CITY _____ STATE _____ ZIP

INSTRUCTIONS

All measurements must be made with a flexible steel tape or measuring cable to the nearest one-eighth of an inch. Wherever it is necessary to change direction of measurement, mark a control point and swing tape at this point. To simplify addition, please enter fractional figures in eighths.

Official measurements cannot be taken for at least sixty days after the animal was killed. **Please submit photographs**, FRONT, RIGHT AND LEFT SIDES are required.

Supplementary Data measurements indicate conformation of the trophy. None of the figures in Lines A and B are to be included in the score. Evaluation of conformation is a matter of personal preference.

A. Tip to Tip Spread measured between tip of horns.

B. Inside Spread of Main Beams measured at right angles to the center line of the skull at widest point between main beams.

C. Length of horn is measured on the outside curve, so the line taken will vary with different heads, depending on the direction of the curvature. Measure along the center of the outer curve from tip of horn to a point in line with the lowest edge of the base.

D-1 Measure around base of horn at right angles to long axis. Tape must be in contact with the lowest circumference of the horn in which there are no serrations.

D-2-3-4. Divide measurement of LONGER horn by four, mark BOTH horns at these quarters even though one horn is shorter, and measure circumferences at these marks. If any portion of the prong occurs at D-3, take this measurement immediately <u>above</u> prong. Should D-2 land on the swelling of the prong, take <u>D-2</u> measurement <u>immediately below</u> swelling of prong.

E- Length of Prong — Measure from the tip of the prong along the upper edge of the outer curve to the horn; thence, around the horn to a point at the rear of the horn where a straight edge across the back of both horns touches the horn. This measurement around the horn from the base of the prong should be taken at right angles to the long axis of the horn.

*Note measurement of each quarter from base (i.e. longest horn = 16'' — quarters should be noted as D-2 =4, D-3 = 8, D-4 = 12.) If adjustments are made for swelling of prong on D-2 or D-3 measurement, note these adjustments in ''remarks'' section.

Photographs: All entries must include photographs of the trophy. A right side, left side and front view photograph will be required for all antlers, horns and skulls. A photograph of the entire animal is requested if at all possible.

Drying Period: To be eligible for entry in the Pope & Young Records, a trophy must first have been stored under normal room temperature and humidity for at least 60 consecutive days. No trophy will be considered which has in any way been altered from its natural state.

THIS SCORING FORM MUST BE ACCOMPANIED BY A FULLY COMPLETED AND SIGNED POPE & YOUNG FAIR CHASE AFFIDAVIT PLUS A RECORDING FEE OF $25.00.

or coming up with the money to secure hunting rights for the day, week or season.

Once such a spot is located, scouting is a must. Topo maps may be beneficial and save valuable time. Regardless, scouting is best accomplished by driving back roads, walking promising terrain and glassing the herds of pronghorns encountered along the way. Animals seen watering at a certain location will likely be back the following day. Also, feeding or bedded animals will generally remain in the vicinity unless harassed. Ravines, rolling hills and brush that could offer concealment for stalking must be noted. Usually a full day or two will be needed to locate the animals and find a suitable ambush site. The remainder of the hunting time may be spent trying to collect a suitable trophy.

Bowhunters who enlist the services of a knowledgeable, qualified guide frequently enjoy good to excellent success. Most often the hunters arrive in a fully equipped camp located on private land in the heart of prime pronghorn country. Pit blinds or similar stands are already constructed and waiting for the bowhunter. All he does is pay the fee, take his place in the stand and wait for action. This method is obviously more expensive than that employed by do-it-yourself hunters; however, it is ideal for the hunter with limited time. Today some guides and outfitters specialize in antelope bowhunts and their clients enjoy excellent annual success. Some camps boast 100% shooting and nearly as impressive success percentages.

The where-to-go sections and advertising pages of most major hunting magazines will give any bowhunter interested in booking a guided hunt numerous leads. Letters or telephone calls—or both—can secure details. Fish and game departments will be able to provide details concerning license fees, season dates, bag limits and game laws. Planning for the hunt should begin a full year in advance.

Practice for antelope hunting should concentrate on accuracy and range estimation. Sight shooters sitting at water holes may choose to pace off various yardages to prominent natural landmarks (the water's edge, a salt block left for cattle, a rock or boulder, a clump of sage, etc.) or to establish their own markers as they construct their stand. A rangefinder comes in handy since such distances can be noted from the blind without needless activity which might alert nearby animals.

Shots taken from crouching, sitting or kneeling positions are common and would-be pronghorn hunters should practice the unorthodox shots they're apt to encounter. Also, it's a good idea to get used to shooting through small openings in brush, typical of pit hunters, or down at sharp angles if a windmill stand is planned. Long, "Hail Mary" shots are attempted each season and pronghorns have been killed by arrows at over 100 yards; however, such kills are pure luck and should not be attempted. Normally the result of such indiscriminate arrow-flinging is a miss or—far worse—a poor hit. Most pronghorns tagged by bowhunters are shot at 30 yards or less.

Another possibility is calling antelope, a practice tried by a handful of bowhunters each season. Innately curious, pronghorns have been coaxed into range by soft bleats and other noises designed to attract their attention. The biggest problem with this tactic is the approaching animal is suspiciously alert, looking for the source of the sound. This creates a less than ideal bowhunting shot.

Trophy Recognition

Antelope horns often appear larger than they really are. Much of this has to do with the fact that pronghorns aren't big animals to start with and even an average buck carries black horns that boast well-developed prongs and project well above the ears. Bowhunters wanting to collect a truly outstanding record book animal should keep the following points in mind:

First, antelope with 15-inch or better horns are truly exceptional trophies. Most Pope and Young candidates have horns at least a foot long. Heavy bases, huge prongs and horn mass quickly add to the overall score.

Second, look for horns that are at least as long

and the inside spread 10 3/8 inches.

The present minimum score for pronghorn antelope is 64. In recent years pronghorns have been second only to whitetail deer in numbers submitted for trophy recognition by the Pope and Young Club.

Judd Cooney's World Record

as the buck's face, have apparent thickness and very long prongs. Exceptionally wide spreads will likely deduct from the overall score.

Third, remember that true trophy pronghorns carry headgear that will "leap out at you." You'll see the animal and immediately **know** you're looking at something special.

Two pronghorns—each with identical Pope and Young scores of 85 0/8—share the World Record title. Back in 1958 Archie Malm shot a huge antelope while hunting near Raleigh, North Dakota. The buck's right horn is 15 1/8 inches long and the left horn 15 inches even. The circumference at the right base is 6 7/8 inches and the left base tapes 6 5/8 inches. The inside spread is 12 6/8. This record endured for many seasons. Then, in 1983, Judd Cooney arrowed an antelope in Moffat County, Colorado that tied the long-standing mark. Cooney's pronghorn has a right horn that is 17 2/8 inches long and a left horn only one-eighth of an inch shorter. Each basal circumference is 6 4/8 inches

<u>Rocky Mountain Goat . . .</u> Peakmaster

21

If bighorn sheep rams are "Kings of the Crags," Rocky Mountain goats deserve the title "Princes of the Peaks." Perhaps no other animal is as comfortable and at ease on the dizzying pinnacles as these denizens of high, bleak places.

Like pronghorn antelope, the showy white Rocky Mountain goat *(Oreamnos montanus)* is unique to North American big game; he is most closely related to the antelope of the Old World. Scientists believe ancestors of these animals made their way to this continent over half a million years ago by crossing the Bering Land Bridge.

Ranging southward from Alaska into the Rocky Mountain states, prehistoric goats soon established themselves among the jagged peaks. Here their descendents generally continue to dwell, living their lives in relative solitude within a home area, often above timberline, of perhaps ten to twelve miles or less. Severe weather and a lack of adequate food may prompt travel to a more desirable location; however, chances are excellent that goats sighted on a remote cliff one year will be located not far away the next season.

Because of the high, remote terrain they favor, mountain goats are one species that escapes the pressures of an ever-expanding human population. Once shot for meat by some Indians and mountain men who called them "white buffalo," goats today are the targets of big game hunters seeking to add a "different" kind of trophy to their collection. Modern goat populations are considered healthy, with British Columbia and Alaska ranking one-two in numbers of animals.

Mountain goats are striking, hump-shouldered animals with long, nearly pure-white coats and coal-black horns, hooves, eyes and noses. The bearded adults stand three feet or more at the shoulder and stretch as much as six feet in length. Weights of 250 to 300 pounds are not uncommon, with an occasional 400-pounder being tagged. Horns, like beards, are present in both sexes and may approach a foot in length.

Goats do not shed their horns and their age may be determined by counting the distinct annual growth rings on each horn and adding one and one-half years. "Spearlike" and "dagger-shaped" are adjectives frequently used to describe a goat's horns and the terms are appropriate. The pointed, slightly sweeping horns are used for defense only on rare occasions; most commonly, a goat will seek to escape its enemies by clambering to safety among the narrow ledges and steep precipices of his mountain home.

Hooves are comparatively small and nearly square, padded with a spongy, rounded material that grips rocks and allows the animals to negotiate the most rugged mountain terrain imaginable.

Goats typically feed on lichens and mountain mosses as well as the available alpine grasses. When winter snows bury the canyon slopes, they do considerable browsing, nibbling at bushes and trees. Goats also seek out higher windswept slopes where vegetation has been exposed. Their fleecy, luxuriant winter coats protect them from bitter mountain winds.

Goat droppings are easily confused with deer and sheep scat. The animals' square-shaped hoofprints are unique but often difficult to find in the high country's rocky terrain. Clumps of hair, snagged on bushes and rocks, offer evidence of goats in the vicinity. Goats commonly use the same bedding areas and these odorous sites are likely to be marked with an abundance of droppings.

Goats depend mainly on their extremely keen eyesight to pick out potential enemies. But like most animals, goats seem to have a difficult time recognizing stationary objects at close ranges. Hearing is well-developed but the sounds of constant wind and the clattering of dislodged rocks are commonplace in the high peaks. Goats possess a good sense of smell and eddying winds can alert goats to the approach of an intruder.

The breeding season for mountain goats is late in the year, typically in November and December. Males, after a summer and fall of solitude, begin seeking out receptive females. Although fighting among breeding billies is uncommon, bluffing and posturing are typical when rivals meet. Rutting billies have been observed rubbing their heads on bushes and trees to mark them with scent from a gland located on the back of each horn.

Nannies begin to breed between their second and third years and have more single than multiple births. Kids are born in May or June, most often in extremely remote and rugged terrain. At birth the goats are perhaps a foot high and weigh six or seven pounds. Each has two small button like bumps on the head where small horns soon sprout. The kids are able to follow their mother almost immediately and develop very quickly. Much of their time is spent cavorting among the rocks while the older animals bed nearby, content to spend hours at a time doing nothing more strenuous than chewing their cuds.

Within a couple of months the kids are weaned and fairly independent; however, bands of nannies and kids often stay together for company until birthing time the following spring. It is common to find family groups of kids, yearlings and nannies at elevations lower than the bachelor billies.

Youngsters often bleat, much like domestic sheep, but adults seldom make any sound other than an occasional grunt.

Natural enemies are few although eagles, wolves, mountain lions and—on rare occasions—a bear may kill and eat a kid. Avalanches and falls may claim a hapless animal, but mountain goats frequently live into their early to mid-teens.

Effective Hunting Techniques

There is no question the best bowhunting method is to get above a feeding or bedded goat and ease down to within good range. Because of their lofty domain, goats do not expect any danger from above and spend considerable time surveying the lower slopes for any hint of danger.

A bowhunter with iron legs and leather lungs who is capable of climbing above his quarry can often work downslope and get a close shot at a feeding or resting animal. Even rocks dislodged by a careless step seldom draw a sidelong glance from the goats since such sounds are common and natural in the terrain above timberline. Of course, getting above unsuspecting animals and into position for a shot is easier said than accomplished. Simply put, a successful hunter must often be in excellent physical condition to collect his intended trophy.

Because of their white coats, goats are not especially difficult to locate in the late summer and early fall seasons. As indicated, getting to them is another matter. Good binoculars or a spotting scope are almost mandatory, not only for locating goats but for trophy evaluation and for planning a suitable approach.

Goats are not nocturnal animals. They typically rise early and feed until midday. Then they seek a resting spot with a good view of the mountainside below them; once bedded, they chew their cud contentedly for several hours. Feeding activity usually resumes in the late afternoon and continues until dark when the animals bed down for the night. Goats dislike rain and wet weather may disrupt their daily feeding pattern.

When a distant goat is spotted, chances are good he'll still be in the immediate area when the bowhunter finally works into position. The problem most bowhunters face is staying out of sight of the goat and locating the exact spot he was last seen. It's essential that a careful study of the terrain be made and recognizable landmarks noted mentally before any stalk is attempted.

Some bowhunters work in two-man teams with one hunter keeping the animal in view across a canyon while his buddy circles and attempts the stalk. This can be effective since one person always keeps the goat in sight. The spotter can give pre-determined signals to help the stalker work into position. In the stalk's final stages the spotter may choose to show himself to attract and hold the goat's attention while his partner closes the final few yards for the shot.

Driving goats is possible under certain conditions although the method is chancy and usually offers a poor target at rapidly walking or running animals. It works best where goat trails lead through some natural crossing. Hunters posted at such ambush sites can get shots at passing animals. Indian hunters once used this technique effectively. The technique is probably left buried in the past.

The final effective bowhunting method is to establish a blind near some natural salt or mineral lick. Such areas act as a magnet, attracting all nearby goats to an area where a patient, well-concealed hunter may have his vigil ultimately rewarded with a close-range shot. Waits near water also could pay off under certain circumstances as during an exceptionally dry year; however, throughout much goat range there is ample water to be found in the seeps, springs or rivulets created by melting snow.

Whenever possible, it's best to locate and stalk a single animal rather than a goat in a group. Since the biggest billies are usually loners by nature, this is seldom much of a problem although small bands of billies do hang together from time to time. The fewer eyes to worry about, the better.

Impatience is always one of the bowhunter's worst enemies. Goats are easy-going, slow-moving, phlegmatic animals that rarely exert themselves. It can be maddening to have a goat stand or lie only partially exposed within bow range for indeterminable periods of time. Minutes may drag like someone pouring cold sorghum and a hunter will wonder if the billy will ever move.

Some hunters have rolled, kicked or tossed rocks downslope in an attempt to get a goat to stand or move into position. Others have purposefully stepped into the open, allowing the goat to see them in hopes of getting a shot at the surprised animal before it bolts.

Goats in heavily hunted areas may bail out at the first glimpse of a nearby bowhunter. Others may stand and stare stupidly at the hunter, apparently incredulous that any enemy could get so close without being detected. Shots at running goats are quite risky. Goats are extremely tough animals and can be very difficult to put down. It's vital that the bowhunter drive a well-honed broadhead through the lungs to ensure a quick kill and recovery. Bows pulling at least 55 to 60 pounds are basic for goat hunters.

Recovering any arrow-hit goat can be difficult. Only a lucky spine shot will anchor an animal and a poor hit is always **trouble**. Even a hard-hit goat that is dead on its feet may cover considerable ground before dropping. And in the vertical terrain common to good goat country, "dropping" is sometimes an appropriate term. More than one goat hunter has watched sickly as his trophy disappeared over the rim of some chasm and cartwheeled hundreds of feet into the rocks below. Such falls can shatter the brittle horns and turn the carcass into pulp. But some goat carcasses have endured such tumbles completely intact with little or no sign of damage to the horns or cape.

Goat meat, especially that of older trophy-class animals, is not considered ideal table fare. It can be tough, stringy and strongly flavored. Consequently, many goats are caped out and packed back to camp along with any choice cuts of meat deemed worthy of saving.

Note: Blood stains should be removed from the

POPE AND YOUNG CLUB
NORTH AMERICAN BIG GAME TROPHY SCORING FORM

P & Y Records Office
1804 Borah
Moscow, ID 83843

BIG GAME   RECORDS

ROCKY MOUNTAIN GOAT

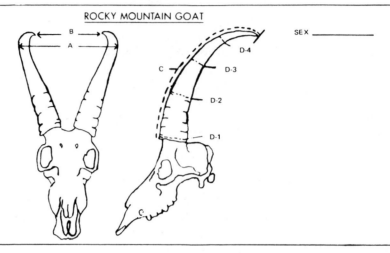

SEX _____

SEE OTHER SIDE FOR INSTRUCTIONS		Supplementary Data	Column 1	Column 2	Column 3
A	Greatest Spread		Right Horn	Left Horn	Difference
B	Tip to Tip Spread				
C	Length of Horn				
D-1	Circumference of Base				
D-2	Circumference at First Quarter (this measurement taken at _____ inches from base)				
D-3	Circumference at Second Quarter (this measurement taken at _____ inches from base)				
D-4	Circumference at Third Quarter (this measurement taken at _____ inches from base)				
TOTALS					

ADD	Column 1		Exact locality where killed	(County)	(State)
	Column 2		Date killed	By whom killed	
	TOTAL		Present owner		
SUBTRACT Column 3			Address		
FINAL SCORE			Guide's Name and Address		
			Remarks: (Mention any abnormalities)		

I certify that I have measured the above trophy on _____ 19 _____

at (address) _____ City _____

State _____ Zip Code _____ and that these measurements and data are, to the best

of my knowledge and belief, made in accordance with the instructions given.

Witness: _____ Signature _____

(To Measurer's Signature)

Pope & Young Club Official Measurer

_____

MEASURER (Print)

_____

ADDRESS

CITY   STATE   ZIP

INSTRUCTIONS

All measurements must be made with a flexible steel tape or measuring cable to the nearest one-eighth of an inch. Wherever it is necessary to change direction of measurement, mark a control point and swing tape at this point. To simplify addition, please enter fractional figures in eighths.

Official measurements cannot be taken for at least sixty days after the animal was killed.

Please submit photographs.

Supplementary Data measurements indicate conformation of the trophy. None of the figures in Lines A and B are to be included in the score. Evaluation of conformation is a matter of personal preference.

A. Greatest Spread measured between perpendiculars at right angles to the center line of the skull.

B. Tip to Tip Spread measured between tips of horns.

C. Length of Horn measured from lowest point in front over outer curve to a point in line with tip.

D-1 Circumference of Base measured at right angles to axis of horn. **DO NOT** follow irregular edge of horn. Circumference measurements must be taken with a steel tape.

D-2-3-4. Divide measurement C of LONGER horn by four, mark **BOTH** horns at these quarters even though other horn is shorter, and measure circumferences at these marks. Mark quarters by starting from base only.

Photographs: All entries must include photographs of the trophy. A right side, left side and front view photograph will be required for all antlers, horns and skulls. A photograph of the entire animal is requested if at all possible.

Drying Period: To be eligible for entry in the Pope & Young Records, a trophy must first have been stored under normal room temperature and humidity for at least 60 consecutive days. No trophy will be considered which has in any way been altered from its natural state.

THIS SCORING FORM MUST BE ACCOMPANIED BY A FULLY COMPLETED AND SIGNED POPE & YOUNG FAIR CHASE AFFIDAVIT PLUS A RECORDING FEE OF $25.00

cape as quickly as possible to avoid staining and to ensure a good mount. Cold mountain water can do the job quickly and efficiently.

Goat hunting should not be considered especially dangerous. The animals themselves, unless wounded and cornered by a zealous hunter, are not likely to pose any threat. Undoubtedly the greatest danger is found in the terrain where goats are typically found and in the exertion required to climb within shooting range. A bad fall could prove fatal. Also, an out-of-shape hunter runs the risk of suffering exhaustion—even a coronary—when he heads for goat country without proper preparation and conditioning.

Close-range shots are possible if the bowhunter has the time, patience and stalking skill. But goat hunting is typically a time-consuming, fairly expensive proposition, especially if the services of a guide or outfitter are required (guides are almost certainly a requirement for the out-of-state goat hunter). And each goat hunter should allow adequate time for his hunt. Goat hunting is seldom a walk-out-and-spot-'em-and-shoot-'em sport.

Bowhunters should practice shooting at extreme downhill angles from a kneeling or crouching position. Chances for a shot employing perfect stance and form are unlikely.

Trophy Recognition

Lone goats located during the hunting seasons in August, September and October are likely to be billies. Goats found in bunches are most often kids and nannies.

Nannies frequently grow longer horns than the billies; however, males typically have thicker, heavier horns and make the best trophies. Horn mass as well as length is vital in chalking up a good score.

Older goats—billies and nannies alike—may appear to have coats with a yellowish cast. Generally the old billies stand out as bigger, creamier animals and merit the most attention. Their horns are typically trophy material.

Sizing up a goat's horns is not the easiest job for a trophy seeker, especially a first-time goat hunter. However, there are several points to keep in mind in determining record book potential. First, average horns are eight to nine inches long and anything beyond this norm is likely to be trophy material if there is sufficient mass to go with the length. Second, horns should be at least three-fourths the length of the animal's face. Third, any horns that appear to be twice the length of the goat's ears are almost sure to be keepers.

The World Record Rocky Mountain goat was killed by Bob Haugen in 1971. Hunting Washington State's Kittitas County, Haugen arrowed a billy that scored 50-0/8. Its right horn is 10-2/8 inches long and 5-7/8 inches in circumference at the base. Its left horn measures 10-1/8 and 5-6/8, respectively.

Sheep . . . Mountain Monarchs

22

The bowhunter who sets his sights on taking any one of the North American wild sheep—Dall, Stone, Rocky Mountain bighorn and desert bighorn—certainly has his work cut out for him. But many of those who have accepted the challenge, especially those who have actually taken a wary ram with the bow and arrow, often claim there is no adventure quite like pursuing these mountain monarchs. The animals themselves are beautiful trophies and the hidden basins and hanging valleys where they live include some of the most spectacular alpine scenery on earth.

For the sake of convenience, this examination will first focus attention on the bighorn sheep and then on the two thinhorn varieties.

Bighorns

The hardy desert bighorn *(Ovis canadensis nelsoni)* of Mexico and the southwestern United States is the only sheep found in lower terrain. But what this sheep country lacks in altitude, it more than makes up for in hot, arid remoteness. Bowhunters generally agree desert sheep are the toughest to take. Licenses are commonly expensive and extremely difficult to come by. But obtaining a license is only the first hurdle to overcome. The desert bighorn's home range has been tabbed "the closest thing to hell on earth" with some justification. Also, although found in huntable numbers today, desert bighorns are not plentiful and simply locating the animals is no easy chore.

Consequently, it should not be surprising to learn that by the time the Pope and Young Club held its fourteenth biennial awards banquet in April 1985 in Bismarck, North Dakota, only **two** desert bighorns had been listed in the records, one from Arizona and the other from Nevada. Others have been taken, however, and it is expected this trophy category will grow in the years to come.

Desert bighorns are small-bodied, thin-necked versions of their mountain dwelling cousins. "Big" rams weigh less than 200 pounds and their horns are generally thinner and shorter. Regardless, the horns of the desert bighorn appear proportionally larger due to the lighter build of the animal wearing them.

Desert sheep have pale, buff-colored coats and light rump patches. Like other members of the wild sheep clan, they have exceptional eyesight and can easily discern a hunter moving two miles away. Favorite foods include common desert plants—even cactus! Natural mineral licks and water holes draw the animals like magnets and could be used as ambush sites by a patient bowhunter.

In the mountains, bighorn sheep are darker, white-rumped specimens. These blockier animals weigh up to 300 pounds and have heavier necks and horns than their desert-dwelling relatives. Ewes of both species are commonly 20 to 25 percent smaller than the rams.

Scientists believe bighorns were the first Asian sheep to cross to this continent when water in the Bering Sea was lowered during the last Ice Age. Theoretically, the animals gradually worked their way south through the Canadian Rockies into the mountainous regions of what would become the western United States. The explorer Coronado reported sighting bighorns during his sixteenth century quest for mythical riches.

Sheep apparently thrived before the coming of the white men, perhaps numbering as many as two million animals. Their original range extended eastward from the mountains into the Dakotas, Nebraska and parts of Texas. But when settlements were established and domesticated stock introduced near sheep country, the wild bighorns began to disappear. Market hunting certainly played a part; however, the competition from livestock, limitation of winter range, disease and similar problems prompted the decline. Today it is estimated that there are perhaps 20,000 bighorn sheep remaining.

Mature rams stand three to three and one-half feet at the shoulder and stretch five feet or more from brisket to rump. Their heavy horns are never shed. The horns, with obvious growth rings, sweep down and curl up, often obscuring an animal's vision. Broomed horns—those with broken tips—commonly result when the rams rub boulders and attempt to wear away the tips to increase their ability to see better to each side.

Bighorn sheep are diurnal animals and may be found moving to favorite feeding areas at first light. They typically feed for a few hours and then choose random beds to enjoy a period of rest and cud-chewing. They often feed briefly at mid-day and again for a longer period each evening before returning to favored bedding areas.

Sheep beds are smelly, easily recognizable depressions marked by mounds of scat. Bighorns use the same nighttime beds day after day—season after season—unless disturbed. These beds are commonly found at the base of rocky cliffs or on protected hillsides with a good view of the lower elevations.

While bighorns rely mainly on their phenomenal eyesight to warn them of approaching danger, they also have well-developed senses of smell and hearing. How they react to human scent and noises varies. If they've been pressured by other hunters,

they may bolt at the first hint of danger. At other times they may simply react with curiosity to the intruder. Regardless, the bowhunter should pay attention to wind direction and avoid unnatural noises when stalking sheep. It's unlikely the bighorns will think twice about rolling rocks dislodged by an approaching hunter—the sound of clattering rocks is common to the high country—but the sound of a human voice or the careless banging of equipment will instantly alert them.

The biggest bighorns are commonly solitary animals, ignoring others of their kind except during the breeding season in November. Groups of bachelor rams are also common; however, most bighorn groups will be comprised of ewes, lambs, yearlings and younger rams. During the days marking the onset of the rut, rams join the nursery groups and frequently engage in head-butting contests for breeding rights.

Wildlife photographers and movie makers have well documented these fights in which the combatants rear up, charge and slam horns together with bone-jarring force. The sound of the impact—a forceful, hollow **clack**—may be heard a mile or more away if weather conditions are right. At other times the big rams simply engage in shoving matches and posturing intended to intimidate lesser rams. Bighorn fights are seldom fatal.

Breeding is usually completed by early December and lambs are born the following May or June. Ewes leave the herd when their birthing time is at hand, seeking out remote spots in rugged terrain. Single births are the norm and at delivery the fuzzy gray lambs weigh 8 to 10 pounds and stand just over a foot at the shoulder. Within a week or so the ewe and her leggy lamb rejoin the flock. Youngsters are quite playful and spend a lot of time cavorting about under the watchful eyes of their mothers. It is not uncommon for bighorn sheep to live to see their mid-teens and the biggest trophy rams are usually those that have survived a dozen or more hunting seasons.

Bighorns frequently have separate summer and winter ranges. Deep snows often force them from the higher elevations into the lower valleys where nutritious forage is more readily available. Movement of the mountain sheep is not a migration in the true sense of the word, yet some of these seasonal treks cover many miles.

Sheep are typically easy going animals, walking about in no apparent hurry. If boogered, they can trot or gallop in a ground-eating gait calculated at upwards of 30 miles per hour. Their leaping ability is legendary and their agility on sheer rock walls borders on the unbelieveable. Hooves have a hard outer edge and an inner cushion of spongy tissue which combine to give them excellent traction on the rocky cliffs.

Quiet animals, bighorns do very little vocalizing. Ewes and lambs bleat and blat to keep tabs on each other. Rams grunt on occasion and utter gutteral blats during the rutting confrontations with rivals.

Sheep hunting not only provides challenging outdoor recreation, it gives successful bowhunters the additional bonus of top-quality meat. Sheep were the staple of some Indian tribes long before the arrival of the white man and early explorers quickly discovered the flavor of bighorn meat and considered it a diet delicacy. Modern hunters commonly save choice cuts and pack out the meat along with the cape and horns.

Trophy Recognition

Both sexes have horns but the ewes' headgear is comparatively smaller, seldom exceeding a foot in length. Immature rams have thin, flat horns with little curl while average adult rams carry horns with heavy bases and more pronounced curves. The old trophies are thick-necked monarchs with massive horn bases and heavy curving horns that sweep below the jaw and upward past the bridge of the nose. Tips are frequently broomed.

The top desert bighorn was shot in Maricopa County, Arizona in 1979. Bowhunter Brad Siefarth's ram has a right horn 31 2/8 inches long and a left horn 31 3/8 inches long. The circumference at the right base is 15 2/8 and 15 4/8 at the left base. Its greatest spread is 19 6/8 inches.

The World's Record bighorn ram was killed in El Paso County, Colorado by bowhunter Gene Moore during the 1983 season. The right horn is 42 3/8 inches long and the left horn is 42 2/8 inches. The basal circumference of the right horn is 15 5/8 and the left is 15 4/8. The ram's total score is 191 3/8. The Pope and Young minimum score for both bighorn species is 140.

Thinhorns

Dall's sheep *(Ovis dalli dalli)* and Stone's sheep *(Ovis dalli stonei)*, a subspecies, are animals of the high, remote regions of Alaska, the Northwest Territories, the Yukon and northern British Columbia. Dall's sheep are pure white while the dark-coated Stone's sheep are bluish-black. Rams of both species have wide, flaring horns—thinner than the bighorn's—that do not obstruct their vision. Typically, a Stone's ram will carry slightly heavier horns than his all-white cousin. Horns are amber and brooming is not as common as among the bighorns.

Any sheep hunter who takes all four North American species of wild sheep is credited with a "grand slam." This term was coined by the late Grancel Fitz, an avid trophy hunter and outdoor writer credited with originating the Boone and Crockett scoring system for trophy class game. At this writing only three bowhunters have successfully taken all four species. The three, all of whom completed their slams in 1985, are Dr. John "Jack" Frost of Alaska, Tom Hoffman of New York and Paul Schafer of Montana. At least one other Montana bowhunter, Paul Brunner, has shot three of the four species.

Dall's and Stone's rams stand slightly more than three feet at the shoulder and weigh an average of 200 pounds. Stone's are slightly larger animals. Big, true trophies may be slightly heavier and stretch as much as six feet from nose to tail. Both thinhorn species are generally lighter, more slightly built animals than their bighorn relation.

These sheep do not migrate although they may

POPE AND YOUNG CLUB
NORTH AMERICAN BIG GAME TROPHY SCORING FORM

BIG GAME   RECORDS

SHEEP

KIND OF SHEEP
_____

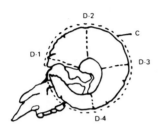 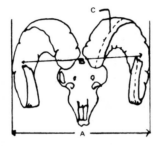 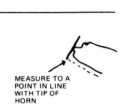

MEASURE TO A POINT IN LINE WITH TIP OF HORN

SEE OTHER SIDE FOR INSTRUCTIONS	Supplementary Data	Column 1	Column 2	Column 3
		Right Horn	Left Horn	Difference
A. Greatest Spread (Is often Tip to Tip Spread)				
B. Tip to Tip Spread (If Greatest Spread, Enter again here)				
C. Length of Horn				▨
D-1. Circumference of Base				
D-2. Circumference at First Quarter (this measurement taken at _____ inches from base)				
D-3. Circumference at Second Quarter (this measurement taken at _____ inches from base)				
D-4. Circumference at Third Quarter (this measurement taken at _____ inches from base)				
TOTALS				

ADD	Column 1	
	Column 2	
	TOTAL	
SUBTRACT Column 3		
FINAL SCORE		

Exact locality where killed _____ (County) _____ (State)
Date killed _____ By whom killed _____
Present owner _____
Address _____
Guide's Name and Address _____
Remarks: (Mention any abnormalities) _____

I certify that I have measured the above trophy on _____ 19 _____
at (address) _____ City _____
State _____ Zip Code _____ and that these measurements and data are, to the best of my knowledge and belief, made in accordance with the instructions given.
Witness: _____
(To Measurer's Signature)
Signature _____
Pope & Young Club Official Measurer

MEASURER (Print) _____
ADDRESS _____
CITY _____ STATE _____ ZIP _____

INSTRUCTIONS

All measurements must be made with a flexible steel tape or measuring cable to the nearest <u>one-eighth</u> of an inch. Wherever it is necessary to change direction of measurement, mark a control point and swing tape at this point. To simplify addition, please enter fractional figures in eighths.

Official measurements cannot be taken for at least sixty days after the animal was killed.

Please submit photographs. Front, right and left sides of horns.

Supplementary Data measurements indicate conformation of the trophy. None of the figures in Lines A and B are to be included in the score. Evaluation of conformation is a matter of personal preference.

A. Greatest Spread measured between perpendiculars at right angles to the center line of the skull.

B. Tip to Tip Spread measured from outer edge of tips of horns.

C. Length of Horn measured from lowest point in front on outer curve to a point in line with tip. **DO NOT** press tape into depression. The low point of the outer curve of the horn is considered to be the low point of the frontal portion of the horn, situated above and slightly medial to the eye socket, (not on the outside edge of the horn.)

D-1 Circumference of Base measured at right angles to axis of horn. **DO NOT** follow irregular edge of horn. Circumference measurements must be taken with a steel tape.

D-2-3-4. Divide measurement C of LONGER horn by four, mark **BOTH** horns at these quarters even though other horn is shorter, and measure circumferences at these marks. Mark quarters by starting from base only.

Big Horn Sheep: In order to accept trophies in this class, we must have complete documentation. We will require a **photograph** of the complete animal if at all possible; photographs of the front, right and left sides of the horns, photocopy of the hunting permit, and certification from the game department of the state or province hunted as to the authenticity of the kill.

Drying Period: To be eligible for entry in the Pope & Young Records, a trophy must first have been stored under normal room temperature and humidity for at least 60 consecutive days. No trophy will be considered which has in any way been altered from its natural state.

THIS SCORING FORM MUST BE ACCOMPANIED BY A FULLY COMPLETED AND SIGNED POPE & YOUNG FAIR CHASE AFFIDAVIT PLUS A RECORDING FEE OF $25.00

be forced from the higher elevations by heavy winter snows. Some hardy animals remain in the high country the year around, seeking out windswept slopes where winter forage is available. Others drop down into the lower valleys, perhaps moving several miles from their summer range.

Gregarious animals, thinhorn sheep are commonly found in groups segregated by sex except during the breeding season. Rams prefer the company of other males although on occasion an old monarch takes up a solitary existence. Ewes, yearlings, lambs and young rams often band together. Such groups are extremely difficult for enemies to approach with so many sets of eyes on the continual lookout for danger. Even the lone rams are exceptionally wary since they seem to understand remaining alert means remaining alive.

Like bighorns, Dall's and Stone's sheep are grazing animals existing mainly on a diet of mountain grasses. They do browse on occasion with the dwarf willow being a favorite. If mineral deposits are available in their home area, the sheep make periodic visits to the licks. Most feeding is a daylight activity.

Thinhorns also have exceptional eyesight and can spot a moving hunter well over a mile away. They possess acute hearing and olfactory abilities as well. When alarmed, the sheep often run for a short distance, perhaps climbing into rugged terrain while keeping a close eye on their backtrail.

All sheep have deer-like tracks but commonly range much higher than any deer that may wander into their territory. Mountain goats may share their range but a goat's tracks are much squarer. Droppings, generally in the form of pellets, are easily found in good sheep country.

The annual rut typically starts in October with rams showing renewed interest in the flocks of ewes and youngsters. Swollen-necked rams join the ewes and do not hesitate to fight for breeding rights. Often the fights are shoving matches but thinhorns also clash in head-smashing confrontations reminiscent of bighorn battles. Rams do not collect harems per se; however, they do hang out with a flock and breed as many willing ewes as possible.

Most lambs are born in May and single births are the norm. Ewes select rugged, inaccessible spots to have their young and remain away from the flock for several days after giving birth. Lambs are perhaps a foot high and six to eight pounds. Dall lambs are snowy white and Stone's appropriately darker. Lambs mature quickly and are extremely active, playing with other youngsters to develop the strength and agility that marks older animals. Sheep may live into their teens with trophy rams reaching their peak after a dozen years.

Thinhorn sheep may fall prey to wolves, cougars and bears on occasion and eagles may snatch a lamb from time to time. Disease claims other animals each year and a few perish in falls. But their largely inaccessible northland home means they have little contact with man except during the hunting seasons and both species are found in healthy, huntable numbers. The total number of both thinhorn species easily exceeds the total number of bighorn sheep.

Trophy Recognition

Truly outstanding Dall's and Stone's sheep have horns that "jump out at you." Simply put, their headgear seems outsized for the rest of their bodies.

Bowhunters in search of good trophies that will rank high in the records listing should concentrate on rams with the following characteristics: heavy bases and horns that curve down past the jaw then sweep up, flaring out, with unbroomed tips projecting well above the nose. Rams with such horns are mature trophy animals and sure-fire record book candidates.

The numero uno Stone's sheep was shot in 1957 by bowhunting legend Fred Bear. Hunting in the Coldfish Lake region of British Columbia, he arrowed a ram that officially scored 158-1/8. The right horn is 40-4/8 inches long with a circumference at the base of 12-4/8 inches. The left horn measures 38-3/8 inches and has a basal circumference of 13-1/8 inches. The ram's tip-to-tip spread is 27 inches even.

Dr. Russell Congdon's Dall's sheep presently heads the Pope and Young listings for that species. Shot in the Delta River area of Alaska in 1961, the ram has nearly symmetrical horns. The right side tapes 38-7/8 inches and the left is 39-0/8 inches. The basal circumference is 12-4/8 inches on each side and the greatest spread is 22-6/8 inches. This Dall's total score is 162-3/8.

The Pope and Young minimum score for both Stone and Dall sheep is 120 points.

Effective Hunting Techniques

Bighorns and thinhorns generally live in remote regions of North America where a bowhunt usually involves packing in, establishing a base camp and then climbing to locate the sheep. Aircraft, horses and shank's mare are often employed by hunters or their guides as prime means of transportation. Consequently, sheep hunting is often the most time-consuming and expensive of big game bowhunting ventures.

Usually sheep hunters spend considerable time sitting and glassing the sprawling, often rugged terrain the animals favor. Good binoculars or a spotting scope are mandatory, probably second in importance only to good legs and lungs. In no other bowhunting activity—except perhaps stalking Rocky Mountain goats—is physical conditioning so important.

Once the animals are located, a stalk is planned that will keep the approaching bowhunter out of sight until he is well within arrow range. The ideal stalk occurs when a hunter works above feeding or bedded rams and moves down on them. Like other mountain-dwelling wildlife, sheep seldom have enemies to attack from above and focus their attention on the lower slopes.

Bighorns and Stone's sheep, because of their coloration, frequently are difficult to locate among the rocks and mountain vegetation. They blend in quite well, even when slowly feeding across open areas, and when bedded may be almost impossible to spot. Even the all-white Dall sheep can blend in surprisingly well at times. Patience is a virtue for any glassing hunter who must slowly, meticulously scan every foot of mountainside in search of his quarry.

As previously noted, all sheep rise early and feed for a period of time early in the day. By mid-morning most are bedded but typically feed for short periods at midday and again in the late afternoon. Mornings are the ideal time to locate feeding sheep and plan a stalk. The whole day is ahead of the hunter and there is no need to rush or push his luck. Late day stalks may become a race against darkness and few sheep guides or hunters relish the idea of getting caught on the high slopes after nightfall.

Sheep may be found at higher elevations—14,000 feet and more—but they also range below timberline and may be extremely difficult to locate in the high, forested basins. While it might be possible to establish a tree stand over a mineral lick, water hole or sheep trail, chances of success would be slim at best. Stalking is the name of the game for most sheep hunters. And getting close to the keen-eyed animals is no small feat.

Some successful sheep hunters locate feeding or bedded animals and anticipate their probable direction of travel. The bowhunters then work into a hiding spot and wait for the sheep to move past. Such tactics sometimes work but they also prove frustrating, nerve-wracking exercises in futility more often than not. Mental discipline and more than a little determination are prerequisites for serious sheep hunters.

Pre-season scouting trips are generally a very good idea for guides or hunters living in or near sheep country. Not only can these scouting expeditions locate scattered bands of sheep but they help familiarize hunters with the terrain and assist in the physical conditioning necessary for this type of bowhunting. Some hunters carry topographic maps on scouting forays, marking where animals were sighted and pinpointing potential stalking routes and ambush sites.

Bowhunters should check out grassy, open slopes on the sunny sides of mountains. Sheep are commonly found grazing in such areas or bedded nearby among rocky outcroppings, escarpments or cliffs.

Sheep hunters should stay off the skyline and always keep out of sight when attempting to approach feeding or bedded animals. Individual sheep react differently to encounters with humans. Some immediately move out while others stand and stare at the intruder. A few animals will run or climb a mile or more before pausing. Some sheep run a short distance and begin grazing, apparently forgetting what prompted their flight. A bowhunter must understand all species have these characteristics and may react in any one of several ways. The point is a bowhunter should remain persistent regardless of the quarry's reaction. Perseverance is a key ingredient to sheep hunting success.

Hunting bows in the 55- to 60-pound range will be adequate for sheep. Hardy animals, they can cover considerable ground even when fatally wounded. Arrow placement is a key consideration with the heart-lung area the primary target. Shots at broadside or quartering away animals are ideal, especially if the sheep are not alarmed. Arrows shot at running game seldom result in fatal hits.

BOWHUNTING

BIG GAME  RECORDS

POPE AND YOUNG CLUB ® FAIR CHASE AFFIDAVIT

To be entered into the Pope & Young Club Records, the animal must meet the minimum scoring requirements, and must be taken in complete compliance with the controlling game laws and the Rules of Fair Chase. The term ''Fair Chase'' shall not include the taking of animals under the following conditions:

1. Helpless in a trap, deep snow or water, or on ice.
2. From any power vehicle or power boat.
3. While confined behind fences as on game farms, etc.
4. By ''Jacklighting'' or shining at night.
5. By the use of any tranquilizers or poisons.
6. By the use of any power vehicles or power boat for herding or driving animals, including use of aircraft to land alongside animal or to communicate with or direct a hunter on the ground.
7. Use of electronic devices for attracting, locating or pursuing game, or guiding the hunter to such game.
8. Any other condition considered by the Board of Directors as unsportsmanlike.

SPECIAL NOTE: For the purpose of the Pope & Young Club, a bow shall be defined as a longbow, recurve bow or compound bow that is hand-held and hand-drawn, and that has no mechanical device to enable the hunter to lock the bow at full or partial draw. Other than energy stored by the drawn bow, no device to propel the arrow will be permitted.

SEARCH & RECOVERY: Was animal recovered on same day as hit? _____ YES _____ NO
(check one)

IF ''NO''give COMPLETE DETAILS of recovery on reverse side.

Falsification of the Fair Chase Affidavit is grounds for dismissal from the Pope & Young Club. Falsification will cause the entry to be rejected, no future entries accepted, and all past entries dropped from the Pope & Young Club records for the individual falsifying the affidavit.

I, _____ attest that my _____
(PRINT)
was taken entirely by means of BOW & ARROW, and in complete compliance with the controlling game laws and the rules of Fair Chase.

_____   _____
HUNTER'S SIGNATURE   DATE

WE THE UNDERSIGNED, DECLARE THAT THE FOREGOING STATEMENTS ARE TRUE TO THE BEST OF OUR KNOWLEDGE AND BELIEF:

_____   _____   _____
Signature of witness to verification of bow kill   Address of witness   Zip
(Does not have to be Eye Witness)

_____   _____   _____
Signature of Guide   Address of Guide   Zip
(if none, write 'None')

THIS FORM MUST BE COMPLETELY FILLED OUT!

REVISED MARCH, 1985

Other Big Game

23

At the 1985 Pope and Young Club general membership meeting in Bismarck, North Dakota, a question was raised why certain other big game species—namely javelina and turkey—weren't added to the list of animals eligible for awards.

Certainly most any bowhunter who has pursued any of the four species of North American wild turkeys might readily agree that a wily gobbler is a challenging "big game" trophy. And even though it's a rare peccary that tops 50 pounds, many bowhunters who have stalked these elusive gray ghosts of the Southwestern deserts could present a sound case for establishing the javelina as a "big game" trophy animal.

True, turkeys are birds and javelina are small, pig-like animals that appear far more ferocious than they actually are. Therefore it could be endlessly debated that neither belongs on the list of big game animals recognized as North American hunting trophies by either the Pope and Young Club or the Boone and Crockett Club.

But the mere fact such a question was raised for consideration is noteworthy. Why? The answer is that modern bowhunters have a chance to hunt and tag practically every species of game animal on earth. Such questions prove there is no single, all-encompassing list of possible bowhunting trophies.

As mentioned in the Preface, this book focuses attention on North American big game; however, no guide to big game bowhunting would be complete without at least a brief mention of other existing possibilities.

The balance of this final chapter deals with bowhunting opportunities for foreign game, the so-called "exotics" and certain North American animals that are attracting increasing attention in bowhunting circles. First comes a look at perhaps the only big game animal that wears feathers.

Wild Turkeys

Once fluttering near the brink of extinction, wild turkeys today number an estimated two million birds. Thanks largely to efforts of wildlife management teams and concerned sportsmen, the noble birds are now found and hunted in growing numbers in most states. This includes some areas where, thanks to transplanting breeding stock in suitable habitat, no turkeys had been previously found. In 1985 only Alaska, Delaware, Hawaii, Maine, Nevada and Rhode Island had no spring turkey season.

Adult gobblers weigh some 15 to 20 pounds on the average while hens run about half as much. All species—Eastern, Florida, Rio Grande and Merriam—appear to be sleeker, more streamlined versions of darker strains of plump domestic birds.

With the return of wild turkeys in huntable numbers came a renewed interest in gobbler hunting with gun and bow. Today a large and growing group of bowhunters awaits the opening of the spring turkey season with as much anticipation as is usually reserved for the fall deer seasons.

Taking a wary, long-bearded gobbler with a hunting bow is seldom easy. With their uncanny

Total camouflage is vital to a turkey hunter. Most prefer mouth calls which leave both hands free for shooting.

ability to detect movement, turkeys represent a definite challenge to the hunter who must come to full draw and release a hunting arrow at close range. Nevertheless, many gobblers fall to well-placed broadheads each year and many more escape untouched. All become the subject of countless hunting tales which fire the imagination and stir the souls of listeners and storytellers alike.

Since turkeys possess the ability to see color, complete camouflage—from clothing to hunting gear and especially the hunter's face and hands—is vital. Many successful bowhunters also use lightweight camouflage netting to create improvised blinds at appropriate calling sites.

Calling is by far the most popular method of getting within good bow range of a spring gobbler and a whole variety of turkey calls awaits selection. Easy-to-use box calls are popular because mastering

one takes relatively little time; however, box calls and slate and striker calls all present a problem for bowhunters: each requires hand manipulation. For this reason most serious turkey hunters favor a mouth operated diaphragm call. Although harder to master, diaphragm calls leave both hands free for handling the bow and arrow.

Where legal, decoys can effectively be combined with calling to tempt a lovestruck gobbler. In the ideal scenario, a caller imitates a hen with romance on her mind. An interested gobbler responds and approaches, fluffing his feathers, fanning his tail and going into an unforgettable wing-dragging strut. The bowhunter remains motionless until the strutting bird passes behind a tree. At this point he comes to full draw and shoots as the bird emerges. The best aiming point is an imaginary spot at the butt of the wing.

If the arrow flies true, the bowhunter must be ready for immediate action. A wounded bird leaves little or no blood trail and should be kept in sight to ensure recovery. Often when a fatally hit gobbler begins flopping about, it's a good idea for the hunter to dash to the bird and pin it to the ground until its struggles subside. Care should be exercised, of course, to avoid contact with the razor sharp broadhead if the arrow remains in the bird.

Indeed, most veteran turkey hunters feel it's best if the arrow does remain in the bird's body. A protruding shaft makes flight difficult. Also, the shaft

Wild turkeys offer bowhunters ample challenge. Many consider the turkey to be a true "big game" animal.

can hang up on undergrowth if the wounded bird attempts to run away. There are, in fact, several washer-like devices now sold which slide onto arrows just behind the broadhead to prevent shoot-throughs on turkeys. At least one company offers a string tracking unit especially for turkey hunters.

Note: Because bowhunters typically share the field with firearms hunters, there is always the chance that a totally camouflaged bowhunter—especially one who is calling—might be mistaken for a bird. Accidental shootings have occurred in the past and more unfortunate incidents are certain as the popularity of the sport increases. Consequently, common sense safety measures always should be taken.

A few bowhunters prefer to hunt turkeys with a companion. Typically one hunter calls while the other hunter, kneeling a short distance away, prepares for the shot if the calls entice a gobbler to investigate. At the next location, the pair often swaps roles, repeating the shooter/caller process again and again until the efforts generate some action.

Most turkey hunting is typically a sit-and-wait type of hunting. Comfort is essential and camp stools, cushions or foam pads can make the waits more bearable. A few bowhunters who prefer to kneel near a tree while awaiting the shot actually wear knee pads. Whatever comfort aid is chosen, comfortable hunters make fewer movements while waiting and are usually better prepared when the shot finally presents itself.

Fall turkey hunting is regarded as more of a hit or miss proposition since the breeding season is long past and calling doesn't work as well in pulling the birds to a hunter. Calling can locate turkeys, however, and it may assist a bowhunter in finding a good ambush spot near a feeding area. A few fall turkeys are shot in accidental encounters as bowhunters pursue deer or other big game species. Regardless, turkeys remain a true challenge—and top table fare—no matter where they're found or how they're harvested.

Bowhunters interested in adding turkeys to their list of seasonal challenges can find a wealth of information available to help them. How-to articles appear seasonally in most outdoor magazines and several turkey hunting books—including a couple written especially for bowhunters—are available. In addition, cassettes and video tapes on everything from calling to hunting methods are now sold.

One national, non-profit organization deserves recognition and support for its efforts in areas of wild turkey research, management and education. For details, write:

The National Wild Turkey Federation
P. O. Box 467
Edgefield, SC 29824

Javelina, Feral Hogs

Collared peccaries, commonly known as the javelina, are a popular bowhunting target from east Texas westward along the Mexican border into central Arizona. Most javelina stand about two feet at the shoulder and are less than three feet in length from long snout to stubby tail. But what these animals lack in size they more than make up for in their fierce appearance. A shoulder mount, with salt-and-pepper neck hair erect and mouth open to expose teeth and tusks, makes a welcome and unique addition to any bowhunter's trophy room.

Javelina typically travel in bands and are most active early and late in the day, before and after the oppressive desert heat settles over their rugged homeland. At such times bowhunters attempt to sight the animals and ease within bow range. Javelina have good senses of smell and hearing so appropriate care is necessary during the stalk. Much of a bowhunter's hunting time is spent glassing distant hillsides—openings in the mesquite thickets and prickly pear patches—or slowly moving through the brush country while keeping an eye peeled for movement or sound which may indicate feeding peccaries. Javelina grunt softly as they move in an effort to keep tabs on each other. They also emit a skunk-like musk which an alert bowhunter may detect before the animals are heard or seen. If alarmed, they grunt or squeal loudly, discharge the

Jim Dougherty hefts a big javelina. The desert pigs are popular targets for bowhunters in southwestern states.

musk and dash away with surprising speed through dense, seemingly impenetrable brush.

Stands taken overlooking popular feeding areas or near caves where the animals seek shelter can result in shots for a patient bowhunter. Some have succeeded in calling javelina. But still-hunting and stalking remains the most popular method of bowhunting javelina. A few Texas and Arizona guides offer their services—at times as a bonus to their deer hunting clients—to bowhunters wanting to add a javelina trophy to their bags. Mid-winter is an ideal season since the desert heat is not as hard on bowhunters as at other times of year. In Arizona, for example, the javelina season typically opens in January.

A well-placed arrow will make short work of any javelina and in truth there is little danger involved in hunting these desert-dwelling animals. A few bowhunters, caught in the midst of an alarmed band of javelina, have claimed they were charged. In most cases they were simply standing where the poor-sighted peccaries wanted to go in their mad dash for safety; however, a wounded or cornered javelina is another matter and deserving of caution and respect.

In certain parts of the United States wild boars and feral hogs may provide bowhunting excitement. Much larger than javelina, the wild hogs may weigh several hundred pounds and reach five to six feet in length. Big boars can stand three feet at the shoulder. Exceptional specimens are even larger and can tip the scales at over 500 pounds.

Wild hogs may be found in small but free-ranging herds throughout certain Southern swamplands, in parts of the Smoky Mountains and in eastern Texas as well as in parts of California including offshore islands such as Catalina and Santa Cruz. These animals are for the most part descendents of native Asian and European wild hogs imported to America and released on private estates. Some hogs are descendents of abandoned, domesticated or half-wild stock.

Most wild hogs are black—and ugly. Some are reddish in color and a few feral hogs are actually spotted. Coats are comprised of sparse, bristly hair. Snouts are long, protruding below small "beady" eyes and erect ears. Jutting, upward curving tushes are often obvious.

It is the wild hogs' wicked-looking tusks—actually elongated canine teeth—that make him dangerous. Combine them with a hair-trigger temper and surprising speed and you have an animal that should not be lightly regarded, especially if wounded or pressured. More than one bowhunter has taken to the safety of a convenient tree to escape an angry boar's wrath. And there are a few unfortunate individuals who will always carry the scars of encounters with slashing tushes.

Note: There are numerous game farms and hunting preserves which offer "wild boars" as part of their hunting menu. These animals are rarely native to the area. Although some preserve owners breed and raise their own stock, most purchase captured or pen-reared hogs and release them inside fenced enclosures to be stalked and shot by hunters. More about this practice appears elsewhere in this chapter.

Wild hogs are gregarious animals. Herds are most active early and late in the day as the animals search for favorite foods, especially tender roots, tubers and nuts. Feeding areas are easily recognizable since the animals' rootings leaves the earth well-turned and tracked.

Still-hunting is one popular method of taking a wild hog trophy. But dense thickets can make stalking difficult and a few bowhunters favor trail-watching or staking out frequently used feeding grounds. Some hunters and boar guides employ packs of hounds to locate and bay the boars.

Boars are tough animals and can be difficult to

The author has bagged several boars while hunting on preserves and public lands where feral hogs range.

kill, especially when excited or angered. Shots should be carefully selected and placed in the heart-lung area. This is easier said than done since a boar's vitals are protected by what some call an "armor plate" of thick muscle and cartilage. Heavier-pulling bows and sharp broadheads are essential.

Both wild hogs and javelina should be considered as suitable table fare although arguments for and against the palatability of the meat will be heard. As is true with most game species, the older trophy-class males seldom make the best eating.

The Exotics

Exotic game is perhaps best defined as un-American. In most instances no hunting license is required for exotic animals since they are privately owned. A bowhunter seeking any of the exotic species generally contacts a ranch or game preserve where the animals are found, books a hunt and pays for what he kills.

Animals typically considered as "exotics" would include certain game such as the European red deer, axis deer, sika deer and fallow deer. Many varieties of sheep and goats are included: mouflon rams, aoudads, Corsican rams and Spanish or Catalina goats. Blackbuck antelope are still another exotic species.

Hunts for exotics may be booked at any time of the year since there are no closed seasons on land where the pay-as-you-go hunting is practiced. The key, quite frankly, is money, since few exotic species come cheap.

The point will be made, "Think of how much it would cost to travel to Africa to hunt an aoudad or to India for an axis deer." Following this line of thought it indeed may be cheaper to travel to Texas—where most exotic game ranches are found—and collect a trophy even when a single animal could carry a price tag of one to two thousand dollars—and more!

But as noted, hunting the exotics is no pastime for the budget-conscious bowhunter. And there are those critics who say there's little challenge in

The author shot this Corsican ram on a west Texas ranch where exotics are kept behind game-proof fences.

entering an enclosure—no matter how many acres it contains—and shooting an animal. Such comments are likely unfair where bowhunting is concerned, especially on some of the sprawling Texas spreads where it's possible to cover miles and never see the high fences that keep the game within a certain area. Still the stigma of shooting "penned up" game remains in the minds of some.

Honestly, bowhunters are unwelcome at many ranches offering exotic hunts. Most often the ranch owners or managers are used to dealing with busy, well-heeled sportsmen who jet in, spend a day or two knocking over several species of high-priced game with a scope-sighted rifle, pay the tab and jet back to their business. There's little fuss, muss or bother involved with such clients. Bowhunters, on the other hand, need to spend time getting close to game and the old "time is money" adage applies to game ranchers as well as Wall Street wheeler dealers. Despite the fact the hunting bow has proved deadly on all exotic species, finding a place to hunt is at times a major hurdle to clear.

Note: Certain exotic species have been introduced in the wild in some parts of the country. For example, bowhunters in the Land Between the Lakes area of Kentucky/Tennessee have had a chance to legally take a fallow deer for years. And bowhunters visiting Assateague Island off the Maryland/Virginia coast have the seasonal opportunity to tag a sika deer. But harvests are strictly controlled and state game laws must be followed in these cases. This makes the situation completely different than a typical hunt for an exotic animal.

Because of the controlled nature of hunting exotics, many times kills are guaranteed. It is noteworthy that usually any wounded animals which are not recovered are counted as a kill.

Hunting Preserves

Like ranches and game farms which offer exotic hunts, hunting preserves are usually open the year 'round and offer a wide range of guaranteed shooting opportunities. Wild boar, sheep and goats are the most common targets and the price tag carried by most preserve game is less than for true exotic species.

Boars called "trophies" may cost several hundred dollars while "meat animals" cost somewhat less. Prices paid for the goats and sheep are comparable.

Hunting is usually conducted under the supervision of a guide who leads one or more hunters through wooded or brushy areas where game feeds or beds. When animals are sighted, stalks are made. Some preserves do have tree stands available along game trails. Often a guide will post a hunter and then circle ahead in an attempt to roust game and push it past waiting hunters. Also, as previously noted, hunting hounds may be used to locate boars and hold them at bay until the hunters arrive.

Hunting preserves come in all sizes from a few acres to several hundred acres and more. Certainly there is little challenge or sportsmanship in entering a small, fenced area and shooting an animal that has no chance of escape. This is bow-killing, not bowhunting. But some preserves do provide quality experiences and lasting memories for bowhunters who want to try something different and are willing to pay the price.

Most preserves offer brief, two- to three-day hunts.

This is ideal for a weekend trip and appeals to people who have little time for the more lengthy, and expensive booked hunts for free-ranging big game.

In addition, many preserves offer limited hunts for exotic and other big game animals. A bowhunter with money could, for example, arrange a "hunt" for a six-point bull elk. The preserve owner would then buy the elk, transport him to the preserve and contact the hunter. Then, for example, if the hunter doesn't mind killing a Montana elk among the hardwoods of a Tennessee ridge, he could return home with a trophy and a hunting tale about his adventure. Obviously, any animals taken in this fashion are not eligible for either Pope and Young or Boone and Crockett competitions.

Preserve hunts are not for every bowhunter; however, they do provide a viable hunting option— and off-season availability—to those who have no problem with the artificiality of put-and-take hunting. It should be clearly understood that preserve hunters are in effect buying animals. Unlike hunts for wild, free-ranging species where

Boars, goats and several species of sheep—like these on an Ohio preserve—are popular animals.

the costs cover the hunt and any animals taken are a bonus, certain guarantees are offered and the kill practically assured.

Foreign Bowhunting

Although hundreds of American bowhunters travel north each year to experience a Canadian adventure, relatively few venture overseas. Most who do go abroad head for Africa.

Time was when an African safari was priced beyond the means of most sportsmen; however, in recent years the cost of many North American hunts has climbed steadily until a hunt on the Dark Continent seems inexpensive by comparison. When you can easily spend thousands of dollars on a single species hunt in Alaska or Canada, it's easy to understand why a multi-species African bowhunt— for the same or even less money—is especially appealing to many.

South Africa is in reality a bowhunting mecca. Per day rates are becoming increasingly reasonable. Even when the various trophy fees are added for game actually taken, the cost remains affordable for an increasing number of people. Year around hunting opportunities exist, but North America's summer months are a popular time for mid-winter African bowhunts (seasons are reversed below the equator).

Although a handful of experienced bowhunters may seek the dangerous African game such as lion, leopard, Cape buffalo and the like, most bowhunters are content to collect a wide variety of plains game. Popular species include kudu, eland, impala, wildebeest, nyala, waterbuck, gemsbok, blesbok, zebra, reedbuck, hartebeest, duiker and warthog.

South African game is generally abundant although it should be pointed out that these animals are found behind fences on working ranches much as the exotic species in Texas. Hunting is generally done from elevated or ground-level stands overlooking watering and feeding areas. All plains game is especially difficult to stalk. Centuries of heavy predation has made the animals continually alert and hard to approach.

Regardless, more and more South African ranches are opening their doors to bowhunters and several North American outfitters cater to booking bowhunters. It's probably a good idea to work with an established agency where knowledgeable hunting consultants are accustomed to working with bowhunters.

Other parts of Africa are open to bowhunting but political turmoil and uncertainty have combined to curtail safari activity. Consequently, South Africa remains the center of bowhunting attention. There are some who feel there is no place a bowhunter can travel—providing he has several thousand dollars to spend—and get more for his money.

While a very few bowhunters have hunted Europe, Asia, Central and South America, the majority of overseas attention outside of Africa is focused on New Zealand and Australia. Bowhunting fever has been burning Down Under for years but recently North Americans have discovered what the Aussies and New Zealanders have known for years—there's ample game and opportunity in this particular corner of the world.

In 1982 the New Zealand Bowhunters Society published a book listing records for various "Australasian" species. Among the categories included in the "South Pacific Rating for Bow Shot Game" were red deer, fallow deer, sika deer, chital deer, rusa deer, buffalo, chamois, thar, wild boar and wild goat. There were also categories for shark, sawfish and stingray.

Several American booking agencies now arrange bowhunting trips to New Zealand and the Australian Outback. Costs are comparable to Africa for both travel and guiding services.

Big game bowhunting today is definitely a worldwide activity. Approaching the dawn of a new century, bowhunters have never had such a smorgasbord of quality experiences and opportunities available. This is true no matter what the choice of destination or species.

Afterword

The future of bowhunting? We talk a lot about it. Some say we overdo it, and that too much mouthing calls attention to things that are best left to run their course. Perhaps.

I think a lot about the future of bowhunting. Maybe I shouldn't, maybe there is no need...because really it is in the hands of the bowhunter himself...and certainly the bowhunter has risen to the challenge before.

There are others—legislators, fish and game personnel and the like—who ultimately make decisions about our hunting, and there are social situations, like attitudes about hunting and the loss of habitat that will certainly strongly affect tomorrow's hunting. But in the end, I believe the most critical decisions about our future will be most affected by you and me. What we do, how we do it, as well as the attitudes and equipment we take to the woods are going to decide our fate in the end. It will, I believe, be how we are perceived by the decision-makers and their constituency that becomes the biggest factor in the future of bowhunting.

Hunting with the bow and arrow caught fire in the '50s and '60s, and by the early '70s was one of the fastest growing outdoor sports in America. I don't think there can be any question that the single most important factor in the growth of this sport was the appeal of the long, separate hunting seasons given bowhunters in those early days. It is important, I think, that we keep in mind that the reason we were given those long special seasons was because of our equipment...**and not for any other reason**.

Because of our equipment it was necessary to get very close to our quarry. Because of our equipment success was very limited. Because of our equipment there was no adverse effect on the daily routines of the animals we pursued. And because of our equipment and the personal effort necessary to master it, our numbers were small and our commitment, of necessity, was intense. It was obvious to the decision-makers that bowhunting was special...it was a more difficult way. We were rewarded with the special long bow seasons we enjoy today.

Today, all forms of hunting—gun, blackpowder, and bow—are being affected by technological development. Many feel it may be the major question mark over all hunting. Technology has contributed mightily to the development of mankind...no question of that. But I do worry about its effect on hunting and on how hunters are perceived by non-hunters. The day of the public's idea of the hunter as a rugged outdoorsman with a pipe in the corner of his mouth and a far away gleam in his eye is gone. In his place is a not very sporting type who will use any advantage, including air-to-ground missiles, to kill an animal. Without question, technology is a double-edged sword...it can be used to help hunting, or it can be used to kill hunting.

Bowhunting is particularly vulnerable, it seems. Because of the difficulty of mastering the bow and arrow and because of the knowledge and experience required for consistent success, sometimes it seems any shortcut should be justifiable and all simplification through technological development, to any degree, is acceptable.

Bowhunters must, I believe, be particularly aware of the need to maintain our touch with the essence of our sport...the more difficult way. It appears that we can allow technology to advance bowhunting to a place where it is no longer seen as a more difficult way.

The future of bowhunting lies perhaps in the cultivation of hunting with the bow and arrow...as opposed to an over-emphasis on modernization and a preoccupation with numbers and successes...and an understanding that method of pursuit is the only difference between bowhunting and other types of hunting. That difference is the key to our future.

Bowhunting, because of its requirement for individual ability, has, more than any hunting sport, created its heroes. Many of these heroes have been instrumental in developing and shaping our sport. In a sport that is very susceptible to the scrutiny of non-participants, it is important that our image shine. And it is critical that our heroes lead and instruct both the beginner and the experienced bowhunter with concern for our future.

Perhaps none has contributed as directly to the development of today's bowhunters, their attitudes, abilities, and their future, as has M. R. James.

As Editor/Publisher of **Bowhunter Magazine** he is one of the principal instruments in educating today's bowhunters. As an old-time, dead-serious bowhunter he has long felt and understood the magic of the forest and the bow. As an educator-outdoor writer with a life-long commitment to our sport, few have equalled his contributions, none his feel for the responsibilities of his position.

M. R. and I each grew up in southern Illinois and Indiana in the '40s and '50s. Perhaps the fact that there were almost no deer and few deer hunters in those days drove M. R., as I suspect it did me, to the vicarious pursuit of hunts and hunters through magazines and books. The writings of Pope, Thompson, Ruark, Hemingway and O'Connor can offer much to a fledgling hunter. Their feel for pursuit and their insistence on sport were strong examples.

M. R. James is more qualified than anyone I know to write a comprehensive book on hunting with the bow and arrow. Few of today's outdoor writers have spent as much time in the woods with bow in hand. Fewer have the ability to present so large a subject in such readable style, and none has as much concern for bowhunting, bowhunters and their future.

G. Fred Asbell
Longmont, Colorado

Bowhunting Organizations

The Professional Bowhunters Society

"The PBS takes pride in its membership, possibly moreso than any other organization in bowhunting history. We have been criticized at times of being discriminatory. Let it be stated here that it is by no means discrimination. We are simply **selective** in our membership. We are no more an 'elitist' organization than a professional football team is an elite group. In a sense, we want you to be to bowhunting what an Olympic athlete, a Blue Angel, a Green Beret or a Special Forces member is to his own field of expertise. In short, we are the **best** and proud of it!"

This paragraph, taken from the Professional Bowhunter Society's Regular Membership application form, explains an attitude which has been present in this organization since its founding in Charleston, West Virginia on September 8, 1963. Founded as a non-profit, fraternal organization, the PBS sought bowhunters of experience, ability and character who were capable of upgrading the status and public image of bowhunters and bowhunting. That goal remains unchanged.

Today two separate membership programs exist. Interested persons apply for Associate status first, vowing to be "professional" in their attitude toward bowhunting; to take bowhunting seriously enough to ensure proper behavior, proper equipment and proper attitude; and to always strive to improve the overall image of the bowhunter. Bowhunters accepted as Associates may later apply for Regular Member status. Regular membership is obtained only through selective review of the PBS Executive Council and is not guaranteed.

It is the purpose of the Professional Bowhunters Society to be an organization whose membership consists only of persons who are considered "Professional Bowhunters" and who vow:

* That by reason of choice, bowhunting is their primary archery interest, and that their ultimate aim and interest is the taking of wild game by bow and arrow of suitable weights in a humane and sportsmanlike matter.

* To share with others their experiences, knowledge and shooting skills.

* To be a conscientious bowhunter, promoting bowhunting by working to elevate its standards and the standards of those who practice the art of bowhunting.

* To provide training for others in safety, shooting skill and hunting techniques.

* To practice the wise use of our natural resources, the conservation of our wild game and the preservation of the natural habitat thereof.

Members receive **The Professional Bowhunter Magazine**, a quarterly magazine published "...as part of the overall program of Professional Bowhunters Society to educate its members and other readers. It is also a purpose of our publication to provide information and opinion that is timely, practical and readable."

In addition, PBSers may participate in PBS-sponsored hunts, programs and contests. They also have free use of the organization's lending library which includes many films and books of interest to hunters.

Interested readers may obtain information and an application for Associate membership by writing:

Professional Bowhunters Society
P. O. Box 5275
Charlotte, NC 28225

Bowhunters Who Care

This organization has several well-defined objectives. Included are the following:

* Neutralize the anti-hunting propaganda with a sound, factual and long-sustained program designed to educate and inform non-hunters.

* Create an awareness among all hunters of the importance of good sportsmanship.

* Open up new areas in which to hunt by improving hunter/landowner relations.

* Influence legislators to give bowhunters a season which is long enough to give them a fair chance to bag their game.

Bowhunters Who Care is a non-profit corporation which invites the support of all concerned bowhunters. A bi-monthly newsletter, **The Tab** keeps members posted on organizational happenings. Membership information may be obtained by writing:

Bowhunters Who Care
P. O. Box 269
Colombus, NE 68601

Bowhunter Education

The stated goal of the International Bowhunter Education Program is "To instill in bowhunters a responsible attitude and to assist them to adopt and follow an acceptable behavior towards people, wildlife, and the environment in which they hunt."

Today several thousand volunteer instructors are qualified to teach the six-hour course. It is estimated between a quarter and a half million men and women have taken and passed the basic bowhunter education course.

William H. Wadsworth is the man generally credited with being the "Father of Bowhunter Education." Besides authoring the manual used to teach the IBEP course, Wadsworth developed many teaching aids and traveled extensively throughout North America conducting clinics and promoting responsible, safe bowhunting practices. From its modest beginnings in New York state in 1969, bowhunter education has grown tremendously under Wadsworth's direction. The National Bowhunter Education Foundation was incorporated as a tax-exempt, non-profit educational foundation in 1979.

The program is now available throughout North America and in several foreign countries. Details may be obtained by writing:

National Bowhunter Education Foundation
P. O. Box 1120
Piscataway, NJ 08854

The Foundation's headquarters facility is located at Land Between the Lakes in Tennessee. Training aids, instructor kits, manuals, flip charts and other materials are warehoused nearby and may be ordered by qualified individuals who write:

International Bowhunter Education Program
Route #6, Box 199
Murray, KY 42071

Bibliography

Bauer, Erwin A. **Treasury of Big Game Animals**. An Outdoor Life Book/Harper & Row, New York, NY, 1972.

Brakefield, Tom. **Hunting Big-Game Trophies**. Sunrise Books/E. P. Dutton & Co., Inc., New York, NY, 1976.

Brakefield, Tom. **The Sportsman's Complete Book of Trophy and Meat Care**. Stackpole Books, Harrisburg, PA, 1975.

Dalrymple, Byron W. **North American Game Animals**. An Outdoor Life Book/Crown Publishers, New York, NY, 1978.

Delaan, Maury. **Everybody's Archery Guide**. Topical Magazines, Inc., Derby, CT, 1965.

East, Ben. **The Ben East Hunting Book**. An Outdoor Life Book/Harper & Row, New York, NY, 1974.

Editorial Committee Boone and Crockett Club. **The Black Bear in Modern North America**. Boone and Crockett Club and the Amwell Press, Clinton, NJ, 1979.

Editorial Committee Boone and Crockett Club. **The Wild Sheep in Modern North America**. Boone and Crockett Club and the Winchester Press, New York, NY, 1975.

Editorial Committee Pope and Young Club. **Bowhunting Big Game Records of North America**, First Edition. Pope and Young Club, 1975.

Editorial Committee Pope and Young Club. **Bowhunting Big Game Records of North America**, Second Edition. Pope and Young Club, 1981.

Elman, Robert (Editor). **The Complete Book of Hunting**. Abbeville Press, Inc., New York, NY, 1980.

Fitz, Grancel. **How To Measure and Score Big Game Trophies**. A Pope and Young Club Book, 1977.

Harbour, Dave. **Hunting the American Wild Turkey**. Stackpole Books, Harrisburg, PA, 1975.

Henwood, Jessie (Editor). **The Game Seekers**. New Zealand Bowhunters Society, 1982.

Hunter Services Division of the National Rifle Association (Editors). **Basic Hunter's Guide**. National Rifle Association, Washington, D.C., 1982.

Koller, Larry. **The Treasury of Hunting**. A Ridge Press Book/Odyssey Press. New York, NY, 1965.

Mays, Buddy. **A Pilgrim's Notebook: Guide to Western Wildlife**. Chronicle Books, San Francisco, 1977.

O'Connor, Jack. **The Big Game Animals of North America**. An Outdoor Life Book/Charles Scribner's Sons, New York, NY, 1977.

Ormond, Clyde. **Complete Book of Hunting**. An Outdoor Life Book/Harper & Row, New York, NY, 1962.

Rue, Leonard Lee III. **Complete Guide to Game Animals**. An Outdoor Life Book/Van Nostrand Reinhold Co., New York, NY, 1981.

Rue, Leonard Lee III. **The Deer of North America**. An Outdoor Life Book/Crown Publishers, Inc., New York, NY, 1978.

Strung, Norman. **The Art of Hunting**. Cy DeCosse Inc., Minnetonka, MN, 1984.

Wadsworth, William H. **Bowhunting Deer**, National Bowhunter Education Manual, National Bowhunter Education Foundation, Murray, KY, 1975.

Wallmo, Olof C. **Mule and Black-Tailed Deer of North America**. A Wildlife Management Institute Book/University of Nebraska Press, Lincoln, NE, 1981.

Waterman, Charles F. **Hunting In America**. A Ridge Press Book/Holt, Rinehart and Winston, New York, NY, 1973.

Whisker, James B. **The Right To Hunt**. North River Press, 1981.

Index

The End

Meet M.R. James

M.R. James is the Editor/Publisher of Bowhunter® Magazine, the most authorative and best-selling bowhunting periodical in the sport's history. This nationally known sportsman and veteran outdoor writer has bowhunted across North America for some 25 years, sharing many of his adventures with a loyal and growing band of readers. James is a Senior Member of the Pope and Young Club, a Regular Member of the Professional Bowhunters Society and a member of numerous national, state and local bowhunting associations. Each year he travels thousands of miles to bowhunt and to conduct instructional/educational bowhunting clinics. He is the author of **Bowhunting for Whitetail and Mule Deer** and served as Editor of the Pope and Young Club's first record book. James has earned both bachelor's and master's degrees in English. Today he resides near Fort Wayne, Indiana with his wife Janet. They are the parents of four grown children: Jeff, Dave, Dan and Cheryl.